SIMULATION AND AI, 1989

Titles in the *SIMULATION SERIES*

SIMULATION AND AI, 1989

Proceedings of the SCS Western Multiconference, 1989
4-6 January 1989
San Diego, California

Edited by
Wade Webster

Simulation Series
Volume 20
Number 3
July 1989

A Society for Computer Simulation International (Simulation Councils, Inc.) publication.
San Diego, California

Rosemary A. Whiteside, Proceedings Coordinator
Lincoln Fish, Assistant

ISBN 0-911801-44-8
ISSN 0735-9276

PRINTED IN THE UNITED STATES OF AMERICA

CONTENTS

Page **Authors**

CONTENTS (continued)

Preface

This Proceeding contains most of the papers presented at the Simulation and Artificial Intelligence Conference held in San Diego, California, in January 1989, under the sponsorship of the Society for Computer Simulation International, as part of the Western Multiconference. By my count, this is the sixth in a series of similar conferences held by SCSI beginning in 1985.

When an ad hoc committee met at the 1987 Multiconference to form an SCSI Technical Activity in AI and Simulation, the committee resolved to see to it that each annual Multiconference include a conference on AI and Simulation, or a similar conference by some other name. At that time several such conferences had been held as part of the annual Multiconference in San Diego or the Eastern Simulation Conference, which has now be renamed the Eastern Multiconference. It has now proven to be quite feasible and effective to hold two such conferences each year, one each at the Western and Eastern Multiconferences.

Now that the AI hype has subsided somewhat, one can see clearly that there is genuine interest and productive activity in the intersection of the AI and Simulation fields, and that this interest and activity is here to stay.

A panel discussion is included in the 1989 conference to explore the relationships among the Simulation, AI, and Neural Network fields. The individual papers included in this conference illustrate the diversity of those relationships.

The papers are organized into the following sessions:

   I.   Neural networks
   II.   Object-oriented simulation
   III. Applications
   IV.   Education and training
   V.   Manufacturing and process control
   VI.   Intelligent simulation tools and environments
   VII. Decision-making
   VIII. Expert system development methods
   IX.   Simulation of computer systems

The papers appear in this proceedings in the order they are listed in the preliminary program, with the intention of making it as easy as possible for the conference attendee to find papers quickly while trying to determine which session to attend at any particular time. This should enable attendees to make the most of the Multiconference format. My apology is offered in advance for any changes that may become necessary between the preliminary and final programs and which may thwart the intent. Apologies are also extended to any author, presenter, or session chairman for any assignment of a paper to a session that he or she may feel is inappropriate. Most of the papers could each be reasonably included in two or more sessions. A major consideration was the achievement of balance among the sessions.

My thanks go to all contributors, session chairmen, and staff members for their hard work to make this conference a success. I am especially grateful for Rosemary Whiteside's efforts and her patience with the rest of us.

Wade Webster, Editor
Lockheed Engineering & Sciences Company

SIMULATION AND AI, 1989

Simulation and AI, 1989
©1989 by the Society for Computer
Simulation International
ISBN 0-911801-44-8

Selective vigilance and ambiguity detection in adaptive resonance networks

Daniel S. Levine
Department of Mathematics
University of Texas at Arlington
Arlington, TX 76019

ABSTRACT

Some modifications of the adaptive resonance theory (ART) networks for binary or analog pattern classification are suggested. These changes add to ART the capacities for selective attention and ambiguity detection.

The ART networks contain two fields of nodes, F_1 for features and F_2 for categories. A vigilance parameter measures how closely an input pattern at F_1 matches F_2-to-F_1 synaptic weights. Two methods for modelling "selective vigilance" are shown here.

One selective vigilance method has been used to simulate frontal lobe damage effects on human sorting of cards that each show a certain number, shape, and color. Frontal patients classify normally on the basis of one criterion, but cannot switch from one criterion to another. In our simulations, F_1 code individual colors, shapes, whereas numbers, and F_2 code card categories. F_1-to-F_2 synapses are gated by reinforcement pathways, and frontal damage is modelled by weakenened reinforcement.

Our second method involves connections from F_1 to a node that resets F_2. If r is vigilance, [I] the number of F_1 nodes activated by the input, and [X] the number of those nodes also activated by a given category node at F_2, match occurs in ART whenever $[X] > r[I]$. If F_1 is divided into *subfields*, each coding some feature class, the term $r[I]$ can be replaced by a weighted sum of the numbers of nodes in each subfield activated by that input.

Ambiguity is modelled by adding to ART another category field F_2· in one-to-one mapping with F_2, and two channels with unequal vigilances r_{max} and r_{min}. If a category is searched and $[X]/[I]$ exceeds r_{max}, the input goes into that category. If that ratio is between r_{min} and r_{max}, the search continues and the corresponding F_2· node is activated. Applications to medical diagnosis and to automatic flight are discussed.

INTRODUCTION AND REVIEW OF ART NETWORKS

The formation of categories among sensory patterns is one of the widest applications of neural networks. Analysis of radar signals, handprinted numerals, speech signals, or any other class of sensory data involves decisions on what are the most important repeatable distinguishing features of the data. Hence the categorization problem is important both for understanding memory processes in the brain and for designing pattern recognizers that deal with variable events.

Most model neural networks for categorization have involved modifiable connections between two layers of nodes, the first layer coding features and the second layer coding categories. Often, there is competition among the category nodes. Some of the more popular categorization models go by the names of competitive learning (Rumelhart and Zipser 1985), back propagation (Rumelhart et al. 1986), brain-state-in-a-box (Anderson and Murphy 1986), adaptive resonance (Carpenter and Grossberg 1987 a,b), and Darwin II (Edelman 1987).

While all of these categorization theories have much in common, the adaptive resonance theory (ART) has, in my opinion, several advantages over competing theories. First, it is a real-time dynamic model that exhibits considerable stability. Various mathematical results show that categorizations of given input patterns are not perturbed by an arbitrary barrage of new inputs. Second, the category prototypes against which an input is tested change over time to reflect the type of patterns that are more frequently observed in the environment. Third, feature and category node layers are influenced by other important neural subsystems external to these layers, such as the motivational and orienting systems. Hence, the theory can be fit in with an interconnected set of psychological theories developed over twenty years (Grossberg 1982, 1987; Levine 1983).

Yet the current forms of the ART models --ART 1 for binary patterns (Carpenter and Grossberg 1987a) and ART 2 for analog patterns (Carpenter and Grossberg 1987b) -- also have several limitations, which are recognized by their authors. This article will suggest modified adaptive resonance architectures that overcome two of these limitations. First, in ART 1 and ART 2, whether an input matches or mismatches an existing category is decided by means of a vigilance parameter that is uniform over the entire field. In living organisms, some sensory features are attended to more than others, and some categories have more rigid membership standards than others. Second, once a decision is made on which category an input belongs to, ART 1 and ART 2 keep no record of how ambiguous that decision was. In living organisms, inputs that are on the borderline between two categories may be tentatively classified in one category but later reclassified if additional evidence arrives.

We shall now give a cursory review of the ART 1 and ART 2 architectures. Figure 1 describes the basic plan of ART 1. Equations governing this network are given in the Appendix. The field F_1 consists of nodes involved in primary processing of input features. The field F_2 consists of nodes that respond to categories of F_1 node activity patterns. Synaptic connections between the two fields are modifiable in both directions, according to two different learning laws.

Inhibition from the F_2 field to the F_1 field (via one of the gain control nodes, which are represented as filled-in circles) serves two related purposes. First, it prevents F_2 activity from always exciting F_1, thus preventing hallucinations from occurring when a category is thought about. Second, it shuts off most neural activity at F_1 if there is mismatch between the input pattern and the pattern expected from the template given by the active category. This occurs because only with a sufficiently large match will the same F_1 nodes be excited both by the input and by the active F_2 category node, which is needed to overcome the nonspecific inhibition from F_2.

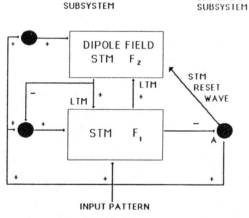

ATTENTIONAL SUBSYSTEM   ORIENTING SUBSYSTEM

INPUT PATTERN

Figure 1. Basic ART 1 architecture: two attentional stages, F_1 and F_2, encode short term memory (STM) activation patterns. Bottom-up and top-down pathways between these stages contain adaptive long term memory (LTM) traces which multiply the signals in these pathways. Gain control nodes (dark circles) modulate STM and LTM. The orienting system generates reset at F_2 when top-down and bottom-up patterns are mismatched at F_1, thus inhibiting active F_2 nodes. (Modified from Carpenter and Grossberg 1987a, with permission.)

The F_2 nodes are also connected to each other in a competitive on-center off-surround network (see Figure 2). Such a network is frequently designed to make choices in short term memory and to contrast-enhance significant parts of a pattern (Amari 1971; Grossberg 1973; Malsburg 1973; Cohen and Grossberg 1983; Rumelhart and Zipser 1985). In this version, the simplest form of choice is made: only the F_2 node receiving the largest signal from F_1 becomes active. This signal is computed by summing input pattern intensities at each F_1 node weighted by the strengths of bottom-up synapses to the given F_2 node.

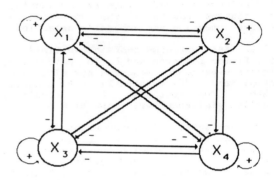

Figure 2. Schematic on-center off-surround network: each node excites itself and inhibits the others.

Hence, total F_1 layer activity is larger in the case of match than in the case of mismatch. If match occurs, as shown in Figure 1, then F_1 inhibits activity of the orienting subsystem node A, stabilizing categorization of the given input pattern in the given F_2 node. If a mismatch occurs, by contrast, F_1 activity is insufficient to inhibit A, which thus becomes active. Activity of the A node leads to reset at F_2 so that the active category becomes inactivated as long as the current input is on. The criterion for mismatch is that the ratio of F_1 activity to total input intensity be less than some prescribed vigilance value.

The short term memory (STM) and long term memory (LTM) equations for this network, shown in the Appendix, embody these considerations along with one additional rule. The *Weber Law Rule* says that LTM size should vary inversely with input pattern scale. This rule is designed to prevent a category node that has previously learned to code a particular binary pattern (1's in particular locations) from also coding every superset pattern (pattern that has 1's in those same locations and some others).

The ART 2 network of Carpenter and Grossberg (1987b), as shown in Figure 3, is designed to categorize analog (or continuous-valued, or gray-scale) input patterns. The architecture builds on the ideas of ART 1 with two layers and modifiable synapses in both directions, but there is more complexity in the processing at the F_1 layer. This processing is designed to contrast-enhance significant parts of the pattern and suppress noise, according to general principles developed in Grossberg (1973).

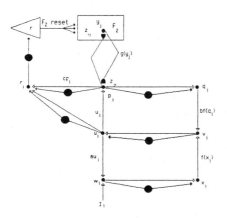

Figure 3. Basic ART 2 architecture. F_1, F_2, and the orienting system are as in ART 1. The single field of nodes at F_1 is replaced by six sets of nodes designed to suppress noise in analog inputs. Open arrows denote specific patterned inputs; filled arrows denote nonspecific gain control. When F_2 makes a choice, $g(y_j)$ is positive if the j th node is chosen and 0 otherwise. z_{ij} and z_{ji} denote bottom-up and top-down LTM strengths; r denotes vigilance. (Modified from Carpenter and Grossberg 1987b, with permission.)

SELECTIVE VIGILANCE AND THE FRONTAL LOBES

The vigilance parameter in the Carpenter-Grossberg model is uniform over the whole sensory field. Yet their model easily permits modification to include selective attention to certain features over others on the basis of significance to the system's goals. Grossberg and Levine (1975) built such attention into a one-level on-center off-surround pattern processing network. This general idea has been refined by Cohen and Grossberg (1987) with their *masking field* that segments features into significant "chunks" such as occur, for example, in speech recognition.

There are many possible approaches to modeling "selective vigilance" in an ART framework, and two of them will now be discussed. An example of one approach was used by Leven and Levine (1987) to simulate data on human patients with frontal lobe damage. These patients (Milner 1964) were given the Wisconsin card-sorting test, where the subject had to classify cards on the basis of one of three criteria (color, shape, or number shown on the card), and at each placement was told whether he or she was

right or wrong without being told why. Frontal patients could classify on the basis of one criterion as readily as normals, but once, say, a color criterion had been established, they had difficulty switching to shape if they could do so at all.

Figure 4 shows the network used by Leven and Levine, some of whose equations are given in the Appendix. There were two levels of nodes, F_1 which coded individual features (colors, shapes, or numbers) and F_2 which coded categories of cards. For simplicity, synaptic weights were not modifiable as in the ART 1 model, but synapses from F_1 to F_2 were gated by attentional bias nodes which caused the network to selectively favor one criterion over the others. These bias nodes were influenced both by the external reinforcement (the experimenter's "Right" or "Wrong") and by habit nodes. The habit nodes were in turn influenced by how often previous matching decisions had been made on the basis of the given criterion.

Frontal damage was modelled by weakening of the gain of signals from the reinforcement node to bias nodes. This interpretation is based on the anatomical fact (Nauta 1971) that the frontal lobes are the major connecting link between the other cortical lobes, which process or associate sensory information, and the hypothalamus and limbic system, which process information about the organism's internal state. The network used here is also suggestive of more recent physiological findings. Mishkin et al (1984) have found evidence that there are brain loci (in the corpus striatum) for motor habits and separate brain loci (in the hippocampus and amygdala) for reinforcement values of events.

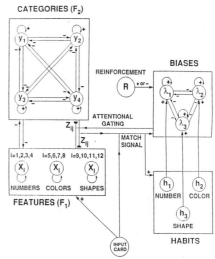

Figure 4. Network to simulate Milner's card sorting data. Bottom-up signals from feature to category nodes are selectively gated by bias nodes. Bias nodes are in turn affected by habit nodes, coding past choice criteria, and reinforcement. Frontal damage is modelled by weakening of reinforcement signals. (Modified from Leven and Levine 1987, with permission.)

The above selective vigilance mechanism did not need modifiable synapses because it was designed to explain attentional changes of short duration. To explain long-term selective vigilance changes, one could combine the habit and bias mechanisms described above with the full LTM laws of the ART network.

But it is also possible that selective attention could influence the connections from F1 to the reset node A of Figure 1. A way for this to occur is suggested by a mechanistic implementation of the Carpenter-Grossberg vigilance rule for pattern matching. Let the vigilance parameter be a number r, $0 < r < 1$, let [I] be defined as the number of F_1 nodes activated by the input pattern and [X] as the number of those nodes also activated by the F_2 node for the perceived category. Then the rule of Carpenter and Grossberg (1987a) is that match occurs, that is, F_1 inhibits the reset node, whenever

$$[X]/[I] > r \qquad (1)$$

holds. A possible network realization of this rule is shown in Figure 5. Let the vigilance be interpreted as the gain of a signal from the input processing level to some other node A_{1a}. There is yet another lower-level node A_{1b}, which has a threshold of 0 and which is excited by F_1 and inhibited by A_{1a}; hence, A_{1b} is active precisely when (1) holds. Finally, A_{1b} inhibits the reset node.

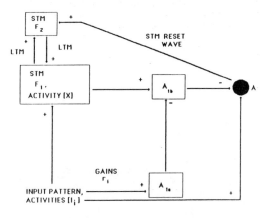

Figure 5. Mechanistic representation of vigilance in a network of ART 1 type. If all gains r_i are equal, this network acts like current version of ART 1. If gains are unequal, the network can exercise selective vigilance.

To adapt the picture of Figure 5 to selective vigilance, divide the field F1 into *subfields*, each responsive to a particular class of sensory features (cf. Grossberg and Levine 1975 or Leven and Levine 1987). Let the gain of signals from each subfield to A_{1a}

be a different value r_1. If $[I_1]$ is the number of subfield nodes activated by the input, the term r[I] in the modified form of (1) could be replaced by $\Sigma_i (r_1 [I_1])$. Such selective inactivation of the reset node, or orienting arousal area, might be related to another frontal lobe function. The frontal cortex seems to reduce nonspecific arousal in the presence of a motivationally salient input, thereby making the organism less distractible (Fuster 1980; Levine 1986). We conjecture therefore that *both* types of selective vigilance mechanism discussed here operate in primate brains.

Vigilance in intelligent organisms or machines is likely to be non-uniform not only across the feature field but also across the category field. Suppose that a system is interested in the presence or absence of two or more classes of objects (say "fish" and "fowl"). Then the criterion for membership in one of the categories to be sought should be more stringent than the criterion for membership in the catch-all category of "neither fish nor fowl". Excitatory or inhibitory modulation from a third set of nodes F3 on F2 could selectively enhance the importance of some categories over others.

DETECTION OF AMBIGUITY

The current ART 1 and ART 2 models always come to a decision as to which category a new input belongs to. The speed of convergence may reflect the amount of ambiguity in deciding between categories, but that amount of ambiguity is not permanently coded. By contrast, some alternative categorization models -- such as the competitive learning (CL) model of Rumelhart and Zipser (1985) and the back propagation (BP) model of Rumelhart et al (1986) -- achieve stability for some input classes but not others. For that reason, the CL and BP models are probably less dependable than ART, but may be better than the current form of ART at registering the degree of "confusion" in the environment.

Ambiguity detection not only is a feature of actual human psychology, but has potential applications to automatic control systems and human-machine interfaces. An automatic pilot system or threat-detection system, for example, could be designed to run by itself if the arriving information is relatively unambiguous, but under more ambiguous conditions transfer control to a human operator or to an expensive (therefore rarely used) specialized subsystem. Ambiguity detection is also applicable to the design of neural network "expert systems" for medical diagnosis. With the inclusion of this feature, it is possible to make tentative diagnoses that can later be revised if additional evidence is introduced.

Figure 6 shows a modified ART 1 network for detecting ambiguity. This network includes an additional field F2' of category nodes which has a one-to-one relationship with F_2. There are *two* vigilance-related channels as in Figure 5, with different gains r_{max} and r_{min}, $r_{max} > r_{min}$. If a category is searched and Equation (1) holds with $r = r_{max}$, the input is classified in that category as before. But if

$$r_{min} < ([X]/[I]) < r_{max} \qquad (2)$$

the search continues via reset, but the F_2· node for that category is activated. Hence if (2) is satisfied for then more than one node, more than one F_2· node has suprathreshold activity. Now if all nodes of F_2· connect to another node B, whose threshold is such that it is activated by two or more F_2· nodes but not by one F_2· node alone, then B serves as an "ambiguity detector".

The two vigilances embodied in Figure 6 can be seen as criteria for "certain match" and for "possible match". If one or more categories are possible but not certain matches for a given input, a tentative classification is made using the best match, but the reset node is not inhibited; hence, top-down weights are not updated. Thus tentative classifications, unlike certain ones, do not cause a shift in category prototypes, and hence do not affect classifications of future inputs.

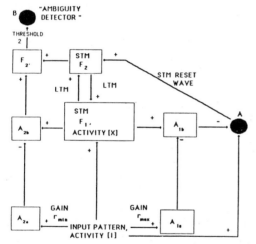

Figure 6. Ambiguity detection architecture. A_{1a} and A_{1b} nodes as in Figure 5, associated with the vigilance r_{max} which determines stable category choices, have analogs A_{2a} and A_{2b} associated with a smaller vigilance r_{min}. If the ratio of F_1 activity to input activity is above r_{min}, the corresponding F_2· node is activated. The ambiguity detector is excited if two or more F_2· nodes are active at once.

REFERENCES

Amari, S. 1971. "Characteristics of randomly connected threshold element networks and network systems." *Proceedings of the IEEE* 59: 35-47.

Anderson, J. A. and G. L. Murphy. 1986. "Psychological concepts in a parallel system." *Physica D* 22: 318-336.

Carpenter, G. A. and S. Grossberg. 1987a. "A massively parallel architecture for a self-organizing neural pattern recognition machine." *Computer Vision, Graphics, and Image Processing* 37: 54-115.

Carpenter, G. A. and S. Grossberg. 1987b. "ART 2: Self-organization of stable category recognition codes for analog input patterns." *Applied Optics* 26: 4919-4930.

Cohen, M. A. and S. Grossberg. 1983. "Absolute stability of global pattern formation and parallel memory storage by competitive neural networks." *IEEE Transactions on Systems, Man, and Cybernetics* SMC-13: 815-826.

Cohen, M. A. and S. Grossberg. 1987. "Masking fields: A massively parallel architecture for learning, recognizing, and predicting multiple groupings of patterned data." *Applied Optics* 26: 1866-1891.

Edelman, G., *Neural Darwinism*. 1987. Basic Books, New York.

Fuster, J., *The Prefrontal Cortex*. 1980. Raven, New York.

Grossberg, S., 1973. "Contour enhancement, short term memory, and constancies in reverberating neural networks." *Studies in Applied Mathematics* 52: 213-257.

Grossberg, S., *Studies in Mind and Brain.* 1982. Reidel, Boston.

Grossberg, S., *The Adaptive Brain, Vols. I and II.* 1987. Elsevier, New York.

Grossberg, S. and D. S. Levine. "Some developmental and attentional biases in the contrast enhancement and short-term memory of recurrent neural networks." *Journal of Theoretical Biology* 53: 341-380.

Leven, S. J. and D. S. Levine. 1987. "Effects of reinforcement on knowledge retrieval and evaluation." In *Proceedings of the First International Conference on Neural Networks.* IEEE/ICNN, San Diego, Vol. II, 269-277.

Levine, D. S.. 1983. "Neural population modeling and psychology: A review." *Mathematical Biosciences* 66: 1-86.

Levine, D. S. 1986. "A neural network theory of frontal lobe function." In *Proceedings of the Eighth Annual Conference of the Cognitive Science Society.* Erlbaum, Hillsdale, N.J., 716-727.

Levine, D. S. and Prueitt, P. S. 1989. "Modeling some effects of frontal lobe damage: novelty and perseveration." To appear in *Neural Networks*, Volume 2.

Malsburg, C. von der. 1973. "Self-organization of orientation sensitive cells in the striate cortex." *Kybernetik* 14: 85-100.

Milner, B. 1964. "Some effects of frontal lobectomy in man." In *The Frontal Granular Cortex and Behavior*, J. Warren and K. Akert, eds. McGraw-Hill, New York.

Mishkin, M.; B. Malamut; and J. Bachevalier. 1984. "Memories and habits: Two neural systems." In *Neurobiology of Learning and Memory*, G. Lynch, J. McGaugh, and N. Weinberger, eds. Guilford, New York.

Nauta, W. J. H. 1971. "The problem of the frontal lobe: A reinterpretation." *Journal of Psychiatric Research* 8: 167-187.

Rumelhart, D. E. and D. Zipser. 1985. "Feature discovery by competitive learning." *Cognitive Science* 9: 75-112.

Rumelhart, D. E.; G. E. Hinton; and R. J. Williams. 1986. "Learning internal representations by back propagation." In *Parallel Distributed Processing*, D. E. Rumelhart, J. L. McClelland, and the PDP Research Group. MIT Press, Cambridge, Mass.

APPENDIX: EXAMPLES OF ART NETWORK EQUATIONS

We will now describe two examples of the types of equations utilized in this work. These examples are from the ART 1 network (Carpenter and Grossberg 1987a) and from the network used to model Milner's card sorting data (Leven and Levine 1987).

In ART 1, the STM activity of the i th F_1 node is labelled x_i and the STM activity of the j th F_2 node x_j. The convention that the subscript "i" relates to F_1 and "j" to F_2 is observed; bottom-up LTM strengths (synaptic weights) are labelled z_{ij} and top-down LTM strengths are labelled z_{ji}.

STM traces at F_1 change quickly under the influence of shunting (multiplicative) excitation from outside inputs and from top-down signals, and shunting inhibition from F_2 (mediated by one of the gain control nodes, the dark circles in Figure 1). Hence

$$\epsilon dx_i/dt = -x_i+(1-A_1x_1)(I_1+D_1\Sigma_j f(x_j)z_{ji})$$
$$-(B_1+C_1x_1)\Sigma_j f(x_j) \quad (3),$$

where ϵ is small (.05 or .1). The function f of (3) is defined by f = 1 if node j of F_2 is active and 0 if node j is inactive. Only one F_2 node is active at a time. After an input comes in, the j th F_2 node receives a bottom-up signal equal to $T_j = D_2 \Sigma_i h(x_1)z_{ij}$, where D_2 is a positive constant and h is the Heaviside step function. The category chosen to be active (that is, to be tested for match between bottom-up and top-down patterns) is the one for which T_j is the largest.

The F_2 STM traces x_j obey the equations

$$\epsilon dx_j/dt=-x_j+(1-A_2x_j)(g(x_j)+T_j)$$
$$-(B_2+C_2x_j) \sum_{k\neq j} g(x_k) \quad (4),$$

where g is a sigmoid function. Equations (4) embody the competitive structure of an on-center off-surround field as in Figure 2.

The LTM trace of the top-down pathway from z_j to z_1 obeys the learning equation

$$dz_{ji}/dt = f(x_j) [-z_{ji}+ h(x_1)] \quad (5).$$

The bottom-up pathway obeys an equation like (5) except that the decay term embodies the Weber Law Rule, a rule designed to prevent access to a category by supersets of the category prototype. This is achieved by reducing signals from input patterns that activate large numbers of F_1 nodes. The design uses competition between LTM traces, resulting in equations of the form

$$dz_{ij}/dt = Kf(x_j) [-E_{ij}z_{ij} + h(x_1)] \quad (6),$$

where $E_{ij} = h(x_1) + L \sum_{k\neq i} h(x_k)$ with L<1.

Equations (5) and (6) guarantee that learning only takes place at synapses to and from active category nodes.

The ART 2 equations, which will not be described here in detail, also involve shunting excitation and inhibition in the manner of equations (3) and (4). Shunting terms in the F_1 STM equations reflect influences of the six sets of input processing nodes shown in Figure 3, designed to suppress noise in analog patterns. The LTM laws are simpler than in ART 1 because supersets are no longer an issue, since patterns consist of continuous values rather than 1's and 0's. Hence the Weber Law Rule is not needed and top-down and bottom-up LTM equations are the same.

The equations for the card-sorting model use a modified ART where synaptic weights are fixed but synaptic signals are gated by attentional biases. The inputs are cards which display one of four numbers (1, 2, 3, or 4) of one of four shapes (triangle, star, cross, or circle) in one of four colors (red, green, yellow, or blue). Hence F_1 contains twelve feature nodes, four each for color, shape, and number, and inputs are binary patterns that activate three feature nodes. The four template cards (one red triangle, two green stars, three yellow crosses, and four blue circles) provided by the experimenter each determine a category encoded at F_2.

The STM traces x_i of the features and x_j of the categories obey the equations

$$dx_i/dt = -Ax_i + (B-Cx_i)(\Sigma_j f(x_j)z_{ji}+I_i)$$
$$-Dx_i\Sigma_j f(x_j), \quad i=1, \ldots ,12, \text{ and}$$

$$dx_j/dt = -Ax_j + (B-Cx_j)(\Sigma_i g(\Omega_r x_i)z_{ij})$$
$$-Dx_j \Sigma_{k \neq j} f(x_k)-I, \quad j=1,2,3,4,$$

where f and g are sigmoid functions; Ω_r are bias node activities (r=1 if the i th feature node codes a number, 2 if it codes a color, and 3 if it codes a shape); k represents category node indices other than j, and I is

an inhibitory signal occurring with any input, designed to suppress the memory of the previous input. Bias and habit node activities obey similar equations, not shown here. The color habit node, say, is activated when the subject (rightly or wrongly) matches the input card to the template card of the same color. The reinforcement signal equals $+\alpha$ or $-\alpha$, with α high in normal subjects and low in frontally damaged ones. The z_{ij} and z_{ji} are fixed at values that are high if feature i appears in template card j, and low otherwise.

In Milner's experiment, 128 trials were run on a random input card sequence. At first, choices based on color were rewarded. Then, after the subject had achieved ten correct responses in a row to color, the criterion was switched without warning to shape. After ten shape responses in a row, the criterion was switched to number, then back to color, back to shape, and so forth. Subjects with dorsal frontal lesions tended never to achieve a stable shape response once color had been established, whereas normal subjects averaged achieving ten correct responses in a row 4 to 5 times.

The explanation of these data in the network of Figure 4 is that with frontal damage, reinforcement signals affect the bias nodes too weakly to overcome the effect of the color habit node once color responses are established. This creates positive feedback whereby color bias gates the F_1-to-F_2 signals, reinforcing the color choices and thus the excitatory effect of the color habit node on the color bias node.

Simulation and AI, 1989
©1989 by the Society for Computer
Simulation International
ISBN 0-911801-44-8

Decomposition of neural network models of robot dynamics: a feasability study

Danilo F. Bassi
George A. Bekey
Computer Science Department
University of Southern California
Los Angeles, California 90089-0782

Abstract

This paper presents a connectionist approach to robot control. In contrast with conventional methods which require the inversion of the robot dynamic equations, in this approach neural networks are trained in order to learn the complete and complex inverse dynamics of the robot, without explicitly solving the equations. The inverse dynamics is represented by simpler functions into which the torque dependence on cartesian acceleration, the joint acceleration-torque correspondence and the velocity-torque correspondence are learned separately, using separate neural networks, each of which requires many fewer training points. After training, the separate networks are recomposed to obtain the solution to the original problem. This approach make possible learning of complete inverse dynamic using several orders of magnitude number of samples less that it would be needed by naive a straight-forward approach. The results show a major reduction in the required number of training points, thus making possible the application of neural networks for learning the dynamic control of a complex, nonlinear system, like a typical six-degrees-of-freedom manipulator. Possible application of the decomposition methods to other problems is discussed in the concluding section of the paper.

1 Introduction

Trajectory control of robotic manipulators has traditionally consisted of following preprogrammed sequences of movement. In order to take full advantage of the inherent flexibility and versatility of these manipulators, there is a need of a correspondingly more flexible and robust control schemes than those used in the past. The difficulty arises from the fact that control is applied at the joints of the robot, while the desired trajectory is specified at its end effector. Thus, control requires the solution of the inverse dynamics problem for a complex, nonlinear system in real time. There have been several approaches to solve this problem, using adaptive control paradigm to find optimal motor command. Nevertheless those approaches, even though they can find an adequate solution, requires large real-time powerful computational resources, owing to inherent mathematical complexity of a complete and detailed model necessary to describe faithfully the dynamical behavior of robotic manipulators (Craig 1986, chp. 8).

Connectionist approach may solve this problem since neural networks can be incrementally trained to learn different relations between variables regardless of their analytical dependency (Rumelhart *et al* 1986). Furthermore, this learning can naturally be enhanced by the associativity and generalization properties of the neural networks. Thus it is not needed to train the system in every possible pattern, a highly desirable property given the potentially large number of distinguishable motor command patterns. In the literature several different distributed architectures can be found to solve this problem statically (Albus 1975; Kuperstein 1987; Josin *et al* 1988; Guez & Ahmad 1988; Elsley 1988), by repeatedly presenting different inputs and desired goals to the neural network. Solutions to the problem of learning control commands in dynamic case, have also been proposed, but they require knwoledge of complex models of the system, and corresponding processing units (Kawato *et al* 1987a,b). However a naive straight-forward connectionist approach for dynamic learning is unpractical due to very large size of input and output spaces. The *functional decomposition* approach allows for practical learning of dynamical control by taking advantage of natural constraints present therewith.

2 Statement of the Problem

The robotic manipulator can be described, mechanically, as an open-loop kinematic chain with programmed movement and controlled by a computer system whose objective is perform desired manipulations with elements presents in its reachable space, so-called work-space. Usually the manipulator performs tasks described in external or global goal frames. But it must ultimately be controlled in its internal, or joint space where lie the actuators. So the system must know the relation between joints coordinates and global or external coordinates (cartesian). Furthermore, usually the movement is specified in terms of goal or final position, and since a manipulator is a dynamic system, a path has to be found in the state space. Since the input to the actuators or motor is usually torque, then it requires the use of dynamic control theory techniques find the appropriate inputs.

The most widely used technique in control is the feedback PID (proportional, integral and derivative) controller, which is adequate in systems with one control variable and with fixed parameters. However in articulated manipulator, its variable geometry implies variable plant parameters and coupling between joints, resulting on PID solutions that are approximative at best and cannot give good performance in the whole space or with higher velocities. A given set of controller gains will be suitable only in a limited region of the space. A suitable approach would be one using adaptive control techniques that gives the optimal solution for different configurations. Since most of parameters may be unknown, a technique that use online learning on the actual system may be well-suited in this case.

Two of the main problems addressed here that should be solved in order to control a robotic manipulator are:

- **Kinematics**: *Given a position vector in the joint space* *find its correspondent position vector in cartesian goal-space.*

- **Dynamics Control**: *Given the state of the manipulator, a path and its derivatives find an actuator torque vector such as the manipulator follow the desired path.*

3 Connectionist Control Learning

The objective of control is to provide the adequate signal to a system in order to obtain the desired response. As indicated above, the common PID controller is well-suited to control a dynamic plant with stationary parameters. But in case of robotic manipulator we have two problems: one is that the dynamic parameters depends on configuration of the robot, the other is the coupling between the variables. Also the complexity of a detailed model in which most of the parameters are unknown makes it impractical to use the complete analytical model. Some kind of learning is required to identify the parameters. A neural network is well-suited in this case because it can handle complex input-output relationships without detailed analytical models, has associative processing, and has learning capability. In comparison, even though traditional analytical approches using adaptive control techniques have achieved good results, they involve high real-time computational power. Since the connectionist approach has the capability to find complex relationship without requiring calculations of model equations, it has the potential of providing a very fast response.

3.1 Previous connectionist approaches

One of the earliest connectionist approaches to robot control is Albus' "Cerebellar Model Articulation Controller" (CMAC 1975). This method uses a three-layer network, the first set of connections being random, and the other one made up of adjustable weights. As stated this model has no apriori knowledge of the structure of the system, and thus can be trained for any kind of system, as long as there are enough units and random connections.

Kuperstein presents (1987) an aproach which incorporates a three-dimensional visual feedback closing the control loop and uses no a priori knowledge of the structure of the system. The architecture of the network consists of an input layer, fed by a stereo pair camera, and connected to three arrays which convert those visual inputs into distributions. The outputs of distributions are connected to a target map which has adjustable weights. The strategy used to trained the network, called the *sensory-motor circular reaction* (Grossberg & Kuperstein 1986). permets to form a spatial representation based upon signals used to orient and move in that space. In other words, given a certain output activity, it is correlated to the sensory pattern that it produces. With this approach, during the training phase, the manipulator receive random patterns of activation, and moves accordingly. At the same time the network receives the visual activation corresponding to the end of the arm and determines an activation pattern, which is compared to the actual pattern. The error so found gives a criterion to adjust the weights. In this case it is used the Hebb's rule (Rumelhart *et al* 1986), which states that the modification of the weights is proportional to the error and the corresponding input. Using this connectionist approach the system learns from the visual feedback the activation motor patterns in order to move to the desired goal.

3.2 Previous connectionist dynamic solution

One complete structured hierarchical model is presented by Kawato *et al* (1987a,b) as an integral solution to this problem. In there, based in biological evidence, the model tries to find the inverse dynamics of the system in order to find the control. The justification is that in biological system the propioceptive feedback is too slow to make an stable feedback loop, in case of rapid (ballistic) movements. The only way to make that control is through a feed-forward model. the feedback is also used though, but mainly to learn. Kawato's model neural structure is nevertheless simple, consisting in only one layer of modifiable weights and a a complete layer of dynamic subsystems composed by an array of non-linear filters, whose components are found in the developed form of the inverse dynamic of the manipulator. In general this approach will require to "guess" or find the kind of function that a inverse dynamic might have. The performance obtained is good, but the system uses a large number of non-linear combination of transcendental function of robotics parameters and its variables, thus it needs a great amount of computational power. Other drawback is that it requires an adequate set of nonlinear subsystems dependent on the particular structure of the robot.

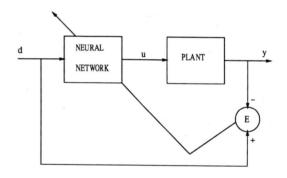

Figure 1: Specialized Learning Architecture

3.3 Dynamic Learning Strategies

Psaltis *et al* (1987) present several architectures of neural networks learning controllers. One particularly well suited to use with a robotic manipulator is the so-called *specialized learning architecture* (fig.1) wherein the neural network is placed at the input of the controlled system, acting as a *feedforward* filter.

In this case the training of the system is based on comparing the desired response with the response produced by the controller. The goal is to achieve zero error for all given input. The main advantage of this method is that it can be used for on-line training, thus leading to a real-time adaption, in the sense that it tracks any variation of the controlled system. But this advantage is effective only if the network has been trained near the operating point of the system, since a random network might not provide a "controlled" set of inputs to train the system. So it is suggested that the network first be trained off-line using the *generalized learning architecture* (Fig.2). Once it converges, it can be put in the feedforward path of the control and thereafter continue adapting to the changes of the system.

Another difficulty that arises is that the widely used back propagation error method cannot be used directly since the error is presented at the output of the controlled system, and not at the output of the neural network. The proposed solution by Psaltis *et al* (1987) is to have the errors propagated through the plant, as if it were an additional, though unmodifiable layer. In this case the error is propagated back using the partial derivatives of the plant outputs with respect to the inputs at the current operating point. Therefore, this method requires some plant parameter identification at the operating points.

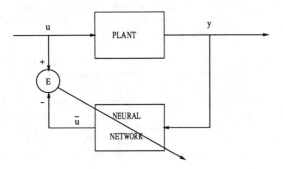

Figure 2: Generalized Learning Architecture

3.4 Robotic Dynamic Learning

We have used simulation to learn kinematic correspondence in a simple articulated manipulator with two degrees-of-freedom (fig. 3). This is one of the simplest manipulators that we could find, but it is relevant by the fact that it presents all the complexities of a generalized manipulator, including non-linearity and coupling . The direct kinematic equations for a two d.o.f planar manipulator are:

$$x = l_1 \cos \theta_1 + l_2 \cos(\theta_1 + \theta_2) \tag{1}$$

$$y = l_1 \sin \theta_1 + l_2 \sin(\theta_1 + \theta_2) \tag{2}$$

where x, y are the cartesian coordinates of the tip of the arm θ_1, θ_2 are the joint angles and l_1, l_2 are the lengths of the links.

In this case the neural network used to find the function above consists of three layers of units, one for input, one for output and one hidden. The hidden layer uses logistic unit (whose function is the sigmoid $f(x) = \tanh(x)$). The output layer uses linear units, since we are looking for a continuous output, not limited to ± 1. Using the back propagation error method, all weights can be used in the learning procedure. It remains to be seen whether this approach is convenient to learn kinematics with higher dimensional spaces and how can it be scaled up. The complete dynamics of a general manipulator is fairly complex. We shall again analyze a simple two d.o.f. jointed planar manipulator. The equations of the dynamic torque (without friction nor gravity and with mass concentrated at the tips of the links) are (Craig 1986):

$$\tau_1 = m_2 l_2^2(\ddot{\theta}_1 + \ddot{\theta}_2) + m_2 l_1 l_2 c_2(2\ddot{\theta}_1 + \ddot{\theta}_2) + (m_1 + m_2)l_2^2\ddot{\theta}_1$$

$$- m_2 l_1 l_2 s_2 \dot{\theta}_2^2 - 2m_2 l_1 l_2 s_2 \dot{\theta}_1 \dot{\theta}_2 \tag{3}$$

$$\tau_2 = m_2 l_1 l_2 c_2 \ddot{\theta}_1 + m_2 l_1 l_2 s_2 \dot{\theta}_2^2 + m_2 l_2^2(\ddot{\theta}_1 + \ddot{\theta}_2) \tag{4}$$

where $c_2 = \cos \theta_2, s_2 = \sin \theta_2$, and m_1 and m_2 are the masses of the respective links.

These equations express the torque at the actuator in order to satisfy the given position, velocity and acceleration vector. Thus, these equations give us the required feedforward function to control the manipulator. However usually the desired trajectory is given in cartesian goal-frame coordinates. Thus we need to transform the path acceleration into joint accelerations which can be fed to these feedforward functions. This transformation can be readily derived from the kinematics equations, the velocity vector being:

$$\dot{X} = J(\Theta)\dot{\Theta} \tag{5}$$

and differenciating over the time, the acceleration vector:

$$\ddot{X} = \dot{J}(\Theta)\dot{\Theta} + J(\Theta)\ddot{\Theta} = [H(\Theta)\dot{\Theta}]\dot{\Theta} + J(\Theta)\ddot{\Theta} \tag{6}$$

where X is the position vector in cartesian (goal) coordinates, Θ is the vector of joint coordinates, $J(\Theta) = [\frac{\partial x_i}{\partial \theta_j}]$ is the *jacobian* of manipulator and $H(\Theta) = [\frac{\partial^2 x_i}{\partial \theta_j \partial \theta_k}]$ is the *hessian*. It can be seen that these matrices relate the acceleration between the two spaces, one giveing the linear dependency and the other the quadratic dependency. We need also the general dynamic equation expressed in the joint space (here we do not consider gravity):

$$\tau = M(\Theta)\ddot{\Theta} + V(\Theta, \dot{\Theta}) \tag{7}$$

where $M(\Theta)$ is the generalized mass matrix and $V(\Theta, \dot{\Theta})$ represents the centripetal and coriolis torques. The solution to the problem of finding the torque vector in such a way as to follow any path given in cartesian external coordinates can be derived from above formulae by substituting the joint acceleration $\ddot{\Theta}$ from eq. (6) into (7):

$$\tau(\Theta, \dot{\Theta}, \ddot{X}) = M(\Theta)J^{-1}(\Theta)[\ddot{X} - [H(\Theta)\dot{\Theta}]\dot{\Theta}] + V(\Theta, \dot{\Theta}) \tag{8}$$

This equation tells us that given any state $(\Theta, \dot{\Theta})$ of the manipulator and a desired path X (in goal space), the required actuator torque can be calculated (computed torque). It is evident that this equation is very complex, even for the simplest jointed manipulator. Our approach is based on using the generalized learning architecture and a convenient neural network to learn the above function (Rumelhart *et al* 1986).

The other problem, seldom addressed,concerns the temporal or dynamic behavior of the connectionist controllers. In many problems, like robotics, the behavior of the system depends heavily on its state, which cannot be controlled directly. For example in the robotic arm, the input torque can only affect the derivatives of the velocity or position. Therefore, the neural network alone cannot control a dynamic system without some special unit that gives derivatives or time delays. In this case, supposing that we have the position, we need the second derivative (acceleration) or, alternately, two time delays (using a discrete-time dynamic model instead). Also we need to know the state of the system $(\Theta, \dot{\Theta})$, that could be measured or identified by some network. We propose the following structure, using the aforementioned specialized learning architecture and some dynamic building blocks (derivatives) (Fig. 4).

We have tried to train a network using the dynamic equation of the robot ($\tau(\Theta, \dot{\Theta}, \ddot{X})$) but we have found some practical problems related to the size of the sample training space. If we require, for example, only ten samples in each dimension, then for a simple two d.o.f. system we shall need 10^6 sample points, a clearly unrealistic solution. This kind of problem also arises in Kuperstein's approach, which needs to visit the whole space in order to learn to move the robot arm to a desired location. In this (dynamic) case this dimensional explosion is exacerbated by the fact that the dynamic equation depend explicitly on the state variables. A practical solution is one that reduces significantly the number of samples needed to learn the complete relationship.

4 Functional Decomposition

The solution proposed here, that is derived from the form of the dynamic equation itself, uses the principle of *functional decomposition*. The idea behind it is quite simple: to decompose and train on simpler relations and then recompose. In the general dynamic equation of the manipulator we find that although the torque depends on everynthing, its terms are decomposable into components which have simpler relationships between them. Specifically, the actuator torque is the sum of the transformed cartesian acceleration minus the second order acceleration and the coriolis and centripetal torque (see eq. 8). Thus we can use a network that will find the coriolis and centripetal terms if the acceleration is kept at zero. Another network could find the second order acceleration term, and yet another one could find the relationship between the torque and cartesian acceleration (with velocities near zero). Then we can recompose the former networks and get the original dynamic function.

Clearly this is an approach that can work in every kind of manipulator, since we are using a general formulation structure. The advantages are twofold: first, we get a more manageable set of data, requiring far fewer samples than the original approach; secondly, the networks themselves are simpler, thus the convergence is enhanced. This approach takes advantage of both connectionist and structural methods, being capable of more generalization than Kawato's (1987a,b), owing to its connectionist structure but, at the same time it is more efficient than a flat, un-structured pure connectionist approach, such as

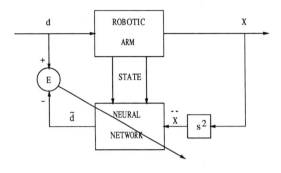

Figure 4: Dynamic Learning

Kuperstein's (1987). It takes advantage of *natural* structure present in *every* dynamic model of a robotic arm. With this approach we get a generalized learning algorithm not restricted to a particular class of arm.

For robotic motion learning we need to train networks in the following equations:

$$\tau_x(\Theta, \ddot{X}_0) = M(\Theta)J^{-1}(\Theta)\ddot{X}_0 \qquad (9)$$

$$\tau_v(\Theta, \dot{\Theta}) = V(\Theta, \dot{\Theta}) \qquad (10)$$

$$\ddot{X}_c(\Theta, \dot{\Theta}) = -[H(\Theta)\dot{\Theta}]\dot{\Theta} \qquad (11)$$

And the actuator torque is given by:

$$\tau(\Theta, \dot{\Theta}, \ddot{X}) = \tau_x(\Theta, \ddot{X}_0 + \ddot{X}_c(\Theta, \dot{\Theta})) + \tau_v(\Theta, \dot{\Theta}) \qquad (12)$$

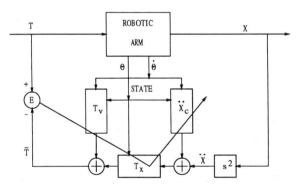

Figure 5: General Learning Architecture using Functional Decomposition

4.1 Results of Simulation

The simulation has consisted of training three different networks on the above equations using the back propagation error method (Rumelhart 1986), with data provided by a simulated 2 d.o.f. manipulator. The constants used for this simulation were the

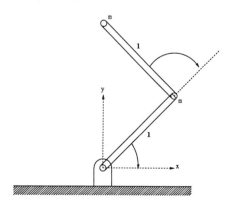

Figure 3: Two degrees-of-freedom manipulator

following: $m_1 = m_2 = 0.5$ [kg] and $l_1 = l_2 = 0.5$ [m]. The range for the arm state were: $-1 \leq \theta_i \leq 1$ [rd] and $-1 \leq \dot{\theta}_i \leq 1$ [rd.s^{-1}] and for acceleration $-1 \leq \ddot{\theta}_i \leq 1$ [rd.s^{-2}].

The neural networks consist of several layers of neural units, fully connected between them. The network structure used for the training is shown in Fig. 6. The output of each unit is:

$$o_i = \tanh(\sum_j w_{ij} i_j - \theta_i) \qquad (13)$$

where i_j are the inputs, w_{ij} are the input weights and θ_i is the threshold.

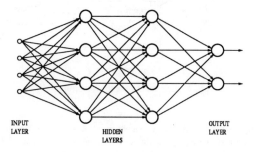

Figure 6: Structure of Neural Networks

The simulation has been carried out by changing different learning parameters as well as the number of units in each layer. In the next table are displayed the results of training:

function	configuration	patterns	η	α
$\tau_x(\Theta, \ddot{X}_0)$	4-16-8-2	75	0.01	0.95
$\tau_v(\Theta, \dot{\Theta})$	4-8-2	81	0.03	0.95
$\ddot{X}_c(\Theta, \dot{\Theta})$	4-16-8-2	81	0.01	0.90

where the configuration corresponds to number of units in each layer (input, hidden, output), η is the learning rate and α is the momentum term. The parameters were chosen after several trials. In particular, the learning rates are high but not enough to cause divergence on learning. The learning curves are shown in Figs 8, 9 and 10.

The result of learning procedures showed also that the global error decreases faster with an increase in the number of units in the hidden layers. For the torque-acceleration relationship, the r.m.s. error achieved for the torque for 75 training points was 1.6 % of full scale after 2000 sweeps. For coriolis and centripetal torque learning the error achieved was 0.04 % of full scale after 1000 sweeps with 81 training points. For cartesian acceleration vs. joint velocity the r.m.s. error was 2.8 % after 2000 sweeps with 81 training points. These results show that the training of neural networks for different parts of a complex dynamic of a manipulator is feasible. Furthermore for certain relationships this learning can proceed very fast as for coriolis and centripetal terms.

Once the networks are trained, the controller can be constructed by combining them according to the function in the torque equation (fig. 7). Further research is required to obtain a suitable method to adjust all the networks simultaneously, by on-line learning, thus allowing control while keeping track of system variations at the same time. Also this research will provide better understanding of the dynamic behavior of the interconnected network when used with manipulators with more degrees-of-freedom.

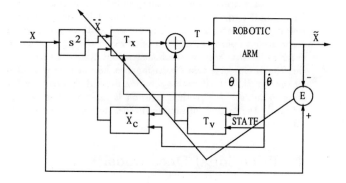

Figure 7: Functional Decomposition Robotic Controller

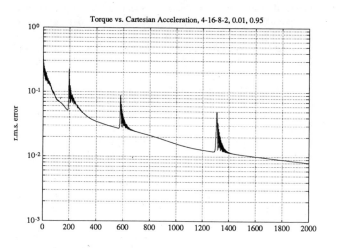

Figure 8: Learning of Torque vs. Cartesian Acceleration

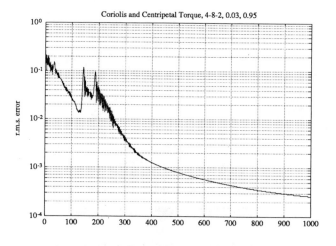

Figure 9: Learning of Coriolis and Centripetal Torque

5 Conclusions

This paper demonstrates the feasibility of decomposing the dynamics of robot manipulator in order to facilitate the application of neural network to robot control. Decomposition into natural components leads to a general approach to learning with fewer training samples. Simulation has demonstrated the validity of the method with a two degrees-of freedom manipulator.

References

[1] Albus, J.S.,"A New Approach to Manipulator Control: Cerebellar Model Articulation Controller", *Journal of Dynamic Systems, Measures and Control*, Sept. 1975.

[2] Craig, John J. *Introduction to Robotics Mechanics & Control*, Addison-Wesley Publishing Company, 1986.

[3] Elsley, Richard K., "A Learning Architecture for Control Based on Back-propagation Neural Networks", *Proceedings of IEEE International Conference on Neural Networks 1988*, Vol II, p. 587-594, San Diego, California, July 24-27.

[4] Grossberg, S. and Kuperstein, M. *Neural dynamics of adaptive sensory-motor control : Ballistic eye movements.* Amsterdam: Elsevier/North-Holland, 1986.

[5] Guez, Allon and Ahmad, Ziauddin, "Solution to the inverse problem in Robotics by Neural Networks", *Proceedings of IEEE International Conference on Neural Networks 1988*, Vol II, p. 617-624, San Diego, California, July 24-27.

[6] Josin, G.; Charney, D. and White, D., "Robot Control Using Neural Networks", *Proceedings of IEEE International Conference on Neural Networks 1988*, Vol II, p. 625-631, San Diego, California, July 24-27.

[7] Kawato, M., Furukawa, K., Suzuki, R., "A Hierarchical Neural-Network Model for Control and Learning of Voluntary Movement," *Biological Cybernetics* 56, 1987a.

[8] Kawato, Mitsuo, Uno, Y., Isobe, M., Suzuki, R., "A Hierarchical model for voluntary movement and its application to robotics", *Proceedings of IEEE First International Conference on Neural Networks*, Vol IV, p. 573-582, San Diego, California, June 21-24, 1987b.

[9] Kuperstein, Michael, "Adaptive Visual-Motor Coordination in Multijoint Robots using Parallel Architecture." *Proceedings IEEE*, 1987.

[10] Psaltis, Demetri; Sideris, Athanasios and Yamamura, Alan, "Neural Controllers", *Proceedings of IEEE First International Conference on Neural Networks*, Vol IV, p. 551-558, San Diego, California, June 21-24, 1987.

[11] Rumelhart, David E., McClelland, James L., and the PDP Research Group, *Parallel Distributed Processing*, The MIT Press, 1986.

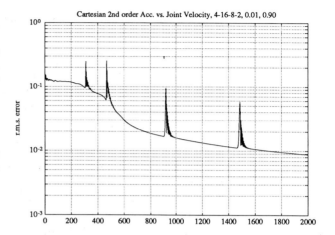

Figure 10: Learning of Cartesian Acceleration vs. Joint Velocity

ISBN 0-911801-44-8

Simulation of a neural network solution to the media selection problem

Virginia H. Clarson and James E. Shimp
ECI Division, E-Systems, Inc.
St. Petersburg, Florida

ABSTRACT

An Associative Search Network (ASN), a type of associative memory system, was trained to make the optimum media selection for a mixed-media network. The ASN employs a reinforcement technique that is a function of the environmental response to the media selected. The ASN is not aware of the "correct" choice but is rewarded or punished by the environmental response reflecting the effect of the resulting message throughput. The learning that is illustrated is called "learning with a critic." After the ASN is trained and the weights are set, a simulation of real-time media selection is performed.

A media is degraded over a time step. When the degrading baud rate approaches a predefined critical value, the ASN alerts the operator of the degradation and prompts him on the best available media. It is shown that as each media is degraded, each occurrence of the alert given by the ASN takes place at a consistent distance from the critical value.

INTRODUCTION

Interoperability between diverse networks has been identified by the DoD as a major objective for communications programs. The significance of interoperability and survivability provided by mixed-media communications has been studied extensively by ECI for the last seven years to develop advanced network and internetworking techniques to interconnect their diverse communication resources [1].

Our work with mixed-media reveals problems that require new and innovative solutions. Special techniques and protocols must be developed to achieve high mission reliability for end-to-end communications and dynamic adaptability to changing media characteristics.

As a result of internal research projects, ECI recognized that a mixed-media approach was an effective means of increasing throughput, reliability, and survivability of comunications networks. Our research led directly to the award of a major contract for a mixed-media communications network which not only used discrete media and media services, but existing networks as media. A subsequent contract utilized this research to significantly automate a world-wide survivable communications integration program which maintains connectivity on five existing networks, using them as media.

The need to automate media selection in a multi-media environment is illustrated in the following typical operating environment:

Current day media and/or media devices are complex with a large number of variables. An example media device has the following variables and options available for correct operation.

1. Bit rate - 6 options
2. Interleaver distance - 2 options
3. Stop bits - 2 options
4. Parity - 2 options
5. Modulation waveform - 3 options
6. Comm activity - 12 options
7. Operator programming - 14 parameters
8. Operator commands - 34 operational commands

The above list represents 75 variables that must be kept track of in order to effectively use this example media device. A typical multi-media environment has five different media that are available for communication at any one time. Extending the above example of variables requires an operator to keep track of 375 different variables and how they relate to the current context of message loading and network performance.

Unskilled operators will make only gross adjustments of these variables, requiring a skilled operator to make any fine adjustments. However, even a skilled operator cannot cope with the number of variables present in a multi-media environment of current day media and/or media devices.

The current techniques used for media selection require evaluation to identify existing algorithms and protocols that are no longer adequate for the more complex communications networks being designed for use in the future. Historically, media selection has been accomplished by a look-up table or complex cost function.

The look-up table approach requires that each component be examined until a match for the current environmental conditions is found. As the number of environmental variables increases, the time required for this exhaustive search may exceed the short time in which answers must be retrieved.

When a cost function is specified, real world data used to evaluate it may not be precise. This is especially true when the characteristics of the environment are not readily discernible. In addition, the weights in a complex cost function are often somewhat arbitrary. These complications imply that the best cost function solution may not be optimal.

As long as media is limited to a manageable number of communications resources, the methods discussed above provide effective, efficient results. But what happens when two or more of the larger military communications programs are required to merge and a single resource has the responsibility of controlling media selection? This implies an immense number of variables and the task of searching for the mathematical optimum of a cost function or the exhaustive search of the look-up table can be of considerable complexity and, hence, time-consuming.

The process involved in media selection can be compared to the process routinely used by the nervous system to solve perceptual problems. Each has an extensive amount of data that is continuously processed; each has only a short time in which the answer must be found. Biological studies indicate that a nervous system solves the computational power and speed dilemma, in part, with parallel processing. In addition, parallel processing provides interconnectivity and feedback necessary for a system to learn to make accurate decisions [2]. This suggests that neuron-like adaptive elements [5] can solve difficult control issues inherent in algorithm development for efficient media selection.

This paper describes the application of an associative memory structure similar to the one described by Barto et al [13], and will also be called an Associative Search Network (ASN). The network that is implemented is not told by some outside process, i.e., a "teacher," the correct pattern to associate with each input, or key. Instead, the network searches for the specific pattern that maximizes some external payoff, or reinforcement. As the learning process develops, each key results in better choices for the pattern that is correctly associated with that key. Within relatively few iterations, the weights are optimized so that each key is answered by the correct media choice.

A brief description of current media selection algorithms is presented in the next section. Section three discusses the historical development of adaptive learning using neural networks. The learning rule used to train the neural network is described in section four and the results of the simulation are analyzed in the section that follows. The conclusion summarizes the procedure and discusses future research in the expansion of the concept of mixed-media management.

MEDIA SELECTION ALGORITHMS

Typical current media selection algorithms are developed during system design time, and do not take into account variable feedback available from the media and network during operation. Media selection is made on the basis of present conditions compared against predetermined conditions, to which a selection decision has been made.

At system design time the link priority and conditions for changing the link priority are established and implemented in the media selection algorithm. The order of link priority and the number and granularity of the conditions for changing the link priority order are largely dependent on the conditions the system is most likely to experience and the complexity of the implementation of the media selection algorithm. Consider the following example:

Between two nodes, there are three media available:

Link A is robust at 32K baud,

Link B is robust at 9600 baud,

Link C is not robust at 300 baud.

The order of link priority would be link A, then link B, and finally link C.

The conditions for changing the priority order might be the absence of the highest priority link, an operator instruction to change the priority based on link performance, or a change in the robustness of individual media. The order of link priority will have been pre-determined for each of these scenarios and simply referencing a look-up table yields a correct solution.

In another example, with the same media as before, traffic is given to all of the media between two nodes all of the time to increase the reliability of delivery. All of the media are selected all of the time. Again, the algorithm is determined before the system is in operation and the advantages of feedback from the acknowledgments of the receiving node are not considered. Knowledge of this information would allow the dynamic reduction of the load on the lower speed media during real-time operation.

Dynamic evaluation of media and/or environmental feedback which results in adjustments to the load on less efficient media or adjustments in the priorities of several media will have the greatest impact when the rigidity of pre-determined solutions is replaced by an appropriate dynamic solution to the conditions. One advantage of the neural network proposed is its ability to recognize any change in the environment that would impact the present media selected. Thus, the neural network can serve as an advisor that warns that the present media selection is deteriorating and to be prepared to change the current choices. This aspect of using the neural network to detect media deterioration will be discussed in the conclusion and is an area of future research.

LEARNING IN NEURAL NETWORKS

Previous studies of neural networks as computational architectures have attempted to explore the structure of intelligent behavior, both natural and artificial [6-9]. One of the first learning rules of associative conditioning was proposed by Hebb [10]. He suggested that synaptic plasticity can be modeled by the following rule:

"Whenever cell A repeatedly activates the firing of cell B, increase cell A's efficiency in firing cell B."

This theory was expanded to include adaptive threshold elements that were used primarily as trainable pattern-classifying systems. When the elements were trained, each input pattern vector had a specified response associated with it. The relevance of the networks in this category to artificial intelligence is that they exhibit forms of problem solving, knowledge acquisition, or data storage that are difficult to achieve by more conventional methods.

The Perceptron [11] performed supervised learning pattern classification by forming linear discrimination rules to adjust a set of weights in an attempt to match their response to a desired or correct response. These networks were composed of adaptive types of elements that could only learn if the environment had a teacher that gave the correct response for each pattern in the training sequence.

The necessity of having the teacher supply the correct answer is the real disadvantage of supervised learning. In some types of problem-solving tasks, the environment that is actually affected by the decisions of the network provides assessments of the consequences of decisions made by all of the adaptive elements. Thus, the internal mechanism of the neural network is not apparent, but a "critic" judges the outcome of a series of decisions made by the adaptive elements collectively [12].

These types of networks are capable of learning to improve performance with respect to an evaluation function that assesses the consequences of the element's actions. The elements in these networks are capable of improving performance under conditions of uncertainty. This uncertainty results from the use of evaluative feedback of the performance of the entire network rather than individual elements. This is a fundamental problem that any learning system faces and is called the "credit-assignment" problem. The credit-assignment problem consists of determining which parts of a complex decision making process deserve credit for improvements in the overall performance of a system, and which deserve the blame for decrements in the overall performance. Current approaches in artificial intelligence for the most part rely on providing the critic with domain-specific knowledge.

The asynchronous binary neural network, or Hopfield associative memory [2-4], is one of the most popular models in today's research. This neural network uses extensive asynchronous parallel processing in the design of a delocalized content-addressable memory or categorizer. The individual neurons and the network itself have relatively simple structures. However, given any subpattern of sufficient size, the collective computational properties of the network model result in a content-addressable memory which correctly categorizes the pattern.

The associative memory structure described herein is patterned after those described as learning with a critic. The environmental feedback is based upon the effect that each media choice has on the total performance of the communications system. Each of the associative search elements (neurons) must discover which responses lead to improved performance. Actions resulting in improved performance when presented with certain key signals become associated with each other. The associative search gives a gradual improvement in media selection and, in relatively few iterations, consistently makes the correct choice.

DESCRIPTION OF MODEL USED FOR MEDIA SELECTION SIMULATION

Adaptive learning is a dynamic process in which the synaptic states, or weights, are driven by the stimulus environment, such that the response characteristics with respect to the same environmental conditions approach some optimizing criterion [14].

Figure 1 illustrates an Associative Search Network (ASN) which is similar to the ASN described in Barto et al. The application is initialized using three media types which will be referred to as Media 1 (M1), Media 2 (M2), and Media 3 (M3). Each of these media has an adaptive element associated with it. Each of the three adaptive elements is comprised of six weights initialized to contain the following information: the processing time required by each media and the priority each media has relative to one another. Thus, the associative matrix has been primed with information that is specific to the domain of the problem.

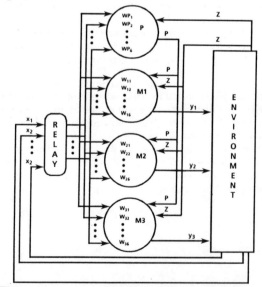

Figure 1. An Associative Search Network Solution to the Media Selection Problem Using an ASN Described in Reference 8

The key is a vector containing the following information: for each media type, an indicator of the current availability and the current baud rate. It is assumed that each medium possesses three baud rate values. See Table 1 for baud rates assigned. During the training stage the availability and baud rate values are randomly generated. The key vector is put through a relaying network which associates numerical values that indicate the set-up time delay for each media. This relaying network corresponds to transformations that take place in sensory pathways. The resulting vector received by each adaptive element in the ASN reflects availability, set-up time, and baud rate for each of the three media. Finally, the input is normalized.

Table I. Media Baud Rates (Bits per Second) Used During Training Stage

Media 1	Media 2	Media 3
4800	9600	2400
2400	4800	1200
1200	2400	600

A second type of adaptive element exists in this network. This element is one that actually predicts what the correct answer should be and is called the "predictor" element. This element has been initialized with six weights that give information on media priority and processing time much like the weights in the adaptive elements.

The inner product of the input vector and the weight vectors is found and a choice is made. (The learning rule used is described later in this section.) The output vector is then evaluated by the environment. If the output maximizes possible message throughput, the reinforcement function from the environment forces an upward adjustment of the weights that produced the firing of the element. Thus, if a certain key leads to an increased reinforcement value, it is desirable to increase the probability that that response will occur again. The predictor element also plays a role in the increase or decrease of the weight values as will be seen. The presence of the predictor is important when training a network where the keys are transitioned at every step.

In general, an ASN can consist of m identical adaptive elements, each of which determines a component of the system's actions. Each adaptive element has n real and positive input pathways x_j, $j=1,2,...,n$, one output y, one real valued reinforcement, z, and one real valued predictor, p. The predictor element learns to predict what the payoff will be for any key presented to the ASN. The predictor element has n real and positive input pathways x_j, $j=1,2,...,n$, one reinforcement pathway, z, and one output pathway, p. Figure 1 illustrates the ASN with m = 3 and n = 6.

Associated with each input pathway is a real valued weight w_{ij} with value $w_{ij}(t)$ at time t. Letting $X(t)$ and $W(t)$ denote the key and weight vectors at time t, the weighted sum $s(t)$ at time t is found by:

$$s_i(t) = \sum_{j=1}^{n} w_{ij}(t) x_j(t) + noise_i(t)$$
$$= W(t) * X(t) + noise_i(t),$$

where w_{ij} is the jth weight for media i and noise is a random variable with mean zero normal distribution. Noise for each element is independent and identically distributed.

We seek the best match between the vectors $X = (x_1,x_2,...,x_6)^t$ and the weight vectors $W_i = (w_{i1},w_{i2},...,w_{i6})^t$. Using Euclidean distance between vectors as the matching criterion, the best match with unit L can be determined by [15].

$$\| X - W_i \|_L = \min_i | X - W_i |$$

This approach is simple mathematically but it can be shown that, using this rule, convergence to optimal weights is achieved in relatively few iterations. The learning rule will then be:

$$\text{If } s(t) = \max_i \{s_i(t)\},$$

then $y_i(t) = 1$ if $s(t) = s_i(t)$,

$= 0$ otherwise.

At each time step t, the adaptive element weights change according to:

$$w_{ij}(t+1) = w_{ij}(t) + c[z(t) - p(t-1)] * [y_i(t-1) - y_i(t-2)] * x_j(t-1).$$

The weights in the predictor element are denoted wp_j, $j = 1, 2, ..., 6$ and the output at time t is:

$$p(t) = \sum_{j=1}^{6} wp_j(t) x_j(t).$$

The weights in the predictor element change according to:

$$wp_j(t+1) = wp_j(t) + cp.$$

The constants c and cp are learning constants determining the rate of learning.

The use of the predictor element in the described learning rule is important when the key presented as input at time t is different than that at time t+1. Consider the worst case situation in which the reinforcement changes for each presented key. If in the learning rule given by (1) and (2), z(t−1) replaced p(t−1), then consecutive values of z would result from evaluating different functions rather than the same function twice and comparing the results. The goal of the predictor element is to adjust its weights until z(t) = p(t−1) for all t. This element gives the best least-squares linear prediction if cp is allowed to decrease over time.

SIMULATION AND RESULTS

The learning rule described in the previous section has been implemented in a computer program. This simulation of associative memory learning has been written in C programming language. The neural network was trained with randomly selected training sets consisting of baud rate and availability for three media. Each training session was allowed to run for 1000 iterations. This was done for 20 sessions. It was observed, however, that it seldom required more than 400 key presentations in any individual session to determine the final weighting values. This consistent convergence is credited to the pre-setting of the weights. After this number of training set presentations, the neural net made the correct decision for the optimum media choice.

The capability of generalization is a highly significant attribute of neural nets. If the neurons respond correctly to input patterns that were not included in the training set, it is said that generalization has taken place [16]. Once the weights were adjusted and the neurons trained, the response of the neural network to various input patterns was tested. The results are shown graphically in Figures 2 and 3 as vectors in 3-dimensional space. Each axis represents each of the three media. The x-axis represents Media 1, the y-axis, Media 2, and the z-axis Media 3. Each of the axes show the baud rates attainable by the media. The dashed lines have been shown to accentuate the 3-dimensional concept.

Two different scenarios were considered. In the first (Figure 2), M2 (the fastest of the three attaining baud rates of 9600 bps) is allowed to degrade over a period of time. The other two media, M1 and M3, are held constant at the maximum baud rates they are assumed capable of attaining, i.e., 4800 bps and 2400 bps, respectively. At each iteration of the simulation, the baud rate of M2 decreases by 300 bps. When the rate reaches 5400 bps, the neural network alerts the operator that M2 is degrading and that M1 is becoming more favorable. An assumption in the training phase was: if M2 drops below 4800 bps and

M1 is running at 4800 bps, then choose M1. Thus, the trained ASN recognized that M2 was moving very close to the critical value of 4800 bps. What is equally important is that the neural net had the capacity to generalize since it continued to choose M2 while degrading over baud rates not used in the training set.

At first, the fact that the degrading media alarm went off so far away from the critical value, i.e., 600 bps, seemed too far away from a realistic warning value. It will be seen in the second scenario that this result is consistent.

The second test (Figure 3) of the trained neural network was to degrade M1 in decrements of 300 bps. The simulation begins with M1 robust at 4800 bps; M2 is held constant at 1000 bps; and M3, constant at 2400 bps. When M1 degrades to 3000 bps, the neural network alerts the operator that M1 is degrading and that M3 is becoming more favorable. The assumption in the training stage was: if M1 drops below 2400 bps and if M2 is also below 2400 bps and M3 is robust at 2400 bps, then choose M3. Again, the degrading media alarm goes off 600 bps prior to the critical value. The consistent warning at 600 bps appears promising and it is felt that the reason that the alarm was in each case given at this time is the coarseness of the granularity of the baud rates during training.

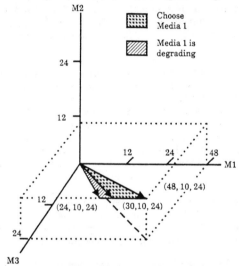

Figure 3. Graphical Representation of Scenario #2

The scope of the media selection problem has been narrowed for this study. In addition, further investigation of other learning rules could result in faster convergence to the optimum weights. However, these results indicate this is not only an innovative solution to the media selection problem, but also shows real promise for revolutionizing the entire concept of media selection. The training of the neural network would take place before any real time application to obtain optimized weights. The weights are then installed in hardware. Media conditions are checked every ten seconds (or less) and the current media choice is confirmed or changed, when necessary.

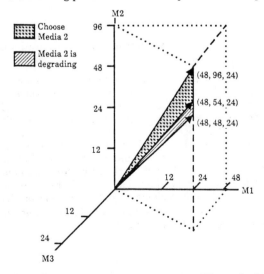

Figure 2. Graphical Representation of Scenario #1

CONCLUSION

Questions about the time required for media selection are just beginning to arise. As has been pointed out, as long as communications systems are relatively small with as few as seven interoperable networks, the present look-up table solutions should suffice. As the requirements for expansion in communications networks or combinations of existing diverse communications networks become more complex, the standard methods of media selection will become inadequate.

The neural network solution is innovative and requires further investigation. The use of neural networks as the avenue to true machine intelligence will become a major area of research of the Defense Advanced Research Projects Agency (DARPA). This supports the continued investigation of refinements to the concept of using a neural network as a monitor of current environment/media conditions. These preliminary results indicate that embedding the neural network in an expert system would result in the most effective solution to efficient media selection. The neural network would be responsible for monitoring and recognizing changes that affect the current media choice and the expert system would interact with and assist the operator in the confirmation of the best new media choice.

Neural networks are a prime technique for developing and controlling the simultaneous data streams which result from battlefield, combat information centers or other crisis management operations. Neural networks not only serve as models for multiple channel processing of critical and support information, but also serve as a gatekeeper technology as a result of the inherent adaptability of their weights and the monitoring of transfer data resulting from changing environmental demands. Neural networks are a key in the large-scale model building and simulation requirements for monitoring large real-time systems that evaluate satellite or launch vehicles. They offer the capability to not only move massive amounts of data for general monitoring and planning, but also to provide interactive linkages for decision making at many levels of a communications system.

The principal value of the expert system is to enable the operator to focus on what is important in his data stream. The expert system partitions this data into meaningful units which the operator can act upon. The expert system combined with the neural network link related incoming information to existing data bases to give the operator a feel of the scope and significance of the overall data confronting him. The combination of these artificial intelligence techniques allows him to make decisions without using data that is superfluous and of little use. Additionally, the final media selection decisions are made with the assistance of an expert with knowledge or experience in a specific situation.

ACKNOWLEDGMENTS

We would like to thank Ron Damer for his support of this research effort and Jerome Kynion for his valuable technical writing contributions.

REFERENCES

1.   R.P. Rice, E.J.Cummins, R.R. Turner, "A Mixed-Media Communications Architecture for Enhanced Interoperability", MILCOM, Vol. 2, July 1986.

2.   J.J. Hopfield, D.W. Tank, "Neural Computation of Decisions in Optimization Problems", Biol. Cybern.,Vol. 52, pp. 141-152, 1985.

3.   J.J. Hopfield, "Neural networks and physical systems with emergent collective computational abilities", Proc. Natl. Acad. Sci. , Biophysics, Vol. 79, pp. 2554-2558, April 1982.

4.   J.J. Hopfield, "Neurons with graded response have collective computational properties like those of two-state neurons", Proc. Natl. Acad. Sci., Biophysics, Vol. 81, pp. 3088-3092, May 1984.

5.   A.G. Barto, R.S. Sutton, C.W. Anderson, "Neuronlike Adaptive Elements That Can Solve Difficult Learning Control Problems", IEEE Sys., Man, Cybern., Vol. SMC-13, No. 5, pp. 834-946, Sept./Oct. 1983.

6.   F. Rosenblatt, Principles of Neurodynamics, Perceptions, and the Theory of Brain Mechanisms, Washington, DC: Spartan, 1962.

7.   N.L. Nilsson, Learning Machines, New York: McGraw-Hill, 1965.

8   J.M. Mendel, K.S. Fu, Adaptive, Learning, and Pattern Recognition Systems, New York: Academic Press, 1970.

9.   R.D. Luce, Individual Choice Behavior, New York: Wiley, 1959.

10.   D.O. Hebb, The Organization of Behavior, New York: Wiley, 1949.

11.   H.D. Block, "The Perceptron: a Model for Brain Functioning, I," , Rev. Mod. Phys., Vol. 34, pp. 123-135, Jan. 1966.

12.   B. Widrow, N.K. Gupta, S. Maitra, "Punish/Reward: Learning with a Critic in Adaptive Threshold Systems", IEEE Trans. Sys., Man, Cybern., Vol. SMC-3, No. 5, Sept. 1973.

13.   A.G. Barto, R.S. Sutton, P.S. Brouwer, "Associative Search Network: A Reinforcement Learning Associative Memory", Biol. Cybern., Vol. 40, pp. 201-211, 1981.

14.   P.W. Munro, "State-Dependent Factors Influencing Neural Plasticity: A Partial Account of the Critical Period", Parallel Distributed Processing, J. McClelland, D. Rumelhart, Eds., London: MIT Press, 1987.

15.   T. Kohonen, Self-Organization and Associative Memory, Berlin: Springer-Verlag, 1984.

16.   B. Widrow, R.G. Winter, R.A. Baxter, "Layered Neural Nets for Pattern Recognition", IEEE Trans. Acoustics, Speech, Signal Processing, Vol. 36, No. 7, pp. 1109-1118, July 1988.

Simulation and AI, 1989
©1989 by the Society for Computer
Simulation International
ISBN 0-911801-44-8

OpEM expert system controller

John R. Clymer
Department of Electrical Engineering
California State University, Fullerton
Fullerton, California 92634

ABSTRACT

Routines to make decisions in simulation programs can be complex. Programming time increases geometrically with complexity of decision routines. Communicating with non-programmers about decision routines can be difficult. An expert system allows the rule independent part of decision routines to be standardized. The amount of programming required to make decisions in simulation programs is greatly reduced. Decision rules, that are expressed in a high level language and input to the simulation in a text file, reduce programming difficulties and facilitate communication with non-programmers. Using fuzzy objects, the expert system is capable of global reasoning and adaptive behavior which is very difficult to implement using traditional programming methods.

INTRODUCTION

At certain events in the operation of a system decisions must be made. Typical decisions determine allocation of resources or choice of alternate actions. In many cases a simple algorithm may make a decision. The algorithm may be a single 'IF' statement combined with a one line calculation. As decisions become more complicated, the algorithm to evaluate the logic necessarily becomes complex. Such algorithms are difficult to write and modify.

As complexity increases, it becomes attractive to employ a formal system for evaluation of rules. One such system is an 'expert system'. Such systems generalize 'IF' statement logic in a way that can be easily modified by input of text data. Logic is data driven rather than 'hard wired' allowing changes in logic to be accomplished by modification of input text files. This is possible, of course, only for the fairly large class of decision making that fits this formal process.

A difficult task for system designers is visualization of system operation. Visualization is essential when building an operational model to experiment with alternate system operation and architectures and to evaluate design tradeoffs. In particular, it is essential in knowledge engineering when developing symbolic objects and rules needed to control and regulate a system.

Operational Evaluation Modeling (OpEM) is a system design and analysis methodology that uses a graphical parallel process language to assist a system designer in visualization of system operation. The purpose of this paper is to discuss an application of OpEM to surface ship warfare using an expert system controller to make decisions.

OPERATIONAL EVALUATION MODELING

Operational Evaluation Modeling (OpEM) is one tool in the larger field of operations research, that employs a collection of modeling and optimization techniques to analyze behavior of systems. A key feature of OpEM that facilitates explicitly defining, visualizing, understanding, and analyzing system operation is the concept of a parallel process expressed using a two-dimensional, graphical language. Some other approaches also use graphical languages. Petri nets describe processes using a graphical language. Data flow graphs describe execution of tasks serially and in parallel where data tokens are created, flow through a network, and are consumed. The SLAM and SIMNET languages describe transactions flowing through a network of queues and resources. The OpEM directed graph language represents system operation using primitives for process flow and interactions among parallel processes such as resource contention and process synchronization. The OpEM language allows a hierarchy of system and model complexity to be described. Only a subset of the language is needed to describe Markov models, and the complete language is implemented for simulation.

Systems analysis is a method of observing a situation, deciding what about it is undesirable, determining candidate solutions that could correct the undesirable aspects, identifying ramifications of each solution, and selecting the best solution. The first step is to recognize a problem exists. This usually occurs when someone in a position of authority decides things in his sphere of influence could be better. Using the systems approach, the current state of affairs is defined precisely. Some form of measurement is applied to the undesirable aspects of the situation to quantify the problem. Next, the desired state of affairs is defined and quantified using the same measures. The difference between the current and desired situation is then defined.

Operational Evaluation Modeling (OpEM) is applied to problems that can be solved by creating a system or organization. To apply OpEM it is assumed the mission, mission objectives, environment, and measures of mission effectiveness can be specified once the problem is defined.

Systems engineering is performed to create a system specification that defines what is to be built. The OpEM methodology for system design and analysis assists systems engineering and provides a structure for system specification. The tasks of systems engineering are: (1) problem definition, (2) functional analysis to understand system operation, (3) definition of alternate architectures based on present and future technology, (4) evaluation of system performance tradeoffs, (5) optimization of system cost and performance, and (6) development of the system specification.

OpEM allows an in depth evaluation of system operation without making limiting assumptions about system structure during concept formulation. The operational model is used as a language to define architectures. It provides a basis for tradeoff studies that compare alternate architectures and technologies for system implementation. The two-dimensional directed graph model describing a system allows system operation to be understood with little difficulty by non-programmers so the customer and design team members can participate in the system design. The input parameters used by the model, called mission attributes, provide the structure for system specification.

For more information about OpEM refer to (Clymer 1988).

CYBERNETIC SYSTEM CONCEPT

System Complexity

A system consists of a set of resources, a set of operations, and a set of goals. An example is a small fish (system) whose environment includes a large fish. The set of operations could be run, hide, or attack. Resources could be fins, teeth, and hiding place. Goals could be survive and protect territory.

A system contends with its environment to achieve its goals. A system must decide which operations to perform to achieve its goals under constraint of limited resources. The fish has resources to either run and hide or attack. What he decides to do depends on his conflicting goals.

Much of the complexity encountered in analysis and design of systems results from the goals. The system goals are often conflicting with many interacting rules for making decisions. Routines to make these decisions in simulation programs are then also complex. Programming time increases geometrically with complexity of decision routines. Communicating with non-programmers about decision routines can be difficult. An expert system allows the rule independent part of decision routines to be standardized. The amount of programming required to make decisions in simulations of systems is greatly reduced. Rules are expressed in a high level language that reduces programming difficulties and facilitates communication with non-programmers.

Rule Based Expert System

An expert system written in Pascal has been modified to interface with OpEM simulation programs. Object oriented simulation routines Send_MSG_to_Object and Read_Object allow symbolic objects to be created and manipulated by the simulation program. A hierarchy of objects can be specified. An object can be associated with a process duplicate, all duplicates of a process, or all processes (the system). Process duplicates allow several entities having the same operations to be modeled using the same code. The inference procedure can pursue goals that relate to objects at any level of this hierarchy.

The controller routine interfaces the expert system with a simulation program. It allows the decision with the highest confidence factor to be executed. If global control has been specified, the controller returns its decision for a goal but does not

execute any associated simulation events to implement the decision. The simulation program can pursue a set of goals and implement the global decision that has highest confidence for the set.

Figure 1 shows a simple rule tree to assign a resource. The goal object to be pursued is Allocate_Res that can be given a value of either 'yes' or 'no'. Two rules are shown that connect knowledge base objects Tgt_Needs_Res and Tgt_Priority to the goal object. If the value of Tgt_Needs_Res is 'Yes' and the value of Tgt_Priority is 'High', the rule on the left side of the figure fires and the goal object is given the value 'yes'. If the value of Tgt_Needs_Res is 'No' or the value of Tgt_Priority is 'Low', the rule on the right side of the figure fires and the goal object is given the value 'No'.

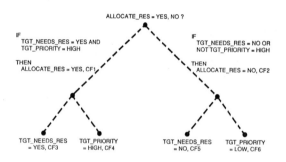

KNOWLEDGE BASE OBJECTS

FIGURE 1   SIMPLE RULE TREE

An object can have several values at a time, each with its own confidence factor. Such objects are called fuzzy. In the above rule tree, if the objects are fuzzy, both rules will conclude values for the goal object. The goal value having highest confidence is implemented. It is believed that a self organizing system can be developed that adapts object confidence factor values to optimize system effectiveness.

A more complex rule tree has intermediate rules that give values to decision objects which temporarily become part of the knowledge base as controller pursues a goal. Decision objects are inferred facts, transient knowledge base objects, that are deleted from the knowledge base after the goal object is given a value. They are deleted to avoid interfering with future consultations.

Using the OpEM Expert System Controller is simpler than conventional programming. An expert in system operation specifies rules and knowledge base objects for the scenario of interest. If no expert exists, the analyst becomes an expert by visualizing system operation assisted by an OpEM directed graph model and timeline analysis. The expert specifies events in the parallel process to be executed when each decision object is concluded with a particular value by controller. The programmer adds code to give each knowledge base object a value or values for fuzzy objects. The programmer inserts calls to controller where decisions must be made. The programmer adds code to modify the knowledge base object values to indicate results of decisions. Decision making in a surface ship warfare simulation is discussed later in this paper.

Cybernetic View of OpEM

The cybernetics view of OpEM is shown in figure 2. This view is based on cybernetic theory as discussed in (Ashby 1956, 1960). The system process is divided into three parallel processes that interact. Control and regulation of the system is accomplished using the expert system controller described above.

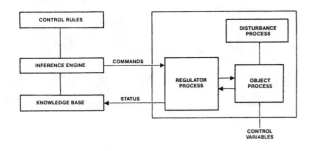

FIGURE 2 CYBERNETICS VIEW OF SYSTEM OPERATION

The disturbance process describes operation of the environment with which the system interacts. With a biological organism, the disturbance process would be operation of all predators and other dangers the organism is forced to contend with to survive.

The object process represents operation of the system. It represents all possible organism behaviors as it obtains its living and contends with predators and other dangers.

The regulator process represents decision making of the system which selects from among all possible system behaviors the action it considers potentially most effective. The regulator describes operation of the system as it performs all decision making tasks. The regulator process receives information from the object process on the status of the disturbance. The regulator considers this information and evaluates possible system behaviors in anticipation of the disturbance. When a decision is made, the regulator process directly executes an event in the object process that starts a system response.

Status information about the disturbance process and system is stored in symbolic objects by the simulation program using object oriented simulation routine Send_MSG_to_Object. Decision rules are provided as input to the model expressed in a high level language. The expert system controller is a computer program that evaluates decision rules using symbolic objects to provide current status in a way that allows implications of the rules to be considered in a decision. Controller can directly execute events in the model to implement decisions.

SURFACE SHIP WARFARE SIMULATION

The Surface Ship Warfare Simulation models attacks by air, surface, and subsurface targets against a warship such as a destroyer or cruiser. This model was developed at California State University Fullerton (CSUF) as a research tool. It is currently used by CSUF graduate students to study advanced simulation topics. Among these are the expert system controller and distributed simulation.

Ship resources for air and surface warfare are Fire Control Systems (FCS), Launchers (LNS), guns (GUN), and Close in Weapon Systems (CIWS). An FCS is required to achieve lockon and FCS track of a target. An FCS track is needed to compute missile and launcher data. A launcher is aimed to achieve the specified missile trajectory against either air or surface targets. A gun is aimed and fired at surface targets, and a CIWS is aimed and fired at air targets within its range. The number, location, and magazine size, if appropriate, are variable for each resource. The current configuration consists of FCS-2, LNS-1, GUN-1, and CIWS-2.

A parallel process is defined as the collection of all possible sequences of system states and events representing the operational behavior of a system or organization. The system states of a parallel process consist of the discrete state of each subprocess in parallel plus the current value of each state variable. The discrete states represent periods of time where either: (1) mission functions are being performed by resources or (2) the process is waiting for a specified logical condition to be satisfied before it can continue. State variables are values that identify the condition of discrete states or represent the structure of the physical system. Events mark points in time where a change of system state occurs.

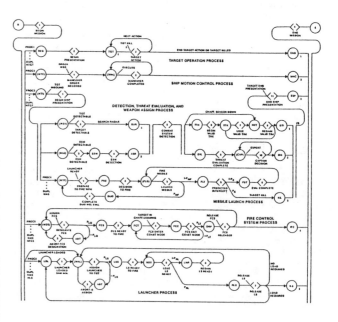

FIGURE 3 DIRECTED GRAPH OF SURFACE SHIP WARFARE

Figure 3 shows a directed graph model of air warfare processes that represents a subset of the surface ship warfare simulation. The circles represent states and the directed line segments represent events. The diagram as shown is reduced too much for detailed study; however, it can be used to obtain an overall impression of the model. The top process describes target operation as it attacks the ship. The motion of each target is described by a motion table that is an input to the model. The motion table specifies the path, speed, and actions of the target. The next process is ship motion control that allows the expert system to order ship maneuvers. The third process models detection and system track, threat evaluation, and weapon assign operations. The expert system controller is used in event E10 of that process to allocate ship resources to targets. Process four describes missile launch and flight. Processes one, three, and four are duplicated for each target in the scenario. Process five models FCS operation and process six models the launcher. These processes are duplicated for each resource in the system. Processes seven (GUN) and eight (CIWS) are not shown.

The directed graph model assists an analyst in visualizing ship operation. Figure 4 shows a timeline of ship operation for a single air target. The directed graph model describes all possible timelines. Timelines differ due to time variation of states and alternate transitions from states. An analyst needs to visualize interactions among parallel processes that degrade performance. Visualization results in insight needed to find optimal control and regulation rules.

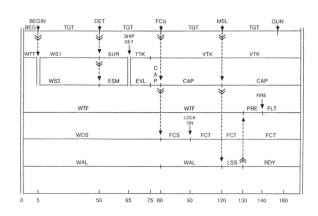

FIGURE 4 TIMELINE OF SHIP OPERATION
OUTCOME

KNOWLEDGE BASE OBJECTS

Shown in figure 1 are rules for allocating a resource. An example rule is:

```
IF
    Tgt_Needs_Res=Yes AND
    Tgt_Priority=High
THEN
    Allocate_Res=Yes, CF=95.
```

The string "Tgt_Needs_Res=Yes" is called an object-value couplet. The string on the left side of the "=" is a symbolic object name and on the right side

is a symbolic value name. Each object value couplet is a stored fact in the knowledge base.

In OpEM, processes are duplicated to model operation of similar entities. For example, in figure 3 the fire control system process models operation of an FCS. Since there are two FCSs in the ship system, two fire control system process duplicates are required. The simulation program has only one routine to model both FCS processes; therefore, the process routine requires distinct state variables and objects to describe the state of each FCS process duplicate. For FCS one, the Dupl2X duplicate value is one and, for FCS two, it is two. A duplicate value identifies state variables and objects required to describe a process duplicate.

Each object is identified by its symbolic name. For a duplicated process, objects with the same symbolic name may be required for each duplicate. Thus, duplicate process numbers (Prc, Dup1, Dup2, Dup3) are also required to identify an object. For example, each object "Tgt_Inside_FCS_Range", having legal values "yes" and "no", is associated with process three and a particular target indicated by Dup1. An object can be shared by a subset of process duplicates by setting some DupX values equal to zero. If DupX is zero, it is ignored in the search for an object. An object can be shared by all duplicates of a process if all Dups are zero. For example, the object "FCS1", having legal values "available" and "busy", is associated with process three. An object can be shared by all processes (the system) if Prc is zero.

The calling sequence of the object search routine contains elements (ProcX, Dupl1X, Dupl2X, Dupl3X). These elements specify the process duplicate under consideration, and they are compared with the object identifiers (Prc, Dup1, Dup2, Dup3) discussed above. The search routine first searches the list specified by ProcX and Dupl1X for a process duplicate level object. If the object is not found, the next list specified by ProcX and Dupl1X=0 is searched for a process level object. If the object is not found there, the final list specified by ProcX=0 and Dupl1X=0 is searched for a system level object. This search procedure allows a hierarchy of knowledge base objects to be involved in a consultation.

An object is stored as a record in dynamic memory as shown in figure 5. The routine Send_MSG_to_Object creates an object record, if it does not already exist, and stores it in a linked list. Combinations of ProcX and Dupl1X, that can be specified in the calling sequence of Send_MSG_to_Object, define a collection of linked lists that store objects. Multiple linked lists reduce search time to locate an object. The calling sequence values (ProcX, Dupl1X, Dupl2X, Dupl3X) for Send_MSG_to_Object also determine the object identifier values (Prc, Dup1, Dup2, Dup3) when an object is created.

The value of an object is stored in a record that is linked to the object record. An object value consists of a symbolic name, three real numbers, and a confidence factor that is an integer between 0 and 100. An object can be multivalued as indicated by a boolean variable in the object record. If an object is multivalued, several value records are stored in a linked list that is linked to the object record instead of one.

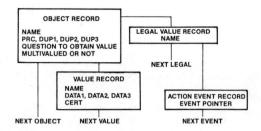

FIGURE 5 STRUCTURE OF OBJECT VALUE COUPLETS

An object has a set of allowable values. Each legal value is stored in a record that contains a legal symbolic name. The legal value records are stored in a linked list linked to the object record. The legal value list is used during a consultation if an object has no value associated with it. The expert system lists legal values and asks the user to select one. During a simulation run, a consultation occurs when the programmer forgets to give an object a value prior to calling controller to make a decision or omits a rule needed to cover a situation.

An example object has the symbolic name 'FCS1'. It is associated with all duplicates of threat evaluation and resource assignment process three. This object has legal values 'available' and 'busy'. Consider this object in the following rule.

```
IF
    Tgt_Needs_FCS=Yes AND
    FCS1=Available AND
    FCS1_Visibility=Can_See_Tgt
THEN
    Designation=FCS1, CF=100.
```

Each legal value can be associated with a list of event pointers. An event pointer provides instructions to an event routine that define how an event will be executed. An action event record consists of Proc, Evtnum, Entry, Dupl1, Dupl2, and Dupl3 numbers. The action event records for a legal value are stored on a linked list that is linked to the legal value record. Action event records associate a set of action events with an object value. An object can be given a value by the Send_MSG_to_Object routine or by controller. When an object is given a value, the set of action events associated with that value can be executed. Events are executed in the order they appear on the action event list.

For example, in the above rule if the premise is true, goal object "Designation" is given the value "FCS1". Associated with this object value is the event (5 1 0 0 1 0). When this event is executed it causes FCS one to be designated to a target. Since the Dupl1 value in the event is zero, the Dupl1X value in the controller calling sequence specifies the target assigned to FCS one.

RULE BASED EXPERT SYSTEM REVISITED

Rule Format

Figure 6 shows the rule format expressed in Backus Naur Form (BNF) notation. The format consists of RULE_NAME:IF, premise, THEN, and conclusion.

RULE_NAME:IF

{{[NOT] OBJ_NAME = OBJ_VALUE (OR)}... (AND)}...

THEN

{OBJ_NAME = OBJ_VALUE [,CF] (AND)}...

- { }... ITERATION OF STRING

- [ ] OPTIONAL STRING

- ( ) SUPPRESS ON LAST ITERATION

FIGURE 6 RULE FORMAT

A premise is a list of object-value couplets (facts) related by OR and AND as shown. A fact is evaluated true if it can be found in the knowledge base. An inverse fact has a NOT in front of it and is evaluated true if it can not be found. Several facts can be combined by the OR operation to form a composite fact. A composite fact is evaluated true if at least one comprising fact is true. The confidence factor for a composite fact is a blend of the confidence factors for its true facts. A blend of confidence factors is greater than either input and less than or equal to 100 percent. Several facts or composite facts can be combined by the AND operation to form a premise. A premise is true if all facts and composite facts are true. The confidence factor for a premise is the minimum confidence factor of composite facts or facts comprising it.

A conclusion is a list of object-value couplets related by AND as shown. If the premise is true, all objects in the conclusion are given a value. The confidence factor for a concluded object-value couplet equals the CF value specified in the conclusion times the premise confidence divided by 100. If an object has been concluded previously with the same value by another rule, new and old confidence factors are blended.

A concluded object can have several values at the same time, each with its own confidence value. A fuzzy object can have partial membership, defined by confidence factors, in several sets at the same time. It is believed that approximate reasoning can be implemented using fuzzy objects. Adaptive control and approximate reasoning are currently being studied using the expert system controller.

Rule Tree Structure

An example rule tree is shown in figure 7. The top of a rule tree is the goal object. All rules that have the goal object in their conclusion form the top branches of the tree. At each level rules connect premises to conclusions. Premises of rules contain either knowledge base objects or decision objects. Objects, other than the goal object, concluded by rules are called decision objects and are temporarily included in the knowledge base.

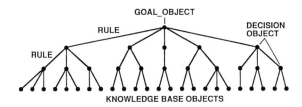

FIGURE 7   AN EXAMPLE RULE TREE

Inference Mechanism

The inference engine used by the expert system controller is based on the one described in (Sawyer and Foster 1986). It is a backward-chaining expert system that begins with a goal object. For the first step of the inference process, the engine scans the rule list for any rules with the goal as the conclusion and tests the premise within each such rule for truth.

The procedure within the program that tests the premise is appropriately called "pursue". It scans the rule list for a rule that has a conclusion that matches the premise of the previous rule or goal for the first iteration. The function that scans the rule list is called "find rule". It searches the rule list from beginning to end for any rule that contains the required object as a conclusion. The inference engine recursively pursues rules in the tree, starting at the goal and proceeding out along branches of the rule tree until a knowledge base object is reached.

As discussed above the goal and decision objects may have multiple values. The controller selects the value for the goal object that has highest confidence. All other values for the goal and decision objects are deleted. These objects are deleted to avoid interfering with subsequent consultations

Rules For Making Rules

The following rules for making rules were derived as the surface ship warfare simulation using the expert system controller was developed.

1. Decision objects in the rule base must have unique object names for each situation. The same name cannot be used for similar situations in different goal trees.

2. All decision objects must be able to be assigned a value. Rules must be included in the rule base to cover all situations. If a situation is overlooked, the expert system will stop and ask for input during a consultation. Rules can be added to the rule base as these situations are encountered.

3. Knowledge base objects must not be concluded during a consultation, but only after return from controller. As was discussed above, decision objects are fuzzy. Many rules fire, but only a few contribute to the goal value selected, having highest confidence. Further, during global reasoning many goals are pursued and compared for highest confidence. Therefore, knowledge base objects (facts) that describe the decision implemented can not be concluded until the decision is actually implemented.

4. Only one goal object can be concluded by controller at a time. One value, having highest confidence, is concluded for a goal object. However, a single goal, object-value couplet, can be associated with a list of action events to be executed.

5. Confidence factors on desirable rule conclusions are set higher than less desirable. The analyst can control decisions made in various situations by selecting rule confidence factors. This fact is the basis of adaptive control discussed in the next section.

CONCLUSION

Expert System Controller

The expert system controller is called upon to pursue a goal or goals when an event of a parallel process must make a decision. The controller has been applied in simple decisions involving a single process or process duplicate and more complex global reasoning. In global reasoning, a set of simple decisions is considered and the decision with highest confidence executed. One example of a global decision is assigning a resource to one of several competing process duplicates. Another example is deciding which task, among several conflicting tasks, should be executed next.

For a simple decision, the system state of the parallel process is provided to the expert system by the event requiring a decision. The Send_MSG_to_Object routine is called to add required information to the knowledge base. As discussed above an object is identified by its symbolic name and duplicate process numbers. The Send_MSG_to_Object routine can create an object or change the symbolic value, data values, and confidence factor of an object value. A object can have more than one value at the same time and each value has a confidence factor. Each object-value couplet is a fact in the knowledge base. For another way of looking at objects, an object can partially belong to several sets at the same time with each degree of set membership determined by a confidence factor, making it a fuzzy object.

After information is placed in the knowledge base, controller is called. Controller pursues a goal object for a process duplicate. If only a simple decision is required, the execute flag is set true and controller will execute the decision having highest confidence. Controller executes all events associated with the selected object value as discussed above. If a global decision is required, the execute flag is false and controller executes no events.

To complete a decision, the Read_Object routine obtains the value given to the goal object. For a simple decision, the Send_MSG_to_Object routine updates the knowledge base to indicate what decision was made. As discussed in the section on rules for making rules, controller can not do this. For a global decision, the confidence factors are compared and the decision with the highest confidence is implemented and knowledge base updated. To implement a global decision, the Send_MSG_to_Object routine executes events associated with the value of the goal object.

One can see that programming a decision is simplified by the expert system routines. What is the benefit of the expert system controller to improve communication with non-programmers? Using the expert system controller, control decisions are specified in terms of fuzzy objects rather than numbers. For example, take the concept of range, a distance separating two entities. Decisions in a conventional simulation are made in terms of numbers. FCS designation occurs when the target comes within a range threshold, range is less than R miles. Consider a fuzzy object Tgt_Range, having legal values "Close" and "Far". The confidence factor for "Close" is a function of range such that as the range decreases the confidence factor for "Close" increases toward 100 percent and for "Far" it decreases toward zero. A fuzzy rule would be:

IF
    Tgt_Range=Close
THEN
    Designation=FCS1, CF=X.

The decision to designate an FCS to a target depends on a symbolic concept rather than a number. Symbolic concepts are used more often by people to make decisions, thus communication about decision rules among people is improved.

Adaptive Reasoning

Some clues about how human genius performs creative thinking is found in (Briggs 1988). The basic idea is that genius seems to be able to consider a number of conflicting facts and rules at the same time. This is similar to fuzzy objects and rules discussed in this paper. For example, Albert Einstein considered a large set of facts and rules about the physical universe to develop his theory of relativity. Through his famous 'thought' experiments he found some of these facts and rules conflicting. He manipulated these conflicting facts and rules in his mind, questioning each one and modifying his belief in them until the implications made sense to him. In particular, his belief in the fact that time is absolute was greatly changed.

It is believed that a discrete event, parallel process system can do creative thinking to adapt its behavior. This can be done by modifying the confidence factor values for facts and rules in such a way that system effectiveness is optimized. From the previous discussion of rule-based expert systems, it can be seen that system operation can be adapted since rule execution is controlled by confidence factors. Experiments in modifying confidence factors have shown that decisions made can be controlled this way.

Confidence factors associated with each rule and object-value couplet (fact) can be controlled. A new function called Fuzzy_Rules is proposed to change rule confidence factors, and Send_MSG_to_Object can change object value confidence factors.

Fuzzy logic routines can assist in manipulating confidence factors. For example, a new routine Fuzzy_Objects is proposed that will compute and modify a confidence factor. This can be done given the object and value names, a state variable value like range above, and a fuzzy logic equation as input. A fuzzy logic equation is a function that relates fact confidence values to state variable values.

Much has been done in the last ten years to develop adaptive, rule-based analog controllers. It is believed that this work may also offer clues as to how to control discrete event processes.

Summary

A rule base for Anti-Air Warfare (AAW) has been developed and included in the surface ship warfare simulation to test the expert system controller routines. The rule format of the expert system was expanded to simplify expression of control rules. Rules for making rules have been formulated to aid in future applications. Sensitivity analysis of an AAW scenario has facilitated debug of these routines and resulted in confidence that they are working properly.

In the near future, research on the expert system controller will focus on fuzzy logic. Fuzzy logic routines to manipulate confidence factors will be written and tested. The expanded expert system controller will be applied to an airport scenario and flexible manufacturing systems to gain further experience with the cybernetic systems concept. The goal of this research is to learn about self organizing systems.

REFERENCES

Ashby, W. R. 1956. *An Introduction to Cybernetics*. Chapman & Hall, London, U.K.

Ashby, W. R. 1960. *Design for a Brain: The Origin of Adaptive Behavior*. Chapman & Hall, London, U.K.

Briggs, J. 1988. *Fire in the Crucible: The Alchemy of Creative Genius*. St. Martin's Press, New York.

Capra, F. 1982. *The Turning Point: Science, Society, and the Rising Culture*. Simon and Schuster, New York, N.Y.

Clymer, J. R. 1988. *Systems Analysis Using Simulation and Markov Models*. John R. Clymer and Associates Inc., Placentia, Ca., P.O. Box 747, 92670.

Kaufmann, A. 1975. *Introduction to the Theory of Fuzzy Subsets, Volume I - Fundamental Theoretical Elements*. Academic Press, New York.

Negoita, C. 1985. *Expert Systems and Fuzzy Systems*. The Benjamin /Cummings Publishing Company.

Okuma, A. 1985. "Software and 'Fuzzy' Logic Let Any Good Programmer Design an Expert System.", *Electronic Design* (Apr): 173-184.

Sawyer, B., and D. Foster,. 1986. *Programming Expert Systems in Pascal*. John Wiley & Sons.

Zadeh, L. A., 1988. "Fuzzy Logic", *Computer* (Apr).

Simulation and AI, 1989
©1989 by the Society for Computer
Simulation International
ISBN 0-911801-44-8

Object oriented models and their application in real-time expert systems

Andreas G. Hofmann, Gregory M. Stanley, Lowell B. Hawkinson

Gensym Corporation

125 CambridgePark Drive, Cambridge, MA 02140 (617)547-9606

Abstract

A principal barrier to more extensive use of model-based reasoning in expert systems is the difficulty of developing and maintaining sophisticated models. A typical way to avoid having to build models completely from scratch is to build libraries of procedures for components in some domain of application. Components and their connections are then specified and the corresponding procedures are invoked in order. Flowsheet-driven simulators for process simulation are an example of this approach (Perkins and Barton 1987).

More powerful abstraction is possible by incorporating object-oriented programming techniques from AI in the simulation algorithms. This approach has already been used extensively in discrete event simulators, but it is applicable to continuous simulation as well. The object-oriented simulator in G2 (Moore et al. 1987) is described and used to illustrate some examples. It is also shown that a real time inference engine can be readily interfaced to such a simulator if the inference engine and simulator share the same knowledge representation structures.

1.   Object-oriented Simulators

1.1   Important Features

Object-oriented simulation involves describing the behavior of classes of objects, each instance of which may consist of many subobjects and variables. This provides a layer of abstraction which allows the user to rapidly develop the simulation of a complicated system without worrying about the details of simulating the basic components. Complicated models can then be built rapidly and reliably (Moore, Stanley, and Rosenof 1988). It is important, however, to provide enough flexibility so that users can specify the behavior of individual instances. The black box approach must provide easy access into the black box if this is desired.

Object-oriented simulation combines techniques from two disciplines: simulation and artificial intelligence. Frames are commonly used in AI to represent objects and their attributes. Attributes can have various types of values and can contain subobjects, allowing for representation of systems and sub-systems. Frames can have methods which describe the behavior of the object. Frames are further organized into a class hierarchy so that classes can inherit attributes and methods from superior classes. Connections between frames can represent both physical and logical relations between objects.

The behavior of objects can be specified generically, at the class level, rather than individually for each instance. This greatly simplifies the task of specifying complicated simulations, since behavior does not have to be specified explicitly for each variable in the simulation.

Object-oriented techniques have been used primarily in discrete applications (Petty, Moshell, and Hughes 1988). Such applications typically use a data-driven approach, where procedures are scheduled in a simulation cycle based on new data and events. The procedures set values of simulation variables as side effects. Such variable updates can, in turn, be new events and can cause further scheduling of activity. This approach is analogous to forward chaining in an inference engine. Typically, only a subset of all the variables in the simulation are updated in any one cycle.

The requirements for continuous simulation are different from those in discrete simulation. Typically, all variables are updated on each simulation cycle, since it is difficult to skip steps when integrating a variable to solve a differential equation. Often, the most natural way to specify continuous systems is by a system of differential and algebraic equations, although procedures are also used for special algorithms or for efficiency reasons.

A weakness of previous equation-based simulators is that equations must be written separately for each variable in the simulation. This becomes tedious for large systems, especially if many of the variables behave in a similar way. Object-oriented techniques can be used in equation-based continuous simulation to overcome this weakness (Elmqvist 1978, 1986).

1.2 The G2 Simulator

The simulator in G2 allows for modelling a wide variety of continuous and discrete systems in an object oriented way. Objects and connections can be defined using tables, as shown in Fig. 1. Note that connections as well as objects can have attributes. This allows, for example, modelling losses through a pipe based on its characteristics and length. Attributes can be constant parameters or subobjects such as variables. The objects can be connected on a schematic to represent complicated networks.

In the G2 simulator, a generic specification of the behavior for some object (the focus object) is expressed in terms of attributes of the object class and of related (usually neighboring) objects. This specification is entered in a natural language form as shown in Fig. 2. Objects related to the focus object are designated using role phrases which specify relations such as connectivity. Thus, in Fig. 2, "the pump connected to valve-1" and "the object connected at the input to valve-1" both designate pump-1, "the pipe connected at the output to tank-1" designates pipe-7, and "the valve connected at the output end of pipe-7" designates valve-4. Port names can also be assigned to connections of objects. Thus, "the object connected at port2 of tank 1" designates valve-3 if the pipe between tank-1 and valve-3 is attached to the port named port2 in tank-1. Furthermore, it is possible to designate more than one related object as in the role phrase "each valve connected to tank-1". Attributes of objects can be designated by role phrases such as "the temperature of tank-1" or "the flow of valve-3".

References to the focus object and to related objects serve as a pattern. When applied to some focus object in the schematic, there is a match if other objects in the schematic are related to the focus object in the manner specified. The first order differential equation in Fig. 2. is an example of generic behavior specification in G2. The focus object class is "tank". Related objects are the pipes connected at the input and the pipe connected at the output. When this equation is applied to the tank in Fig. 2, the focus object is tank-1, the output pipe is pipe-7, and there are two input pipes. Note, however, that this equation could be applied to many similar instances in a larger schematic, even if there are some variations. As long as a tank has one or more input pipes and one output pipe, the pattern matches and the equation can be used to determine the level of the tank.

Behavior can be specified generically at different levels in the class hierarchy, since each class inherits generic specifications from superior classes. The equation in Fig. 2 can be applied to all instances of subclasses of tank. It is possible, however, to override this equation for any of the subclasses; a different equation could be used for water tanks, for example. It is also possible to override the generic specifications for an instance by writing equations for the instance. Instances can also be treated individually by giving them attributes that are parameters of the object and by using connections of the object to other objects.

As a result, modeling can be done in a top-down style with the most general objects being defined first. When a new class of object is added to the library, it is necessary only to focus on the differences between the new class and existing classes. This modelling by difference is fundamentally more maintainable than traditional techniques using libraries of Fortran routines.

1.3 Equation-based Simulation in G2

In G2, simulations are specified using first order differential and difference equations and algebraic equations.

During the initialization process, generic equations are combined with the schematic to produce specific equations to be executed at runtime. Pointers are kept from objects and connections in the schematic to any variables they affect, so that if the schematic is edited while the simulation is running, the affected equations can be immediately rederived.

Often the resultant set of specific equations is simultaneous and non-linear. In general, it is necessary to solve a non-linear differential-algebraic system. This could be accomplished using a Newton-Raphson method. However, this method is computationally expensive since it involves, among other things, the solution of a set of linear algebraic equations. It is therefore important to take advantage of a number of simplifying characteristics that are typical of many applications.

It is often possible to break a large system of equations into sets of smaller ones. This is because the large set often consists of smaller sets that are decoupled. It is much less expensive to solve several sets of simultaneous equations than to solve one big set. Another important characteristic is that the system of equations is often sparse. Components are usually affected only by their neighbors, resulting in a sparse Jacobian. Taking advantage of sparseness greatly reduces the time required to solve a set of simultaneous linear equations.

The Jacobian often has characteristics that allow for further simplification. Portions can usually be computed by symbolic partial differentiation. This is often more efficient and accurate than numerical differentiation. Furthermore, portions of the Jacobian are often linear or change slowly and therefore have to be computed only once or infrequently. Finally, since tables are often used to specify non-linear characteristics (pump curves for example) and since the internals of such tables are accessible in G2, it is easy to determine the partial derivative of a tabular function at some operating point.

The Newton-Raphson mechanism can also be used in implicit integration techniques which are useful for solving stiff systems of differential equations common in many applications (Petzold 1982).

Fig. 3 shows a simulation using standard control blocks such as integrators, summers, and gains. Note that these are all specified at the class level by differential and algebraic equations.

2.   Applications in Real-time Expert Systems

2.1   Interface to the Inference Engine

Interface of the G2 simulator to the inference engine is simplified by the fact that the inference engine and simulator can share the same schematic. The inference engine can access variables via the same role phrases used by the simulator. Thus, the inference engine and simulator may use the same language to designate variables. Data service from the simulator to the inference engine can be controlled by switches in variables.

The fact that G2 is intended for real time on-line applications puts additional requirements on the simulator. The simulator is often run in an interactive mode rather than a batch mode. It is therefore important to have animated displays, such as readouts and graphs, which show values while the simulator is running. It is also important to be able to edit the knowledge base while the simulator is running and observe the effects of such edits. The simulator must be not only fast,but also suspendable. It cannot consume all the computer time if there are other tasks of high priority to be executed. Finally, the inference engine should be able to control when simulations are run.

2.2   Applications

One important use of simulation in real time expert systems is to test the knowledge base before going on-line, especially in applications where the real time expert system is actually controlling the plant in a closed loop fashion rather than just monitoring data and presenting conclusions to the operator. This is especially important after changes have been made to an existing knowledge base of rules. Fault conditions as well as normal operation can be simulated. This allows for testing that is often impossible when the expert system is on-line. In G2, it is easy to switch the inference engine's data service from simulated values to live sensor data.

Fig. 4 shows a portion of a schematic and some generic rules for a liquid flow application. Note that the rules are expressed in a natural language form and use the same role phrases used in the simulator. The rules shown diagnose pump failure based on the flow sensor and the position of the valve. It is easy to simulate various kinds of pump failures. For example, the simulated pump can be turned off by setting its "manual-switch" attribute to 0. This exercises the diagnostic rules that should inform the operator that the pump has failed.

More interesting applications are possible when the simulator is run in real time in an on-line mode. In such applications, one or more simulated models of the plant being controlled are run in parallel with the plant. Each model must be kept aligned with the plant using sensor data and heuristics from the inference engine. Such a model is useful for a number of reasons. It can be used to deduce internal states of the plant which are not directly measurable by sensors. It can also be used both to check if sensors are failing (by comparing sensor data with model data), and to filter noisy sensor data.

If the model is aligned with the plant, then parameters which cannot be measured directly can be computed. Thus, drifting of these parameters can be detected and the control system adjusted accordingly. This is usually now done by human operators, but it could be done by an expert system that uses knowledge and heuristics about the plant and the control system. Such an expert system could be used as an auto-tuner, to adjust control parameters based on plant response to test inputs during an initialization or calibration period when the plant is not in normal operation. The expert system could also be used as an adaptive controller which adjusts control parameters continuously while the plant is in normal operation (Astrom 1987).

Another useful application is possible if simulations can be run faster than real time. A simulation could be run some length of time into the future to predict results based on the current state of the plant and a set of control settings and strategies. The inference engine could try several such simulations with different control strategies to explore alternatives and choose an optimal control strategy. This idea could be extended to allow for genuine state space search using AI search techniques. The inference engine would run a simulation for some length of time to generate a new branch in the search tree. The new node at the end of the branch would represent the state of the simulated plant at the end of the simulation run. The tree could be expanded in a depth first or breadth first manner and could be pruned (branches abandoned) using heuristics.

Heuristics can also determine which quantitative models are most appropriate given a current operating point. This extends the range of operation for quantitative models and control systems based on them. In general, the closer cooperation of quantitative models and heuristic knowledge embodied in rules will yield more robust and efficient control systems.

References

In a Conference Proceedings:
Astrom, K.J. (1987)
"Adaptive Feedback Control."
In Proceedings of the IEEE Vol. 75, no. 2 (Feb.)

Technical Report:
Elmqvist, H. (1978)
"A Structured Model Language for Large Continuous System."
Ph.D. Theses, Report CODEN: LUTFD2/TFRI-1015,
Department of Automatic Control, Lund Institute of Technology, Lund, Sweden

In a Conference Proceedings:
Elmqvist, H. (1986)
"A Simulator for Dynamical Systems Using Graphics and Equations for Modeling."
In Proceedings of Third Symposium on Computer-Aided
Control System Design, IEEE Control System Society

In A Conference Proceedings:
Moore, R.L., Hawkinson, L.B., Levin, M., Hofmann, A.G., Matthews, B.L., David, M.H., 1987
"Expert Systems Methodology for Real Time Process Control
In Proceedings of the 10th World Congress on Automatic Control, Volume 6

Technical Report:
Moore, R.L., Stanley, G.M., Rosenof, H., 1988
"Object Oriented Rapid Prototyping with G2."
Gensym Corp., Cambridge, MA

In A Book:
Perkins, J.D., and Barten G.W., 1987
"Modeling and Simulation in Process Control."
In Computer Aided Process Operations
G.V. Reklaitis and H.D. Spriggs eds. Elsevier

Journal:
Petty, M.D., Meshell, J.M., Erigler, C.E., 1988
"Tactical Simulation in an Object-Oriented Animated Graphics Environment"
Simuletter, Vol. 19, no. 2 (June): 31-46

In a Conference Proceedings:
Petzold, L.R. (1982)
"A Description of DASSL: A Differential/Algebraic System Solver"
In Proceedings of the 10th IMACS World Congress on System Simulation and Scientific Computation 430-432

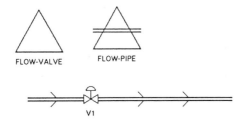

p1, a flow-pipe	
Notes	OK
Names	P1
Length	none
Thermal loss	none
Input temperature	a quantitative-variable: not activ
Output pressure	a quantitative-variable: not activ

flow-valve, an object-definition	
Notes	OK
Name of class	flow-valve
Name of superior class	throttling-valve
Attributes specific to class	flow-rate is given by a quantitative-variable; input-pressure is given by a quantitative-variable; output-pressure is given by a quantitative-variable; position is given by a quantitative-variable
Capabilities and restrictions	none

v1, a flow-valve	
Notes	OK
Names	V1
Flow rate	a quantitative-variable: not act
Input pressure	a quantitative-variable: not act
Output pressure	a quantitative-variable: not act
Position	a quantitative-variable: not act

Fig. 1 Object and Connection Definition

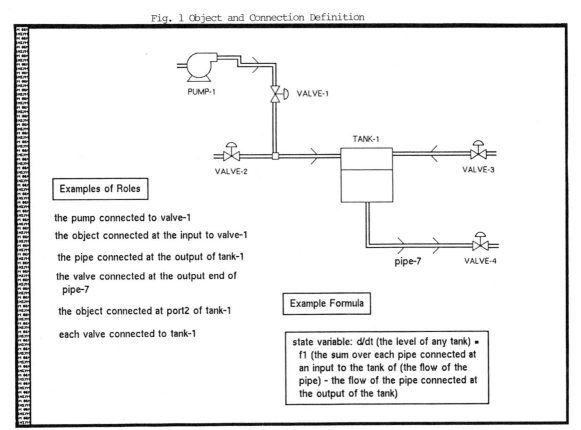

Examples of Roles

the pump connected to valve-1

the object connected at the input to valve-1

the pipe connected at the output of tank-1

the valve connected at the output end of pipe-7

the object connected at port2 of tank-1

each valve connected to tank-1

Example Formula

state variable: d/dt (the level of any tank) = f1 (the sum over each pipe connected at an input to the tank of (the flow of the pipe) - the flow of the pipe connected at the output of the tank)

Fig. 2 Designation Using Role Phrases

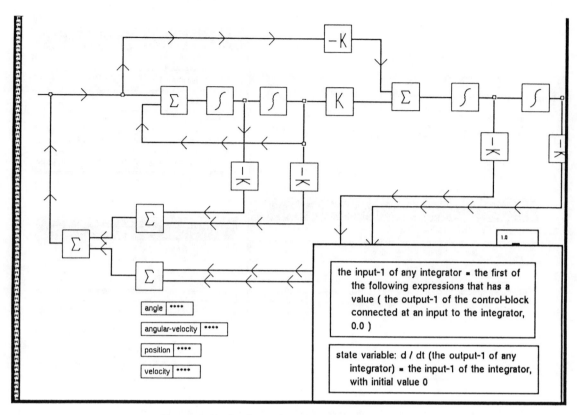

Fig. 3 A Simulation Using Control Blocks

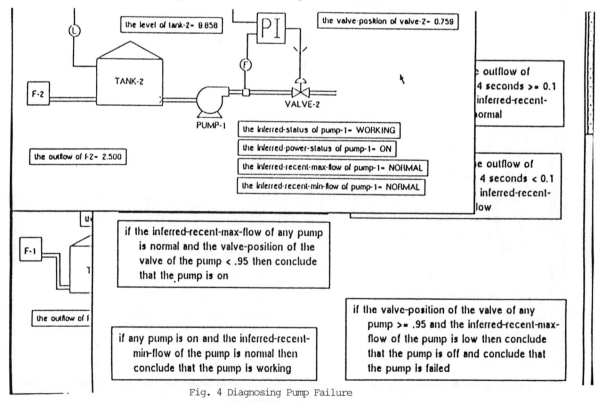

Fig. 4 Diagnosing Pump Failure

Contribution of an object-centered representation for computer aided modeling in biology

Christine PIERRET-GOLBREICH
INRIA- BP 105
78153 LE CHESNAY cedex FRANCE

ABSTRACT

Recent progress in Computer-Science, particularly in Artificial Intelligence, has led to the design of a new type of software for computer-aided modeling. The goal of this work is to make use of all the possibilities of knowledge-based systems in order to provide the biologists with a computer environment that can assist them to solve a biological modeling problem. An original aspect is the use of an object-centered knowledge representation (OCR). Knowledge is described using interdependant units called "schemes" without any other type of description unit. In particular, no rules are needed because the knowledge bases management system, Shirka [RECHENMANN 85], has its own inference mechanisms. Firstly, the reasons for this choice are presented, then their implications for the design of the knowledge-base will be given. The point developed in this paper deals more precisely with the model formulation step. Throughout, the benefits of using an object-centered representation will be stressed.

INTRODUCTION

Over recent years biologists have been becoming increasingly interested in modeling. This growth of interest is directly linked to the advances that have been made in the development of powerful computer tools. However, as biologists may well be unfamiliar with both Computer-Science and modeling, difficulties may arise when they use classical computer tools. These tools are often scattered, and despite efforts to provide integrated software, a great deal of time is often necessary to put them into operation or even to decide which of the available methods is appropriate. Moreover, although these software discharge the user from programming efforts, several important steps of the modeling process are ignored. For these reasons, the aim of the EDORA project is to develop a system which can provide original and efficient assistance for **each** step of the model's construction, from its formulation to its simulation or validation.

The analysis of dynamic systems began in the engineering sciences. The goals concerned prediction, command, or numerical control. In biology, however, the objectives are more diverse: understanding the behaviour of a biological system (cognitive aspect), anticipating a future state (prediction), controlling the behaviour in order to optimize or influence it, trying to estimate a variable that cannot be found by direct measurement (instrumental aspect), etc. [PAVE, 1987]. In most cases, the goal is explanatory or decisional, and generally concerns understanding the biological laws that govern the phenomenon under study. The biologist is not looking for precise numerical results, but is often more interested in the qualitative significance of the results obtained. As R. MAY [MAY 76] pointed out: " One broad aim in constructing mathematical models for populations of plants and animals is to understand the way different kinds of biological and physical interactions affect the dynamics of various species. In this enterprise, we are relatively uninterested in the algebraic details of any particular formula, but are instead interested in questions of the form : which factors determine the numerical magnitude of the population; which parameters determine the time scale on which it will respond to natural or man-made disturbance.... Accordingly, attention is directed to the biological significance of the various quantities in the equations, rather than the mathematical details; to do otherwise is to risk losing sight of the real world in contemplation of mathematical trees."

After a quick review of the existing tools for modeling, it will be looked at their characteristics and shown why they are not well suited to satisfy the aim purchased in biological modeling. The basic concepts of OCR and the design of the knowledge base are then presented.

COMPUTER-AIDED MODELING: THE STATE OF THE ART

Classical software in computer-aided modeling

At present, different types of software, covering a variety of functions, are in use :

Software "made-to-measure": the most usual method adopted by consultants working with biologists consists of designing specific programs as the need arises. In favourable cases, common programming standards are set by one laboratory, which makes it possible to build up a program library. The advantage of this method is that the products correspond to local needs. These programs, however, remain isolated from one another. If a biologist uses them in succession, he must therefore go through the stages of learning how to put each one into operation (due to differences in data form, etc.). The effort that this requires can be discouraging and often leads to lost time or bad use of software. As the user interfaces are often rudimentary, either a consultant must be brought in, or else only a circle of initiates can use the software. More importantly, its use frequently leads to an inflexible methodology as there is no other product on hand to solve a given task (e.g. the systematic use of linear regression, of one given integration scheme, or of one optimization method). Not only is the user unaware of the limitations of the method that he has, but no other method is available to him.

Specialized Software and Program libraries: these libraries have been developed to provide a certain function independent of a particular field of application. For example: Numerical integration (*LSODA*, [HINDMARSH 83]) Identification (*HARWELL*; *NAG*), Optimization (*MODULOPT*, [LEMARECHAL 80]), Symbolic calculus (*MACSYMA*; *REDUCE*), Sensitivity analysis (*SAP*, [ARNAUD 84], *HEQS*, [DERMAN 85]), Bifurcation analysis (*AUTO*, [DOEDEL 85]), Data analysis (*CLAVECIN* [DEMONCHAUX & 85]), Graphic representation (*GRAPHIQUE*, [AUDA 85]). Apart from presenting the same difficulties as those mentioned above, a notable lack of documentation on a given method's conditions of use, means that no assistance is available for choosing the appropriate method. Owing to their general nature, such software is bulky, expensive, and, as they are often developed to run on specific machines, their transportation is generally either long or else impossible.

Integrated software: a great deal of software has been designed with the aim of integrating, in a single computer environment, the tools that are necessary to construct and/or simulate models. It is possible to distinguish between two main types:
- Firstly, there is a large variety of simulation languages, most of which were designed for a large class of problems and created to simulate general ordinary differential equations (*CSMP* [SPECKHARD 80], *ASCL*, *DYNAMO* [PUGH 81], *SIMNON* [ELMQVIST 77]). Such languages have a number of characteristics and advantages. One could refer, for example, to CELLIER [CELLIER 86], [CELLIER 84].

- Other systems have been developed more specifically for biology: *COSMOS* [HAMROUNI 79], *MLAB* [KNOTT 84], *BIOMOD* [DELAND 82], *DYNAMAC*, *CROISSANCE* [ROUSSEAU 88]. Each of these brings a positive contribution to a given aspect of computer-aided model. In particular the DYNAMAC software, (for the interactive graphic study of differential systems), CROISSANCE, (for hand-drawn identification of growth models), and STELLA [LEWIS 86], have notably extended man-machine interaction by taking advantage of the new communications concepts offered by MACINTOSH. This is not a question of simple gadgets at the interface level. Such approaches can be the basis for totally new mechanisms in the modeling process. For its part, MLAB is a good illustration of how the tools necessary for mathematical modeling can be integrated in a single environment: it incorporates a wide variety of mathematical, graphic and statistical operators, as well as including an extensive collection of operators necessary for data analysis.

Although the modeling strategy is complex and not well formalized it includes at least important phases such as the model's formulation, test, identification and validation steps. Certain common characteristics of classical software become apparent when looking at each of the steps that make up the modeling process [PIERRET 88a]:

For the *formulation* of the model, classical software generally uses the mathematical formalism directly, and is based on a command language that allows operations to be carried out or methods to be applied on the data and the models. In this case, two major criticisms may be made: the use of such software requires the user to learn the command languages which, despite great improvements, remains a relatively difficult task; no assistance is available for defining the mathematical expressions that are used to define the model. These two handicaps may prove overwhelming for an inexperienced user, which may well be the case of a biologist who is familiar with neither Computer-Science, nor mathematical modeling. Other software uses specific formalisms in order to represent systems, examples of this type of software being that of Forrester [FORR 61], for DYNAMO, STELLA, that of ECL (Energy Circuit Language) [ODU 72], [ODU 82], and that of compartmental formalism for COSMOS [HAMROUNI 79]. The current trend towards products with user-interfaces to make communication with the machine easier, encourages the use of intermediate formalisms which have clear graphic isomorphic representations and partly solves the problems of using description languages with complex syntax. In this second case, there is certainly more assistance in the model's formulation, but the following problems still remain: first, a given formalism is adapted to a special class of systems and a particular modeling technique. Forrester's formulation, for example, was designed to represent models in the field of industrial dynamics. As a consequence of such formalisms, the user must represent his system in a way that may be quite unnatural for him (for instance in terms of compartments and flows of materials), and he must adopt a given modeling approach which may be inappropriate to his problem. Moreover, certain more complex structures cannot be represented by these formalisms (e.g. models with subdivisions in age-class, or models whose components are created or destroyed). In conclusion, the user may find himself in difficulty during this important step of the model's formulation. In fact this step involves either selecting a model from a prototypical models catalogue or else constructing a specific model. The choice of model may depend on a number of inferences made from the specifications previously obtained about the biological system (e.g. the form of the data curve, the biological family of the populations, or the type of the biological situation). If no prototype is suitable, the solution is the result of long chains of deduction which allow the model to be constructed step by step from the specifications. Thus the choice of a prototype or the design of a new model requires different kinds of knowledge: **biological and mathematical, qualitative and quantitative knowledge**.

The next stage, *testing* the model, can be broken down into several phases: simulation and qualitative analysis: seeking steady states and studying their stability, periodic solutions, bifurcation points, and sensitivity analysis of the model. In fact as most aspects of the model's analysis are generally absent, this step is often limited to simulation. But even for this, no information is provided on the choice of methods available (e.g. for integration). One reason for this is that it implies the use of sophisticated **numerical methods** for ordinary differential equations. The qualitative analysis requires **various mathematical competences:** numerical analysis, symbolic calculus, etc...

The *identification and validation* steps also require **competences in various fields (numerical analysis, control, statistics,** etc.) for instance when studying the identifiability or giving the correct statement of the problem (the choice of criterion etc...), when choosing the suited estimation method. The lack of assistance is even more pronounced in this step concerning the identification of the model. There is no phase involving a study of the model's identifiability. The user receives no advice to help him formulate the problem of identification properly: the choice of the type of criteria, or its expression (weights), and the choice of the optimization method, are entirely left up to him. These problems, which are difficult for an expert in mathematics, numerical analysis or statistics, can lead to false results without the biologist knowing. Neither is any assistance given to validate the model, or to choose experimental protocols, despite the fact that they are important phases in the modeling process.

Expert Systems and modeling

A long list of expert systems in scientific computation can be drawn up (particularly in data analysis or in statistics). In the field of Control, several institutes have begun or are seriously studying the possibility of developing expert systems (Department of Automatic Control at Lund Institute of Technology in Sweden, Engineering Department at the University of Cambridge in England, Laboratoire de signaux et systemes at the University of Nice, project Meta2 at INRIA in France). However, while the necessity of using Artificial Intelligence techniques is clearly admitted in the field of modeling, much more projects than realizations can be found. The difficulties mentionned above about classical software have led to the consideration of using expert systems as consulting systems. In the field of continuous system simulation, such systems could [KERCKHOFF 87] :
" - give user's support in the synthesis of differential models or help in defining them from schematic representation
    - provide knowledge on the known mathematical properties
    - do formal manipulations, such as symbolic differentiation or symbolic solving of equations
    - give user's support in selecting algorithms, such as numerical integretion or parameter estimation algorithms;
    - give user's assistance in the interpretation of mathematical expressions."
Even less realizations are devoted to the specific area of modeling applied to biology. ECO project [MUETZELFELDT 87] and EPX system [SOO 87], [GARFINKEL& 88] are the two projects which can be brought nearer to Edora.

In conclusion, the system which is being developped, while offering the functions of classical software, is marked off from those by the introduction of important specificities to aid, guide, and explain the choices of objects or methods through a knowledge-based system approach. Through this quick review the characteristics that are essential for such a system have been brought to light: it must allow the **coexistence and management of diverse bases** i.e. objects bases, methods bases, and a knowledge base; it must have a flexible dialogue system, as the system must allow initiatives to be left either to the user or to the system. These priorities lead to a certain number of basic choices: the choice of an object-centered representation, the system is intended for use on workstations of the SUN, APOLLO, and MACINTOSH type.

KNOWLEDGE REPRESENTATION

There is not a fundamental difference about *what* knowledge-based systems and classical programming can achieve but rather about *how* they do it. The basic distinction is the separation of the knowledge base and its management mechanisms. The advantages are that the base can evolve and be updated more easily, and that it provides means of obtaining explanations and a better control of the management mechanisms. These two points are important for an expert system as they allow expertise to be brought to light more efficiently.

Once the knowledge has been separated, the question arises of how to represent it. The efficiency of a knowledge representation model can be judged by its power of expression, its accessibility and its power of explanation [PIERRET 88b]. In a context such as biological modeling, the formalism must be adapted to the representation of such diverse object bases as those for mathematical objects (arithmetic expressions, equations, models, etc.) and objects from the real world (i.e. in biology: animal, population etc.), as well as a methods base (numerical algorithms, symbolic manipulations) and a knowledge base.

The different representations in KBS

The methods used range from the most declarative to the most procedural: sentences in natural language, production rules, structured objects: units, frames, schemes, and semantic networks.

Examples stated in different representations:

natural language :	the wolf eats the sheep	(L1)
	the wolf is a predator	(L2)
	the sheep is the prey	(L3)

| calculation of predicates : | eat (wolf, sheep) | (P1) |
| | preadator (wolf) | (P2) |

schemes:	{p1		
	isa	=	predation
	who	=	wolf
	what	=	sheep}

Production rules and structured objects are the most used representations. They correspond to two distinct "philosophies": the production rules correspond to classical relational formalism. An object does not exist in its own right but only in so far as it is part of a set of scattered statements in the knowledge base. It therefore does not exist as an entity, but it is defined only through its various properties in the base. Using a system based on production rules consists of asking questions about statements. The reasoning process therefore involves finding answers by manipulating the statements in the base and those that have been inferred using the "modus ponens". In object formalism, on the other hand, the emphasis is placed on the representation of the object as a well-defined, structural entity. Using an object-centered system therefore consists of asking questions about the object's slots. Here, the reasoning process involves finding answers by using the knowledge contained in the objects, assisted by the system's own inference mechanisms. These inference mechanisms act on objects and not on statements, which therefore requires specific reasoning mechanisms. The approach based exclusively on the use of rules appears somewhat inefficient when dealing with static relations between such concepts as taxonomies, or when dealing with information by default, but it is, however, optimal for all aspects of representing dynamic knowledge. The advantages of the object-centered representation are considerable: it is an economical means of representing objects and their relationships, and it is well-suited to the experts' way of reasoning. In fact, the current trend is towards hybrid representations using rules and objects: for example, LOOPS [STEFIK& 83], KEE [FIKES& 85], CENTAUR [AIKINS 84].

Object-centered representations (OCR)

In rule-oriented systems the representation of knowledge complies with a relational model based on rules. In object-oriented systems, on the other hand, the representation is based on a single type of entity: the object.

The origins of OCR.

Object-centered representations owes its origins to various ideas: semantic networks [QUILLIAN 68], Minsky's work on frames [MINSKY 75], as well as the development of object programming (SIMULA [BIRTSWISTLE 73] and SMALLTALK [KAY 76] being the forerunners). A quick review will show the essential ideas that each has contributed: the notion of an *object* regrouping the sets of data that share the same characteristics into entities, the notion of a *hierarchical* organization with an inheritance mechanism, and the notion of a data structure representing a *prototypical* situation.

- Object programming has played an important role in contributing to the concepts of object and the inheritance mechanism found in all object-centered representations. For the object programming an object is comparable to a virtual machine [RECHENMANN 85]. It has a local memory and is able to respond to messages using the adapted methods that it posseses. The methods appear in the description of the class to which each object belongs. The classes themselves are objects. Each element of a class is provided with the methods associated to the class. The definition of a sub-class leads to the inheritance of the methods and variables of the class.

- In semantic networks a concept is connected to the network or the family to which it belongs by two types of link: the isa link which means that an object belongs to a particular family of objects; the ako link which means that a network is a sub-network of a family of objects. Through these two links came the idea of a hierarchical structure and the top to bottom inheritance of properties and the notion of instance [BRACHMAN 77].

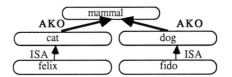

Figure 1: An example of a network.

- It is worth noting that this inheritance mechanism was, however, totally absent from Minsky's article [MINSKY 75]. His essential contributions were the notions of *frame*, data structure representing a prototypical entity, and the notion of viewpoint. A frame is a generic concept which describes a prototypical entity or a class of objects. It arose from the established fact that an individual does not build up new structures to represent a new situation, but tries to find in his memory a structure that represents a similar or closely related situation. After having found a situation that identifies the new situation adequately, the individual uses the extra information that this provides to decide how to behave appropriately. This concept had already appeared in the field of psychology: from observations carried out on the behaviour of subjects who were trying to recognize an object (or a situation), BARTLETT established that the subjects perceived some properties of the object from which they inferred a scheme of the object. This scheme was then used to check the object's missing properties, [BARTLETT 32]. The notion of viewpoint was first introduced by MINSKY about change of position in vision and for change of amphasis in language but also about problem solving : "sometimes in problem solving we use two or more descriptions in a more complex way to construct an analogy or to apply radically kinds of analysis to the same situation. *For hard problems, one 'problem space' is usually not enough!*" [MINSKY 75]

Thus these different trends led to the creation of both the original structures and the specific reasoning mechanisms that support them: inference by inheritance or instantiation, object identification, classification etc... It is important to recall the basis for frames and/or schemes because, as shown above, they were introduced to represent a certain type of behaviour or reasoning. The OCRs that were derived directly from this are thus well suited to solving problems where the method is similar, as is the case for different steps in the modeling process. For example, the modeler, starting with a certain amount of perceived information (data form, the biological description of the situation, etc.) can seek the model that has the same characteristics from the set of models that are listed in his knowledge base. Then he can check the mathematical properties that are attached to this model (steady points, stability, etc.).

Common structural characteristics in OCR.

Whatever the formalism and the implementations adopted, the schemes in SHIRKA [RECHENMANN 85], the frames in various representation languages such as FRL [GODSTEIN& 77], KEE [FIKES& 85] or UNITS [STEFIK 79], units or prototypes in KRL [BOBROW& 77], [AIKINS 83], scripts, etc., representations by structured objects all present certain common characteristics. The formalism and the syntax used in the following examples are those of the SHIRKA schemes, and the examples are from EDORA.

- the basic concept in OCRs is the object. An object is a data structure which makes it possible to mimic the conceptual entities of the universe to be modeled. Thus an object or a class of objects can be represented in a structured way (fig. 3 and fig. 4). The term 'object' should be taken in its widest sense: it may be a physical object (an animal, a cell, etc.), a concept (a variable, a differential equation, an enzyme, a predator, etc.), a situation or a context (the growth of a population, situation of predation etc.), an algorithmic method (integration), etc. It is defined by its name and a set of slots which describe all the characteristics of the conceptual entity that it represents. For example, a circle is characterized by its center and its radius, a date by the month, the day and the year, a cell by its diameter. The slots themselves can refer to other objects. Depending on the models, the slots may or may not be typed. The slots, in their turn, are described by facets. In most OCRs there are certain standard types of facets, for example : "default" makes it possible to attribute a default value to the slot in question, and "restriction" specifies the set of values allowed for the slot, etc. Thus an object is a structure at three levels (fig. 2) allowing the knowledge base designer to describe the "profile" of the objects.

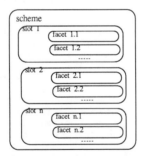

Figure 2: A scheme, the syntactical unit of representation of Shirka

The object's profile can refer to different aspects of the object. For example, the object "variable" can be considered in different ways : from the formal point of view it is a symbol that can be assigned with a value, the biological significance is kept with its implications for the range, dimension, etc. Details of the integration of the different semantic levels concerning a minimal kernel of symbolic calculus are given in [PIERRET 87]. In the same way, the generic object "system" brings together biological and mathematical semantics as certain of its slots refer to mathematical objects (model, data), and others refer to biological objects (situation, process) :

```
{system
    model       $one        model
    process     $one        process
    curve       $one        curve
    situation   $one        situation}
```

- Class and instance are other basic concepts. A class corresponds to the notion of a *generic* object (close to the notion of Clancey's scheme or Minsky's frame) while the concept of instance corresponds to the notion of a *particular* object: an instance is a sample of a given class (fig. 3, fig. 4).

```
{variable
    meaning     $one        string;
    value       $one        reel;
    range       $one        interval;
    unit        $one        string;
    dimension   $one        symbol}
```

Figure 3: Example of a class scheme

```
{x
    isa         =       variable;
    meaning     =       rat-size;
    value       =       50;
    range       =       [0 60];
    unit        =       cm;
    dimension   =       L}
```

Figure 4: Example of an instance scheme.

It is possible to define classes of prototypical objects and EDORA's catalogs of models, differential equations and biological processes were designed in this way. For example, the class of autonomous linear equations was defined using a prototypical instance :

```
{dif-linear-autonomous
    kind-of     =       linear-quadratic-autonomous
    prototype   =       dif-equ#1}
with

{dif-equ#1
    is          =       differential-equation
    lhs         =       diff#1
    rhs         =       plus#1}
```

(diff#1 and plus#1 are predefined instances representing $\frac{dx}{dt}$ and $ax+b$ respectively.)

- The concept of specialization and hierarchy: a sub-class corresponds to the notion of a more *specific* object. The classes are organized in a lattice structure in which each class inherits the slots of the classes that it specializes (fig. 6). In this way a class inherits, in so far as it does not redefine it, the knowledge that is attached to the classes above it. The knowledge base designer can describe each class as a specialization (sub-class) of a more general class by using a specialization link (fig. 5).

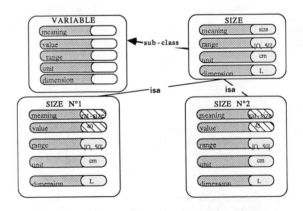

Figure 5: Concepts of class, sub-class, instance

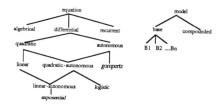

Figure 6: Examples of a lattice structure for equations, models

- Procedural attachment: object-representation allows a combination of procedural and declarative approaches by permitting certain slots to have procedural attachments. In general, two forms of procedural attachment can be distinguished. In KRL these two forms are called "domestic" and "daemon" methods (known respectively as methods and active methods in KEE). The first generally correspond to LISP procedures which allow, for example, the value of a slot to be found. The second are triggered as soon as certain conditions have been satisfied: when recording or accessing the value of the slot.

The role of OCR in reasoning.

The facilities introduced by OCRs have an important place in reasoning. The inferences based on the structural properties of the objects and the taxonomies generally play a major role in reasoning. As the knowledge is encoded on the objects themselves, the inferences are faster than with general deduction methods (such as those of production rule interpreters). The way of using an object-centered system usually consists of creating instances and asking questions about these instances. In general those are incomplete and the inference mechanisms have precisely to derive from the information provided by the instance class scheme the unknown values of the slots. These mechanisms are quickly presented:

- inference by value: if the value v of a slot s is defined in the class scheme C, then each instance of C inherits this slot value v. Example: for each instance of *size* , if the *dimension* is asked, the value L is automatically provided (fig. 7)

```
{size                              {size N°1
    kind-of    =      variable;        is      =    size
    meaning    $default  size;          meaning  =    rat-size-1;
    range      $default  [0, +∞];       unit    =    cm}
    unit       $default  m;
    dimension  $value    L}
```

Figure 7: A class scheme with default and class values

This type of reasoning is frequently encountered: an expert can often only access an object's partial properties from which he identifies a class scheme, then he deduces more information from that scheme.

- inference by default: if the value v of a slot s is defined by default in the class scheme C, then each instance of C inherits this slot value v unless different information is given: by lack of more information the value of the slot *unit* is "m", however its value is "cm" for the instance size N°1 (fig. 7). This mechanism permits to express a very usual type of reasoning: most human reasoning is carried out despite a shortage of information. This lack of information does not block the process as information is substituted by default. The problem of reasoning by default can be regarded in the same light as that of exceptions. The assertions that can be made are rarely universal but rather of the type: most of the objects P satisfy the property Q. For example, "most birds fly" means that all birds fly apart from certain exceptions (the ostrich, the penguin). The systems based on the calculation of predicates must explicitly specify the list of exceptions:

$$\forall x \quad bird(x) \wedge \neg ostrich(x) \wedge \neg penguin(x) \ = > flies(x)$$

But this representation does not make it possible to conclude that a bird, in general, flies as the intermediary facts -ostrich and -

penguin could not be proved due to lack of information. This is why such systems generally add an extra rule stating : if $\neg P(x)$ cannot be deduced, then infer $P(x)$. On the oher hand, OCRs offer a simple means of dealing with this question of reasoning in the case of incomplete information. Thus, for example, to translate the fact that a bird, in general, flies, OCRs use the $default facet in the description of the bird class.

- inference by pattern-matching: this mechanism permits to find all the instances x from a class C which satisfy a particular pattern described by a filter F

- inference by inheritance: if there is a specialization link from a class A to a class B, the knowledge base's management system will find that B is a specialization of A without having to use any other reasoning mechanisms (pattern-matching, etc.). It uses the ako links, and the prototypical descriptions of the class to gain more information about the object. Thus the sub-class B inherits all the slots of A. For instance as "*size*" specializes "*variable*", it inherits the *meaning, value, range, unit* and *dimension* slots of this class. Sub-class can even inherit from a set of values or the value of these slots. The ako link also transmits the inference mechanisms of the class A to the sub-class B. If one class specializes several classes, it will inherit all the slots of these classes as well as adding its own slots to them. The inheritance mechanism is a basic inference mechanism in OCRs.

- inference by procedural attachment: if a slot s of a class C owns a method M which permits to obtain the value of s then, whatever the instance x of the class C, this method is called to compute the value of this slot for x, when this is necessary. This is an economical means of linking the objects and the methods. It allows the integration of procedures in a declarative context. The following example, expressed in the formalism of the schemes from SHIRKA, illustrates how a specific method of computation can be attached to each model, for example, the "logistic software" method for the logistic model, the "gompertz-software" method for the Gompertz model. These methods are only triggered by the system when the value of the simulation is required. The appropriate method for an object is encoded directly on the object.

```
{model
    kind-of     =         object
    equations   $list-of   equation
    simul       $one       chronic}

{logistic-model
    kind-of     =         model
    simul       $sib-exec
                {logistic-software
                    equ  $var-list < -    equations
                    res  $var- >          simul}

{gompertz-model
    kind-of     =         model
    simul       $sib-exc
                {gompert-software
                    equ  $var-list < -    equations
                    res  $var- >          simul}
```

The other type of procedural attachment mentioned above, the daemons, make it possible to call procedures which do not give a result, but which have side-effects. These daemons can be used to activate an alarm when a critical threshold has been passed. SHIRKA maintains the consistency of the base by using procedures linked to slots which are called when adding, suppressing, or modifying the value for these slots.

- Inference by classification: let x an instance of a class C of a hierarchy; this mechanism permits to find all the most specialized classes of the hierarchy to which x can belong. Thus working with the base's organization by hierarchy, another type of reasoning is proposed which corresponds to a very frequent human type of reasoning. The most obvious applications are those concerned with classification in taxonomies. This aspect of comparing an object with a prototype is particularly used for medical or other problems of diagnosis [POPLE 82] [CLANCEY 84]. The characteristics of OCRs are especially useful for piloting such diagnostic processes: the prototypical description of a class provides, in a declarative way, a means of knowing whether an object belongs to a class or not. Moreover many other types of problems (choice, recognition etc.) can be solved by identifying the appropriate class of an object in a hierarchy. For instance, this is the approach that has been used to select a model from those contained in the model base (see below). This mechanism appears to be of the utmost importance in OCR.

STRUCTURATION OF THE KNOWLEDGE BASE

The design of the knowledge base by the use of schemes is now presented. More attention is spent on the model formulation which consists of deriving a structural description from the behavioral description of the biological system.

Separation of the universe into structured objects

A biological system can be seen from different viewpoints: biological or mathematical viewpoints, qualitative or quantitative viewpoints. These different conceptual viewpoints lead to dividing the universe into for families of objects: *model, process, curve, situation* (fig. 8). *Model* and *process* are the two objects which have been abstracted to represent the deep knowledge (i.e. knowledge about the internal mechanisms of the sytem, the principles that govern its behavior). The object *model* represents the system in the mathematical formalism i.e. by a set of differential equations while the objet *process* represents it in the pseudo-chemical formalism i.e. with a set of pseudo-chemical reactions (fig. 10). *Curve of response* and *situation* have been selected for the surface level (i.e. knowledge concerned by the findings about the sytem).

viewpoint	biological	mathematical
surface	situation	curve
deep	process	model

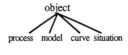

Figure 8: Different families of objects

The structure of each generic object has been defined by a class scheme (fig. 9):

```
{model
        var-ind         $one      independent-variable;
        state           $list-of  state;
        parameter       $list-of  parameter;
        equation        $list-of  dif-equation;
        initial-cond    $un       reel;
        prototype       $one      model;
        steady-points   $list-of  steady-pnts;
        simulation      $one      chronic }
```

Figure 9: Model scheme

BIOLOGICAL FORMALISM
"a population growth limited by substratum"

```
{situation#0
        is           =    situation
        growth       =    true
        regulated    =    true
        nb-factors   =    1
        factor-type  =    substratum}
```

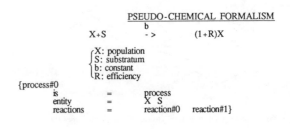

PSEUDO-CHEMICAL FORMALISM

$$X+S \xrightarrow{b} (1+R)X$$

$$\begin{cases} X: \text{population} \\ S: \text{substratum} \\ b: \text{constant} \\ R: \text{efficiency} \end{cases}$$

```
{process#0
        is          =    process
        entity      =    X S
        reactions   =    reaction#0   reaction#1}
```

MATHEMATICAL FORMALISM

$$\frac{dx}{dt} = bRxs$$

$$\frac{ds}{dt} = -bxs$$

```
{model#0
        is          =    model
        state       =    x s
        parameter   =    b R
        equations   =    dif-equ#0  dif-equ#1}
```

Figure 10: Different aspects of knowledge about a system and their representation by schemes

Each of these objects has needed the definition of other schemes as their slots can refer to objects. For instance, the object *model* has required to represent by schemes other different concepts: *variable, parameter, differential equation*. Each one in its turn has needed to define new objects: *expression, operator* etc. Thus the base has been structured in a progressive way.

Organizing the universe through the specialization links

Each generic object is the root of a hierarchy. The different object bases in EDORA have thus been organized hierachically, with hierarchies for models, equations, processes, shapes of a curve (fig. 11), situations, etc. For example two branches stem from this root: the branch containing the catalog of pre-defined models, and the branch of compound models (fig. 6). The compound models are obtained by pre-defined operations that make it possible to link the input-output variables of the components (sub-models). The components can all be from the catalog or any other model. This hierarchical organization has the advantage of allowing different consistency tests to be made during a model's construction. For example: if model B succeeds model A, the time horizon of B must be included in that of A the linked variables must be compatible concerning their dimension and unit; the initial states of A and B must be compatible if there is any feedback; the constructed network must not have any loops.

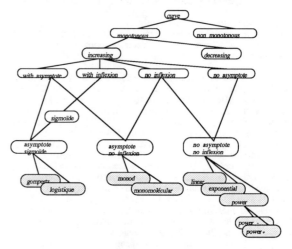

Figure 11: Hierarchy of curves

Organizing the universe through the causal associations: agregated objects

There are causal associations between the different objects *process, model, curve, situation*. A process is associated with a biological situation, a curve with a model, and a model is derived from a process. But the associations network between these knowledge is complex: one curve can be associated with several situations, one situation wit several curves. Moreover, neither the descripion of the situation, neither the description of the curve is sufficient to select a process or a model. A model cannot be straight derived from the biological description of the situation or from the shape of a data curve. Therefore, a "higher level " object (called *system*) has been defined which agregates these different viewpoints about the system into a single object. This object synthezises the causal associations. Each sub-class of this object is "a world of consistent knowledge".

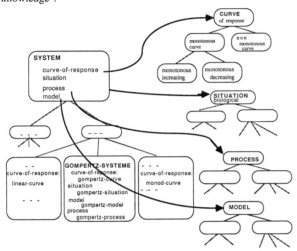

Figure 12: Lattice organization, support of a "multi-classification reasoning"

This organization in multiple hierarchies linked together by a higher level hierarchy is the support of an original reasoning mechanism which recursively calls classification (fig. 12): an instance of the class system which corresponds to the problem under study is created by the user and the classification of this instance is asked to Edora managing system. In order to identify its position in the *system* hierarchy, Shirka asks the user to provide the values of the slots *curve* and *situation*. To help the user answering, the classification is then recursively called, successsively on the *curve* and *situation* hierarchies. The descriptions of the data form and of the situation are thus given by the user. Consequently a set of possible or sure classes of *curve* and *situation* are proposed by the system among which the user can chose his answers. Finally, a list of sure, possible, impossible classes is returned for the so defined instance of *system* . This design of the base is also the support of the construction of new models. Combining operators which permit to compound elementary systems have been defined therefore.

CONCLUSION

This paper has attempted to show the benefits of an Object-Centered Representation :

- it is a simple and concise means of representing the knowledge that is needed throughout the modeling process.

- this type of representation is the basis for reasoning mechanisms that approach those of the modeler. In particular, the inference by classification on multiple hierarchies seems to be a type of reasoning of major importance. It has been presented how this technique can permit to solve the problem of the model formulation. Partial answers to the questions raised by classical simulation tools have been given using examples. Although certain

aspects of the problem have not been dealt with here, they may be found in [PAVE 86] [RECHENMANN 85]. In particular, the recognition of models is presented in [PIERRET 87], the formulation of a model from an intermediate representation using what is known as pseudo-chemical formalism in [PAVE 86] and [PIERRET 88b]. Further developments will concern the other steps of the modeling process (test, identification, validation). The design of the methods base is tackled in [PIERRET 88b]

The design of a knowledge base in this formalism of representation is a long and exacting undertaking. The benefits, however, go beyond the field of biology: such an approach may be used each time it is necessary to use methods for manipulating mathematical objects while keeping the significance of the objects that are manipulated.

ACKNOWLEDGEMENTS: The author wishes to extend her gratitude to RECHENMANN F. and PAVE A. for providing the computer tool and the biological framework which made this work possible.

BIBLIOGRAPHY

[AIKINS 84]
Aikins J.S.
A representation scheme using both frames and rules.
In Rule-Based Expert Systems, Buchanan B.G. and Shirtliffe (eds) Addison-Weslay, Reading,Mass.,1984, pp 424-440.

[AUDA 85]
Auda Y.
Logiciel graphique pour l'analyse des données (Fortran 77)
Laboratoire de Biométrie, Lyon 1, ronéo, 107 pp

[ARNAUD 84]
Arnaud M., Lamarre H.
Un logiciel pour l'analyse de sensibilité de systèmes dynamiques
Rapport année spéciale ENSIMAG 1984

[BARTLETT 32]
F.C. Bartlett
Remembering: a study in experimental and social psychology
Cambridge Universu-ity Press, London,1932

[BRACHMAN 77]
Brachman R.J., Schmolze J.G.
What's in a concept: structural foundations for semantic networks
Int.J. Man-Machine Studies , 1977, 9, 127-152

[BIRTSWISTLE 73]
Birtswistle G., Dahl O., Myhrhaug B., Nygaard K.
SIMULA begin
Oetrocelli Charter, New-york, 1973

[CELLIER 84]
F.E. Cellier
How to enhance the robustness of simulation software
In Oren T.I., Zeigler B.P., Elzas M.S. (eds). Simulation and Model Based Methodologies: An integrative view. Springer Verlag, 1984 pp.519-536

[CLANCEY 84]
Classification problem solving
AAAI 84 pp. 49-55

[DELAND 83]
Deland E.C.
Conceptual models in physiology, where are we?
Proc. of The IFIP WG 7.1 Working Conference on Modelling and Data Analysis in Biotechnology and Medical Engineering ,Brussels 82. Holland Publishing Company, Amsterdam , 1983, pp 11-17

[DEMONCHAUX & 85]
E. Demonchaux, J. Quinqueton, H. Ralambondrainy
Clavecin: un système expert en analyse des données
Rapport de recherche INRIA N°341, juil 1985

[DERMAN 85]
Derman E., Sheppard E.G.
HEQS: A Hierarchical Equation Solver
AT&T Technical, Vol 24, N° 9, pp. 169-176, 1985

[DOEDEL 81]
Doedel E.J.
Auto: A program for the automatic bifurcation analysis of autonomous systems
Cong. Num., 30, pp 265-284,1981

[ELMMQVIST 77]
Elmqvist H.
SIMNON: An interactive Simulation Program for Nonlinear Systems.
Proceedings Simulation '77, Montreux, 1977

[FIKES & 85]
Fikes R., Kehler T.
The role of frame-bases representation in reasonning.
Communications of the ACM, Vol 28, sept 1985, pp 904-920

[FORRESTER 61]
Forrester J.W.
Industrial Dynamics.
MIT Press, 1961

[GARFINKEL & 88]
D. Garfinkel
Construction of metabolic models using Artificial Intelligence Technique
12th IMACS World Congress, july 18-22 1988, Paris, pp. 545-547

[HAMROUNI 79]
    Hamrouni M.K.2 :
    Etude et développement d'un système informatique d'aide à l'élaboration de modèles en biologie.
    Thèse de 3eme cycle , Université Pierre et Marie Curie, Paris, 1979
[HINDMARSH 83]
    Hindmarsh A.C.: *Odepack, a systematized collection of ODE solvers.*
    Scientific Computing, STEPELMAN et al. (eds), North-Holland Publ., Amsterdam, pp. 55-64,1983
[KAY 76]
    Kay A., Goldberg A.
    SMALLTALK-72 instruction manuel, SSL 76&é`
    Xerox Palto Alto Research Center, Palto Alto,California, 1976.
[KERCKHOFFS 86]
    Kerckhoffs E.J.H., Vansteenkiste G.C., Zeigler B.P.
    A.I. applied to Simulation.
    Simulation Series, Vol 18, N°1
    The Society for Computer Simulation Publication,San Diego/California, USA, February 1986
[KNOTT 84]
    Knott G. and al
    MLAB Reference Manuel
    Division of Computer Research and Technology, National Institute of Health, Bethesda, Maryland, 1984
[LEMARECHAL 80]
    Normes modulopt 1
    Rapport interne INRIA Aout1980
[LEWIS 86]
    Lewis J.
    STELLA: A Model of its Kind
    Practical computing, september, 66-67
[MAY 81]
    May R.M. : *Theoretical ecology , principles and applications..* Blackwell scientific publications, Oxford.
[MINSKY 75]
    Minsky M. :
    A framework for representing Knowledge .
    The Psychology of Comp Vision P.H. Winston ED., McGrawHill1975.
[MUETZELFELDT & 87]
    Muetzelfeldt R., Robertson D., Uschold M., Bundy A.
    Computer-Aided construction of Ecological simulation programs.
    Intern. Symp. on A.I., Expert Systems and Languages in Modelling and Simulation, Elsevier Sc. Publ. Barcelona, 1987
[ODUM 72]
    Odum H.T. :
    An energy language for ecological and Social ySstems: its physical basis.
    Systems Analysis and simulation in Ecology B.C.Patten Academic Press 1972, pp.139-211
[ODUM 82]
    Odum H.
    Systems Ecology: an introduction
    Wiley&sons, 1982
[PAVE & 86]
    Pavé A., Rechenmann F.]
    Computer aided modelling in biology:an artificial intelligence approach.
    Artificial Intelligence and Simulation, SCS Rev , 1986
[POPLE 82]
    Pople H.
    Heuristic methods for imposing structure on ill-structured problems: The structuring of medical diagnositics.
    In Szolovitts P., ed., Artificial Intelligence in medecine. Westview Press, Boulder, Col, 1982.
[PIERRET 87]
    Pierret-Golbreich C.
    Object-centered Knowledge Representation for biological Modeling.
    International Symposium on A.I., Expert Systems and Languages in Modelling and Simulation, Elsevier Sc. Publ. Barcelona, 1987

[PIERRET 88a]
    Pierret-Golbreich C.
    Knowledge Representation for computer aided modelling in Biology.
    12th IMACS World Congress 88, Paris, July 18-22,1988
[PIERRET 88b]
    C. Pierret-Golbreich
    Vers un système à base de connaissances centrée-objet pour la modélisation de systèmes dynamiques en biologie.
    Thèse de doctorat, Université de Compiègne, 1988
[PUGH 81]
    Richardson P. and Pugh L.
    Introduction to Systems Dynamics Modeling with Dynamo
    M. I.T Press, 1981
[QUILLIAN 78]
    Quillian M.R.
    Semantic Memory
    Semantic Information Processing, Minsky M. Ed, MIT Press, Cambridge,1968, PP227-270.
[RECHENMANN 85]
    Rechenmann F: *SHIRKA: Mécanismes d'inférence sur une base de connaissances centrée-objet.* Cinquième congrès AFCET-ADI-INRIA. Reconnaissance des formes et Intelligence Artificielle, Nov 1985
[ROUSSEAU 88]
    B. Rousseau
    Vers un environnemnt de résolution de problèmes en biométrie
    Thèse de doctorat, Université Claude Bernard Lyon 1, 1988
[SOO 87]
    V.W. Soo
    A Qualitative Matching Scheme for Postulating Enzyme Kinetic Models and Experimental Conditions: Reasoning With Constraints
    Ph.D. Thesis, Rutgers University, 1987

[SPECKART 80]
    Walter L. G., Speckhart F.H.
    "CSMP"
    Simulation, Vol 34, N° 34, 1980
[STEFIK 83]:
    Stefik M., Bobrow D.G., Mittal S., Conway L.
    Knowledge programming in LOOPS: report on an experimental course.
    The A.I. magazine, Vol.4, N°3, 1983, pp 3-13

HSKB: an architecture for embedded reasoning in
simulation systems

D. Castillo, M. McRoberts, S. Green, B. Sieck
McDonnell Douglas Astronautics Company
P.O. Box 21233
Kennedy Space Center, Florida 32815

ABSTRACT

Object oriented simulation (OOS) provides a natural
means for organizing and controlling simulation models.
Recently, expert systems (ES) have been embedded within
OOS environments as a means for performing heuristic
reasoning during simulation. The problem with this coupling
is that traditional rule based ES paradigms lack the organizing
principles of object oriented design. This generally forces
inference control to be a function of constructing the
knowledge base. Recognizing the potential benefits of
embedded reasoning systems, including the difficulties
associated with employing conventional ES technology, we
propose Hierarchical Segmented Knowledge Bases (HSKB).
Consistent with OOS, HSKB provides a means for building a
knowledge base from locally known knowledge segments
which are organized according to the taxonomy of objects.
This results in the object's ability to reason within its specific
context and provides an enhanced capability for focusing on
local modeling without defining global control strategies. In
this paper, we discuss both design and implementation details
of the HSKB architecture.

1. INTRODUCTION

Object oriented programming (OOP) paradigms are fast
becoming attractive vehicles for constructing simulation
models of real world systems. The popularity of OOP stems
from the close relationship between program objects and real
world processes (Stefik and Bobrow 1986). Program objects
are declarative representations of real world entities, each
characterized by their attributes, behaviors, and relationships
to other objects. Interactions between objects are performed
via message passing protocols.

Current research in object oriented simulation is
directed toward the development of *knowledge based object
oriented simulation environments*. The most popular attempts
involve coupling Expert System technology with OOS
technology. Many of these coupling arrangements conform
with O'Keefe's (1986) taxonomy of topologies; embedded,
parallel, cooperative and intelligent front/back ends. Within
this taxonomy, the embedded expert system (EES) approach is
becoming increasingly popular as a means for performing
knowledge based simulation.

The popularity of EES arises from the ability to
support heuristic and qualitative reasoning *during* the
simulation process (Kitzmiller 1988). This is especially
desirable when modeling complex decision processes, where
quantitative representations are often infeasible and
unavailable (Castillo, McRoberts and Sieck 1988b).

Despite their popularity, EESs are not without cost.
There are often significant penalties in both overhead and
performance associated with the integration of rule based
systems and object oriented systems. Other difficulties
include nonoptimal solutions, reasoning under uncertainty,
error handling, availability of expertise, validation and truth
maintenance.

Recognizing this, we propose an architecture, called
Hierarchical Segmented Knowledge Bases (HSKB), designed to
simplify many of the difficulties associated with EES.
Section 2 begins with a brief overview of previous work in
the area of EES. Section 3 describes the motivation for the
HSKB approach. Section 4 gives a perspective on the
simulation environment using the HSKB architecture. Section
5 details the design and implementation aspects of HSKB.
Section 6 presents an example illustrating the reasoning
process. Finally, Section 7 discusses our conclusions and ideas
for future research.

2. OVERVIEW OF PREVIOUS WORK IN EES

Much of the previous work in EES (ROSS, Smalltalk,
Eric, KBS, ORIENT84/K, Omega, Smallworld etc.) follows a
similar paradigm for performing embedded reasoning. In this
paradigm, the object itself contains the knowledge required
for responding to a particular message. Also, in many cases,
messages are patterns that utilize pattern variables in the
message template of the behavior definition. Pattern
variables act as wildcards matching against *atoms*, *lists*, or
consecutive *forms*. Thus, each time a message is sent, a
unification process is activated, returning all objects matching
the message pattern. After the message is received, the
appropriate behavior is invoked. Adelsberger (1986) gives an
detailed comparison of the above mentioned systems.

2.1 Problems with the Early EES Work

Much of the previous work in EES represents a
significant contribution to the area of embedded reasoning.
There are, however, some areas in which obvious improvement
is possible. These include but are not limited to:

- *reducing the amount of pattern matching that
  occurs during message passing,*
- *providing a simplified means for performing
  backtracking,*
- *using a conventional knowledge based architecture
  for storing IF-THEN logic.*

As described in Section 2, many OOS systems execute a
pattern matching process during message transmission. While
this approach is consistent with the concept of pure object
oriented programming, it is often extremely inefficient.
Since, messages are the central protocol for all objects, they
are responsible for invoking various types of object responses
(ie. procedural as well as rule oriented behaviors). This
implies (as we will demonstrate in Section 4) that a
unification or matching process is not always necessary.

Many previous EES paradigms provide a complex and
cumbersome means for performing backtracking. Generally, a
large number of messages are required for implementing a
detailed search. In many cases, each clause within the current
message is itself another message. This process is often
inefficient.

Much of the early EES work describes behaviors in
terms of IF-THEN logic which is essentially *hard coded* on the

object. This is often inconvenient for rule editing and modification, particularly if one desires to view the entire knowledge base.

3. MOTIVATION FOR HSKB

HSKB is a means for performing embedded reasoning during simulation. Unlike much of the previous work in EES, HSKB attempts to minimize pattern matching, provide a robust backtracking facility, and utilize a conventional knowledge base for storing IF-THEN rule logic.

Associated with this paradigm are a number of difficulties, most of which are associated with the integration of rule based systems with OOS systems. Other problems include those normally associated with many rule based systems. We now address these issues.

Coupling rule based systems with discrete event simulation is often complex (see Figure 1). The nature of discrete event simulation implies that state changes occur *only* at discrete points in time. Inference over rules, however, may *asynchronously* affect the state of an object. The problem becomes even more complex when rule based architectures employ private data structures. Pattern matching on external representations often requires an intermediate process whereby the object is converted to a separate representation suitable for inference. Furthermore, in many systems, rules are global, potentially able to fire at any time during the rule firing cycle.

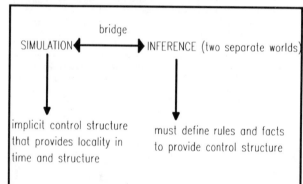

Figure 1: Integrating Simulation and Inference

Another principal concern is that OOS systems generally do not require strict control structures as do rule based systems. In rule based systems, control is written in terms of rules and assertions. This is often difficult even for the experienced programmer.

Hierarchical Segmented Knowledge Bases attempts to address these potential problems by providing a rule based architecture whose mechanical operation is consistent with OOS. Before we address the details of HSKB, a look at the simulation environment, particularly the knowledge representation, is warranted.

4. SIMULATION ENVIRONMENT

HSKB is an integral part of a large scale object oriented simulation system, called the Advanced Ground Analysis Planning Environment (AGAPE), in use at NASA Kennedy Space Center (Castillo et al. 1987). Within the AGAPE architecture, HSKB structures and directs the inference process. This requires a tight coupling between the object oriented nature of AGAPE and the syntactic structure of HSKB.

4.1 Knowledge Representation

The AGAPE system is supported by an object oriented frame representation language, called McDofs (McDonnell Douglas Object Frame System). McDofs is a programming environment built upon a conventional frame system. Two message passing functions, *TELL and ASK*, provide a syntactically unified interface to the underlying frame system. All communication with an object is handled via TELL and ASK as demonstrated by the following syntax:

(**tell** *object message* [*args***]*])

Messages themselves, are objects within McDofs. When a message is defined for an object, an instance of the class *Messages* is created. This new instance stores all information pertaining to the newly created message. The message is compiled, loaded into the LISP environment, and stored in the object's *message hash table*. The following macro template illustrates the message syntax:

(**defmessage** *object message-name args body* [*documentation*])

McDofs is designed in a layered fashion within the LISP environment. A set of base messages that are common to all objects are defined for each newly created object. These messages access direct frame calls.

Domain specific messages are defined *above* the base message layer. These messages are generally *procedural* and specific to the application domain. Messages that require rule based or *condition-action* logic are defined as *HSKB messages*. HSKB messages contain rule bases that are accessed through the same message protocol as *procedural* messages, but provide an alternative rule based format for defining condition logic. This eliminates *hard coding* the condition logic directly on the message (details are explained in Section 5).

4.2 Simulation Process

AGAPE utilizes a *script driven* simulation paradigm (Castillo et al. 1988a). Scripts are analogous to Schank and Abelson's (1975) theory of *plans*. A script is a series of temporally ordered *activities*. Activities are declarative representations for tasks, procedural messages, HSKB messages, or other scripts.

During simulation, objects send messages to other objects in the environment. Each object then responds with the appropriate behavior. Behaviors are defined on the local object or inherited according to the object taxonomy. State changes occur as a result of performing a behavior.

Most behaviors are defined in terms of scripts. When a message is sent to an object, say *object-A*, the object determines if a script is associated with the incoming message. If so, *object-A* tells itself to post the script event on its event calendar. An *after-demon* then sends a message to the *Event-Manager* informing it that at time *tnow* (or whatever time the script is scheduled to fire), an event on *object-A* is to occur. When the Event-Manager receives this message a *before-demon* inserts *object-A* onto its event list. All event insertion utilizes a heap algorithm and is modeled after Hilton's (1987) distributed event paradigm.

The *Event-Manager* only knows that an event on *object-A* will occur at *tnow*. It does not know the event type, nor does it care. After *object-A* is inserted on the *Event-Manager's* event list, an after-demon then determines the object scheduled for the next event. A second *after-demon* tells this

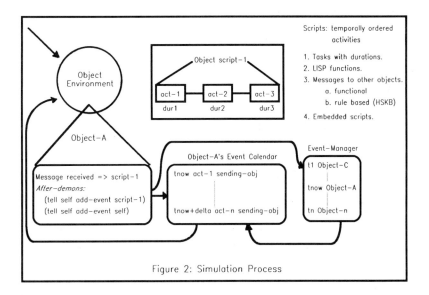

Figure 2: Simulation Process

object (*object-A*) to *execute-your-next-event*.

Upon receiving this message, *object-A* fires off an *after-demon* that removes the next event from its event calendar. In this scenario, the next event is a script. The script then executes the appropriate activity within its activity structure. Possible actions include scheduling a task, executing a procedural message, or invoking an HSKB message. Based on the activity type, the procedure repeats. The entire process in controlled by firing *before* and *after* demons. Figure 2 illustrates this process.

5.0 HSKB ARCHITECTURE

In knowledge based object oriented simulation systems, rules are primarily used to effect the simulation model and environment. Rules may be used to perform simple calculations, alter or create object classes, alter or create specific objects or object instances, determine an object's status, control object animation, and, alter and control the actual simulation.

The number of rules created for a single simulation may be enormous given the range of capability mentioned above. A single list of rules, which must be searched each time a rule requires invocation, is computationally expensive during model development and simulation.

Some rules operate only in specific situations and consequently there is little that can be done to speed the search to execute these rules. However, the bulk of rules operate on whole *categories or classes* of objects and functions, and if these *categories* are already known to the system, search time *decreases*.

HSKB, as shown in Figure 3, proposes to keep all rules in a general collection called the Knowledge Base. The categorization or Rule Sets, are lists of specific rules belonging to that rule set. Unification and search, will occur over these predetermined Rule Sets.

While a set of rules is automatically incorporated into the environment governing the system level model building and simulation constraints, the user determines the mapping of rules to rule sets prior to simulation for those rules created by the user. A single rule may belong to more than one rule set.

In addition to an increase in search speed for invocation of rules, other benefits are derived from this approach. Rules are arranged and grouped *naturally* in the simulation environment according to the modeler. The ability to reason about which rules appear in which rule sets (or not at all) provides the system, and hence the operator, a clear optimization path.

A detailed description of the architecture and implementation of HSKB follows.

5.1 Rule Language and Syntax

Rules in HSKB are fired in a backward chaining manner similar to PROLOG (Sterling and Shapiro 1986). Both the antecedents and consequents of rules are made up of patterns containing variables. A unification algorithm adapted from Charniak et al. (1987) is used to match these patterns. Goals are maintained in a stack, where the top goal is matched against the consequents of all applicable rules. When a rule matches, its antecedents are then pushed onto the stack of goals.

Rules are defined using the *define-HSKB-rule* macro. A rule's definition includes its name, a consequent pattern and any number of antecedent clauses. The following template illustrates the syntax:

(**define-HSKB-rule** *name* **:lhs** *consequent* **:rhs** *antecedents*
　　　　　:documentation *doc-string*)

Each rule is implemented as a frame instance with a unique id; however, several rules can share the same name. This is to allow for individual rule shadowing as we shall see later.

The consequent of a rule consists of a single pattern, which is matched against the active goal. Patterns are made up of a symbol called the *predicate* followed by some number of arguments according to the predicate. Arguments can be literal atoms, pattern variables or list structures. Pattern variables appear as symbols preceded by a question mark (e. g. *?width*).

The antecedent of a rule may contain any number of clauses. The inference engine attempts to satisfy each clause in the antecedent whenever the consequent is matched. These clauses may be of several types: patterns, lisp predicates,

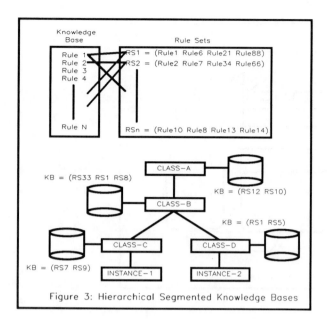

Figure 3: Hierarchical Segmented Knowledge Bases

function calls, and special HSKB functions. The inference engine will attempt to satisfy each clause in turn and the rule will fail to fire when all clauses have not succeeded and no more backtracking is possible.

Patterns have the same syntax as they do in the consequent. Pattern clauses are satisfied by making the pattern into a goal to be proven after substituting the variable bindings established by the prior clauses and the consequent. If the new goal cannot be satisfied then the clause will fail.

Lisp predicates can be used as clauses provided they have been previously declared. Lisp predicate declarations resemble:

(define-HSKB-predicates *predicates**)

Before a lisp predicate clause is matched, any pattern variables are replaced by their current bindings. The result is then evaluated as a lisp expression. If the predicate returns *nil* then the clause fails, otherwise it succeeds. An error occurs if the clause contains a pattern variable which is not bound when it is evaluated.

Any LISP function can be executed for its side effects by using the *Call* syntax. Such a clause contains the symbol *Call* and a LISP expression to evaluate. This works much like evaluating a lisp predicate clause except that *Call* always succeeds and does not require an explicit declaration.

Several special functions are provided by the HSKB rule language which affect the inference process. One of these is *Bind*, which accepts a pattern variable and a LISP expression and binds the variable to the value of the expression. Another is *Bind-in-list* which is analogous to bind except that it expects the value to be a list and binds the variable to successive elements of the list whenever the clause is reached in backtracking. The last of these is *Return-value* which causes the top-level query to return the value of its argument.

5.2 Rule-set Concepts and Syntax

A rule set is simply a set of rules. A new rule-set is created using the *define-HSKB-rule-set* macro and rules are added to rule-sets by executing an *add-rule-to-rule-set* form.

These templates illustrate the syntax:

(define-HSKB-rule-set *name*)

(add-rule-to-rule-set *rule rule-set*)

Rule-sets are implemented as frames with each rule-set keeping track of its member rules and vice versa. A rule-set is linked to a specific object and message name using the *use-rule-set-for* macro as shown:

(use-rule-set-for *object rule-set message-name-list*)

Rules-sets are indexed within objects by the names of the messages in which they are used. When an HSKB-method is invoked by a message, one or more rule-sets become active and only rules from these rule-sets can be used to satisfy the message.

5.3 Association of Rule-set, Messages and Goals

Using HSKB, methods can be defined for an object which consult a local knowledge base. Such methods are constructed by calling *define-HSKB-method*, and are distinct from standard procedural methods that are created via *defmessage*. The format is shown here:

(define-HSKB-method *object message-name arg-list*
 goal-pattern)

They are, however, used in the same way (that is, the message sender cannot tell the difference). An HSKB method definition specifies which object (class) it belongs to, the message name it implements, the parameters for the method and a top level goal pattern. The method's parameters become pattern variables bound to the message arguments. These values are then substituted into the goal pattern and inferencing is invoked to try to satisfy the resulting goal.

The return value of an HSKB method can be provided through the execution of a *Return-value* statement otherwise it is defined to be the bindings returned by the goal.

5.4 Inheritance of Rule-sets

When an object receives a message which is implemented by an HSKB method, it uses any rule-set attached to the object that is applicable to that message. In addition, rule-sets associated with this message which belong to the object's ancestors become available. Thus a combined set of rules is formed, made up of all the rule-sets from the object's hierarchy which apply to the message.

The rules governing the combination of rule-sets are as follows: rules from objects which are closer to the message recipient have precedence (that is they are always tried first); if two or more rule-sets each contain a rule with the same name, then only the one closest to the recipient object is used (called rule shadowing); there is no defined precedence between rule-sets attached to the same object, and sharing a rule name among such rule-sets is prohibited.

The rule-sets thus inherited and combined form a local knowledge base, which is then used by the inference engine while trying to satisfy the message. That is, the entire backward chaining inference process utilizes this knowledge base, excluding messages and functions called from within rules. This inheritance mechanism provides for general rules to be defined for abstract classes and for more specialized rules to be defined for more specific classes. Also, rule shadowing allows for inherited rules, which do not apply to a lower class, to be overridden.

5.5 Overall Inference Process

This section summarizes the entire HSKB process. A hierarchy of objects are defined before any messages are sent. Rules are defined and grouped into rule-sets and each rule-set is attached to an object in the hierarchy. Each rule-set is then associated to one or more messages and HSKB methods are defined, including a top level goal for inferencing. The following steps are then performed:

1. The object receives a message.

2. The method for this message is found either in the object or in an ancestor.

3. If this method is not an HSKB-method then it has a compiled function definition and is directly executed.

4. Rule sets which apply to the current message are taken from the object and inherited from its ancestors. These rule sets are combined into a single knowledge base.

5. The message arguments are substituted for pattern variables in the top-level goal pattern for the HSKB-method.

6. The inference engine tries to satisfy the resulting goal pattern using the combined (inherited) knowledge base.

6.0 A SIMPLE HSKB EXAMPLE

Consider a simple example where an HSKB-message, called *request-resource*, requests five Digital Technicians for processing a task. The decision logic for allocating Digital Technicians is defined as follows:

1. If the technicians are available, assign them to the task.

2. If there are not sufficient Digital Technicians available, then attempt to acquire Mechanical Technicians with digital certification (alternate resources).

3. If there are no alternate resources available, then find all tasks that are being serviced by Digital Technicians (or Mech. techs with digital certification) and determine if any of these tasks can be preempted. If so, suspend the task's processing and acquire this resource. Reschedule the task for processing when the resource becomes available.

4. If there are no alternate resources and/or tasks that can be interrupted, then notify the current task to wait until enough of the requested resource becomes available.

Now suppose, the following HSKB top level rules are defined for the above decision logic:

```
(define-rule p8 generic-resource-rule
    :lhs (request-resource ?res ?task)
    :rhs ((number-available ?res ?task))
    :documentation
        "Checks if resource is available")
```

```
(define-rule p9 generic-resource-rule
    :lhs (request-resource ?res ?task)
    :rhs ((look-to-alt-res ?res ?task))
    :documentation "Checks if alternate resource available")
```

```
(define-rule p10 generic-resource-rule
    :lhs (request-resource ?res ?task)
    :rhs ((bind ?time-to-resume
                (+ *current-simulation-time*
                    (ask ?task duration)))
          (bind-in-list ?task-to-suspend
                (ask ?res tasks-currently-using-res))
          (ask ?task-to-suspend is-interruptible)
          (tell ?task-to-suspend interrupt ?time-to-resume)
          (return-value (ask ?task-to-suspend resource)))
    :documentation
        "Determines all tasks using the desired
        resource and finds if any are interruptible.
        If so, returns the desired resource.")
```

```
(define-rule p11 generic-resource-rule
    :lhs (request-resource ?res ?task)
    :rhs ((call '(add-task-to-wait-queue ?res ?task)))
    :documentation
        "Tell task to wait for resource to
        be available")
```

These rules are then placed in the rule-set, *digital-technician-assignment-rules*, attached to the object *Resources* and associated to the *request-resource* HSKB message.

For our example, a task requests 5 Digital Technicians. The Digital Technician object has an attribute called *rule-set-hash-table*. The rule-set-hash-table's keys are the associated HSKB message names, in this case *request-resource*. In our example, the Digital Technician object does not have a rule set related to the *request resource* message. However, Digital Technician's parent, the class object *Resources*, contains the rule-set *digital-technician-assignment-rules*. This rule-set is collected and now forms the local knowledge base.

The rule-set is then searched for a :lhs matching on the goal generated by the *request-resource* message. The first goal that is tested on the :rhs is *number-available*. For our example, let us say there are two more Digital Technicians requested then are available. This condition causes this rule to fail.

The next condition of *request-resource* attempts to satisfy the *look-for-alt-res* request. For the purposes of our example, we will assume that this request also fails. The inference process then proceeds to *rule p10*.

Rule p10, utilizes the HSKB special functions, *bind and bind-in-list*. The variable *?time-to-resume* is bound to a point in time when the task, if interrupted, may continue processing. The :rhs then binds the variable *?task-to-suspend* to those tasks currently using the required resources. These tasks are then individually queried to determine if they are interruptible. The process backtracks through the successive candidate tasks until an interruptible task is found or all candidates are exhausted. If successful, the desired resource is returned, otherwise, the rule fails and the fourth rule is tried.

7.0 CONCLUSION

This paper has described the HSKB paradigm for performing embedded reasoning in OOS. HSKB utilizes a central knowledge base for defining IF-THEN rule logic. This knowledge base is then segmented into rule-sets that are organized according to categories or themes and later attached to the appropriate objects. Inference is invoked by special HSKB messages that correspond to specific situations. Thus, only rules pertaining to these situations are inferenced over during simulation. This approach differs from much of the previous work in knowledge based simulation, where decision logic is actually *hard coded* directly on the object. With HSKB, the benefits of expert systems to simulations are realized and the performance penalties on simulation due to expert systems are reduced.

8.0 FUTURE RESEARCH

Future research is directed toward the development of an enhanced demon driven inference engine that supports both forward and backward reasoning. Faster match algorithms and a more robust rule language are also required. Applications of HSKB to adaptive simulations will be investigated. Other efforts include applications of HSKB outside of OOS.

REFERENCES

Adelsberger, Heimo H. 1986 "Rule based object oriented simulation systems." INTELLIGENT SIMULATION ENVIRONMENTS Vol. 17, No. 1, pp. 107-112.

Castillo, D., McRoberts, M., Sieck, B. 1988a. "Embedded Expert Systems Improve Model Intelligence in Simulation Experiments." In Proceedings of Summer Simulation Conference (Seattle, WA, July 24-26).

Castillo, D., McDaniel, M., Sieck, B. and Tilley, R. 1988b. "Coupling Artificial Intelligence and Simulation for Analyzing Payload Ground Operations at Kennedy Space Center." In Proceedings of First Florida Artificial Intelligence Research Symposium (Orlando, FL, May 4-6).

Castillo, D., Ihrie, D., McDaniel, M., Tilley, R. 1987. "An AI Approach for Scheduling Space-Station Payloads at Kennedy Space Center."In Proceedings of Third Annual Conference on Artificial Intelligence in Space Applications (Huntsville, AL, Nov), pp. 361-370.

Charniak, Eugene, Riesbeck, Christopher, McDermott, Drew, Meehan, James 1987. Artificial Intelligence Programming. Lawrence Erlbaum Associates, Hillsdale, NJ.

Hilton, Mike 1987. "The Eric User's Manual." Griffiss AFB, New York.

Kitzmiller, C.T. 1988. "Simulation and AI: Coupling symbolic and numeric computing." In ARTIFICIAL INTELLIGENCE AND SIMULATION: The Diversity of Applications (San Diego, CA, Feb), pp. 3-7.

McArthur, D., Klahr, P. 1982. The ROSS Language Manual, N-1854-AF, The Rand Corporation, Santa Monica, CA.

McRoberts, Malcolm, Fox, Mark, Husain, Nizwer 1985. "Generating model abstraction scenarios in KBS." In Proceedings of AI, Graphics and Simulation (San Diego, CA, Feb), pp. 29-33.

O'Keefe, Robert 1986. "Simulation and expert systems- A taxonomy and some examples." SIMULATION 46:1, (Jan): 10-16.

Reddy, Y.V. Ramana, Fox, Mark S., Husain, Nizwer, McRoberts, Malcolm 1986. "The Knowledge-Based Simulation System. IEEE Software (Mar): 26-37.

Schank, Roger, Abelson, Robert P. 1975. "Scripts, Plans and Knowledge." In Proceedings of 4th IJCAI, pp. 151-157.

Shannon, Robert E. 1986. "Intelligent simulation environments." INTELLIGENT SIMULATION ENVIRONMENTS Vol. 17, No. 1, pp. 150-156.

Stefik, M., Bobrow, D. 1986. "Object-Oriented Programming: Themes and Variations.", The AI Magazine, p. 40-62.

Sterling, Leon, Shapiro, Ehud 1986. The Art of Prolog. The MIT Press, Cambridge, Mass.

Simulation and AI, 1989
©1989 by the Society for Computer
Simulation International
ISBN 0-911801-44-8

A revisitation of the erlang-b formula and an algorithm for its easy computation

Peter D. Rizik, Sc.D
Booz, Allen & Hamilton, Inc.
4330 East-West Highway, Bethesda MD 20814

Horst Ulfers
Defense Communications Agency
C4S-A710, Arlington VA 22212-5409

ABSTRACT

The following paper is a revisitation of the Erlang-B calculation used in telecommunications management. An algorithm that dramatically reduces computation time from the direct approach is illustrated. A review of the formula derivation and a discussion of the assumptions has been prompted by a view of a general misunderstanding among practitioners of the calculation and its applicability in the industry.

INTRODUCTION

The massive telecommunications industry boom has affected technology throughout the world and shows no sign of slowing down in the near future. This growth has also created a demand for the technical practice of all aspects of telecommunications engineering - planning, design, operations, transmission, and maintenance - in the management of the large telecommunications infrastructures that thread together information and communities around the globe. Simultaneously, the computer revolution, which predated the telecommunications revolution by nearly a decade, has brought powerful personal computers to the desks of management, making computer literacy a must for managers in all industries. In fact, accredited business schools in the United States are required to provide minimal computer instruction to today's business degree candidates - the managers of tomorrow. Computer applications to management problems are no longer the sole domain of electrical engineers, economists, and operations researchers. The unfortunate trend of a general mathematics competency decline in the United States as shown by the National Iowa Standardized tests, the National SAT and National GMAT scores, raises concerns about general computer application aptitude. One concern involves the application of an often used computer simulation decision aid for telecommunications management. Proper management of telecommunications assets requires sound engineering/economic decisions regarding numbers of switches, personnel telecommunications trunks, and channels within trunks. Many practitioners rely on computer simulation decision aids based on operations research application methodology to guide decisions on complex or computationally intensive management problems.

One such problem arises in the figuring of the optimal trunk sizes to service communications demands. A standard operations research application to telecommunications is generally used. The application is the Erlang-B traffic blocking calculation.

Since the post-divestiture telecommunications growth, an epidemic misunderstanding or misbelief of the basic principles of traffic engineering has plagued the telecommunications industry. Principles laid down by the Danish mathematician A. K. Erlang in 1917 are just as valid today as they were 71 years ago; these methods are widely applicable and cited as standard recommended procedures by the CCITT, Vol. 2, red book, 1976. Many practitioners correctly use the application. More, however, do not.

Some of the applications of the Erlang-B formula are akin to the following scenario. A manager purchases a PC for management applications. The manager usually writes application programs where he finds use of a formula with the term n!. Instead of finding out what the term n! is and writing his own subroutine to access whenever n! is needed, the manager purchases a package to access a look-up table of n! instead of writing a single subroutine to compute n!. This is an apparent waste of money for the manager and the company.

This paper is a revisitation of the assumptions and derivation of the Erlang-B formula. An extensive list of sources and other significant references are provided in the bibliography. An illustration of a quick and easy algorithm for its computation with few memory or computational requirements is also provided.

Background

The following provides the background for the derivation and attempts to highlight areas of observed confusion.

The most fundamental assumption of classical traffic theory, and stochastic process applications in general, is that call arrivals are independent, one from another. Independence of arrivals produces a random statistical pattern. The random arrival assumption provides a mathematical formulation and allows for solutions to many telephony problems that are otherwise mathematically intractable and only approximated by computer simulation. Although there are many instances in telecommunications where this assumption may not be entirely true, resulting solutions can be modified to more closely approximate cases where correlation between sources of call arrivals occurs. The randomness of call arrivals results in the distribution of the number of calls in a fixed, small period of time to be Poisson distributed. This probability distribution is simply a function of the mean arrival rate of traffic. That is, from the mean arrival rate, estimates can be made for the probability of no arrivals, one arrival, two arrivals, etc., in a given period of time. If 200 calls arrived in 1 hour, the average arrival time is expressed as 200 per hour.

The Erlang-B formula makes no assumption as to the pattern or distribution of call service rates. (The Erlang-C solution, however, assumes a negative exponential service time distribution.) Service rates are usually expressed in number of calls per unit time per channel. For example, if 6 channels serviced a total of 300 calls in one hour, the average channel service rate would be 50 calls per hour.

Another source of confusion has been in the use of the term 'Erlang'. The Erlang-B formula is an equation that computes the probability of blocking on a single connection. An Erlang distribution, on the other hand, is a statistical distribution used to characterize traffic holding times. It is a special case of a gamma distribution where one of the parameters is restricted to the set of positive integers. A final distinction is that an Erlang is a unit of traffic. The total number of Erlangs through a system in a given time period is the mean arrival rate divided by the mean service rate. This ratio is called the traffic load. So, for example, if one call arrives in 1 hour, and occupies the line for one hour, the mean arrival rate is one per hour and the mean service rate is one per hour; so the load is 1 Erlang for the trunk group for the hour (which may have more than 1 channel). On the other hand, if 60 calls arrive in one hour and the trunk group services each one for one minute, the average arrival rate is 60 per hour the service rate is 60 per hour; so the load is also 1 Erlang. A single Erlang is also described as to 3600 call seconds, regardless of how it is composed (e.g., 3600 1-second calls, 60 1-minute calls, or 1 60-minute call). A single Erlang therefore is a distribution of arrival-holding time combinations. The blocking problem can be envisioned as dropping balls in adjacent time slots. If there are 60 calls randomly arriving in an hour, and each will require exactly 1 minute in service, logically more than one trunk will be required to reasonably carry the traffic because the chance of

each of these balls falling in exactly different slots is very small.

The Erlang-B formula is:

$$P_{\mathbf{B}}(\rho, c) = \frac{\dfrac{\rho^c}{c!}}{\displaystyle\sum_{x=0}^{c} \dfrac{\rho^x}{x!}}$$

Given ρ the traffic load in Erlangs and c to be the number of channels on a trunk group, the Erlang-B formula calculates the probability of blocking for the offered traffic. This is the percentage of call arrivals not receiving service because all available channels were occupied when they arrived. No queue can form, blocked calls are cleared.

Another common use of the formula among traffic engineers is to compute the minimum required number of channels on a trunk group to maintain a probability of blocking given a traffic load. For example, given a load of 20 Erlangs and a requirement of probability of blocking not to exceed .01, use of the formula allows for computation of the minimum required number of channels at 30.

The system, shown in exhibit 1, is the single connection for which the Erlang-B formula applies. Often this segment is part of a larger network. Offered traffic is assumed to enter, for example, node A on the left. If a channel is unoccupied, the call arrival enters into service instantaneously. If all channels are occupied, a newly arriving call is dropped from the system. Serviced calls exit at node B. Service time at each of the nodes is assumed neglible, the application only involves the serving channels in the trunk group.

Exhibit 1:
The System: A c Channel Trunk Group

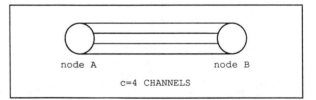

node A   node B

c=4 CHANNELS

The following presents the derivation of the Erlang-B formula and attempts to identify points in the mathematical steps where key assumptions are made which the telecommunications practitioner should realize.

The Derivation

Let c be the number of channels connecting nodes A and B. Let $P_n(t+\Delta t)$ be the probability of n calls being in the system, at time $t+\Delta t$. Assume no queue can form if the number in the system is the number in service. Let λ be the average arrival rate of calls to the system. The probability of a call arrival occurring between time t and t+Δt is $\lambda\Delta t + 0(\Delta t)$. Define Δt so small that the chances of more than one arrival in Δt is zero. $o(\Delta t)$ is the probability that more than one arrival occurs in Δt and is a quantity that becomes negligible as $\Delta t \to 0$; that is,

$$\lim_{\Delta t \to 0} \frac{o(\Delta t)}{\Delta t} = 0$$

We have chosen Δt small enough that $(\Delta t)^n = 0$ for n>1. Call arrivals are assumed independent one from another.

Similarly, the probability of a service completion between t and Δt is $\mu(n)\Delta t + 0(\Delta t)$. Where μ is the average service completion rate on a single channel, and if n channels are occupied, the probability of exactly one service completion is $\mu n \Delta t + o(\Delta t)$.

To have n in the system at time t+Δt, either one arrival occurred between t and Δt when there were n-1 in the system, or one service of n+1 calls was completed between time t and t+Δt, or with n in the system neither an arrival nor service completion occured between time t and t+Δt.

STEP 1:

For $0 \le n \le c-1$

$$P_n(t+\Delta t) = P_n(t)(1-\lambda\Delta t)(1-\mu n\Delta t) + P_{n-1}(t)\lambda\Delta t + P_{n+1}(t)(n+1)\mu\Delta t$$

For $n \ge c$,

$$P_n(t+\Delta t) = P_n(t)(1-\lambda\Delta t)(1-\mu c\Delta t) + P_{n-1}(t)\lambda\Delta t + P_{n+1}(t)(c)\mu\Delta t$$

For n = 0,

$$P_0(t+\Delta t) = P_0(t)(1-\lambda\Delta t)+P_1(t)\mu\Delta t$$

STEP 2:

For $0 \le n \le c-1$,

$$P_n\frac{(t+\Delta t)}{\Delta t} =$$

$$\frac{[P_n(t)(1-\lambda\Delta t)(1-\mu n\Delta t)+P_{n-1}(t)\lambda\Delta t+P_{n-1}(t)(n+1)\mu]\Delta t}{\Delta t}$$

then

$$\lim_{\Delta t \to 0} \frac{P_n(t+\Delta t)-P_n(t)}{\Delta t} = \frac{dP_n(t)}{dt}$$

$$= -P_n(t)(\lambda+\mu n) + P_{n-1}(t)\lambda + P_{n+1}(t)(n+1)\mu$$

For $n \ge c$,

$$\frac{P_n(t+\Delta t)-P_n(t)}{\Delta t} =$$

$$\frac{[-P_n(t)(\lambda+c\mu)+P_{n-1}(t)\lambda+P_{n+1}(t)c\mu]\Delta t}{\Delta t}$$

then

$$\lim_{\Delta t \to 0} \frac{P_n(t+\Delta t)-P_n(t)}{\Delta t} = \frac{dP_n(t)}{dt} =$$

$$-P_n(t)(\lambda+c\mu) + P_{n+1}(t)\lambda+P_{n+1}(t)c\mu$$

For n = 0,

then

$$\lim_{\Delta t \to 0} \frac{P_0(t+\Delta t)-P_0(t)}{\Delta t} = \frac{dP_n(t)}{dt} = -P_0(t)\lambda+P_1(t)\mu$$

STEP 3:

A stationary solution implies $P_n(t)$ is to be independent of time, $P_n(t)=P_n$. There are no changes over time, so,

$$\frac{dP_n(t)}{dt} = 0$$

then,

For $0 \le n \le c-1$,

$$-P_n(\lambda+n\mu)+\lambda P_{n-1}+P_{n+1}(n+1)\mu = 0$$

For $n \ge c$

$$-P_n(\lambda+c\mu)+\lambda P_{n-1}+P_{n+1}c\mu = 0$$

For n = 0

$$-\lambda P_0 + \mu P_1 = 0$$

STEP 4:

So for $0 \le n \le c-1$,

$$P_{n+1} = P_n \frac{(\lambda+n\mu)}{(n+1)\mu} - P_{n-1}\frac{\lambda}{(n+1)\mu}$$

For $n \ge c$

$$P_{n+1} = P_n \frac{(\lambda+c\mu)}{c\mu} - P_{n-1}\frac{\lambda}{c\mu}$$

For n = 0

$$P_1 = \frac{\lambda}{\mu} P_0$$

STEP 5:

Iteration yields the following where the load $\rho = \frac{\lambda}{\mu}$,

$$P_1 = \rho P_0$$

$$P_2 = \frac{\rho^2 P_0}{2!} \qquad n = 1$$

Since $P_2 = P_1 \frac{(\lambda+\mu)}{2\mu} - \frac{\lambda}{2\mu}$

$\qquad = \frac{\lambda P_0}{\mu} \frac{(\lambda+\mu)}{2\mu} - P_0 \frac{\lambda}{2\mu}$

$\qquad = \frac{P_0}{2} [\rho (\rho+1) - \rho]$

$\qquad = \frac{\rho^2 P_0}{2}$

then

$$P_3 = \frac{\rho^3 P_0}{3!} \qquad n = 2$$

$\qquad \vdots$

$$P_m = \frac{\rho^m P_0}{m!} \qquad n = m-1 \leq c-1$$

$\qquad \vdots$

$$P_c = \frac{\rho^c P_0}{c!} \qquad n = c$$

$$P_c = \frac{\rho^{c+1} P_0}{(c!) c} \qquad n = c+1$$

$\qquad \vdots$

$$P_c = \frac{\rho^{c+r} P_0}{(c!) c^r} \qquad n = c+r$$

So in general,

$$P_n = \frac{\rho^n P_0}{n!} \qquad n \leq c$$

$$P_n = \frac{\rho^n P_0}{(c!) c^{n-c}} \qquad n \geq c$$

STEP 6:

Since we discard any arrivals from the system if all c channels are servicing calls, then the only equation of interest is when n≤c.

Then the only equation characterizing the system is:

$$P_n = \frac{\rho^n P_0}{n!}$$

since n cannot exceed c.

Since

$$\sum_{n=0}^{c} P_n = 1, \quad \sum_{n=0}^{c} \frac{\rho^n P_0}{n!} = 1.$$

So $P_0 = \left[\sum_{n=0}^{c} \frac{\rho^n}{n!} \right]^{-1}$

Therefore the Erlang B formula for load ρ and c channels is

$$P_c = \frac{\rho^c}{c!} \left[\sum_{n=0}^{c} \frac{\rho^n}{n!} \right]^{-1}$$

and is interpreted as the probability that an arrival is blocked. $P_n = P_c$ because a blockage can only occur if n = c (i.e., the system channels are all occupied.) which is the Erlang B blocking probability formula.

Review of Limitations:

This section provides a review of the more important limitations or assumptions concerning Erlang B applicability. Many telecommunications practitioners commonly misinterpret or misquote the application and argue against its use.

The first limitation or restriction is that this formula applies to one link as shown in Exhibit 1 — application to an entire network is more complicated.

Secondly, Δt was chosen conveniently small with respect to λ and μ so that the chance of more than one arrival or service completion in Δt is zero. In Step 1, the terms $\mu n \Delta t$ and $\mu c \Delta t$ represent exactly one service completion for n and c respectively. So Δt is chosen with respect to the larger c as well. But, in Step 2, Δt goes to zero in the limit so this is not a real limitation for practitioners.

The largest outcry concerns Step 3, where a stationary solution is chosen to change $P_n(t)$ to P_n. This allows the derivative to be set to zero to solve for P_n to begin the iteration. In telecommunications trunking the assumption that the state probabilities do not change over time, although not realistic, is reasonable because   estimates for the load ρ over the busy hour is used to estimate maximum demand for which we calculate the minimum number of trunks which satisfies a pre-specified probability of blocking for the link. The Erlang B formula assumes that P_n does not change over time; in fact, P_n is stationary. For erratic systems, the probability of blocking estimate should be qualified as to only hold true over small time periods. Areas of application, however, are often point-in-time, crisis control characterizations.

In Step 6, the exact meaning of P_c is the probability that the system is in state $n = c$, after which a call must arrive in order to be blocked. The proportion P_c is the Erlang B formula.

Finally, the Erlang-B calculation can be used to calculate trunk sizes for data applications where no queues can form. However, more often, packet switching networks carry data applications where queues are permissable and therefore Erlang B does not apply.

Exhibit 2:
A1; Direct Computation for c Channels, ρ Load

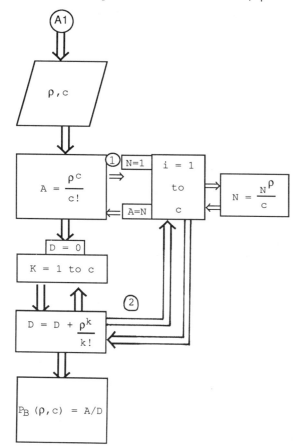

Exhibit 3:
A2; Iterative Computation for c* Channels, ρ Load

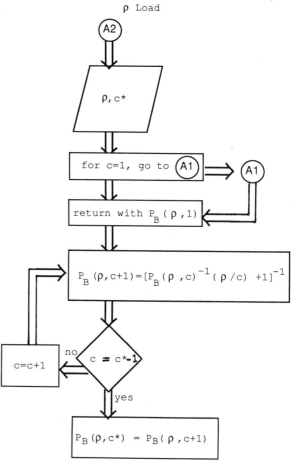

Algorithms:

Algorithm A1 in Exhibit 2 illustrates the computational steps of direct calculation of Erlang-B. This algorithm takes longer to process for each successive step as ρ or c gets large. For large c or ρ (e.g., ≥ 20), the computation time is dramatic and many desktop PCs cannot hold such large numbers in buffer space without overflow errors. To prevent these errors, routine 1 is a subroutine for piecemeal computation of $\rho^c/c!$ which can be used when overflows occur. The same subroutine is accessed in Step 2 for the same reason. The output is the probalility of blocking for ρ and c. This algorithm is still very slow for even modest applications concerning, for example, Defense Communications Systems' traffic loads over 20 Erlangs.

Algorithm A2 performs the same output calculation given the same inputs, but is much more efficient, and, as illustrated in Exhibit 3 is simpler. This algorithm skips to algorithm A1 to compute the starting probability of blocking for ρ and $c = 1$, then iteratively computes the blocking probability for c = 2, c = 3, and so on until c = c*, where c* is the input number of trunks. The recursive relationship takes advantage of the summation in the denominator of the Erlang B formula by taking the inverse. Computation time for c = c* is similar to the time it takes to do c* inverse operations. It is fast, simple, and does not rely on approximation functions.

Conclusions:

An enormous body of literature illustrating the derivation of and expansion to the Erlang-B formula exists today. Most of it was written between 1917 and the 1970's. The relatively recent telecommunications boom experienced worldwide has prompted this revisitation of one of the most often used, and sometimes misused, calculations in telecommunications engineering. This paper has served to clarify some of the assumptions in the derivation and illustrate a simple means of computer simulation of the calculation. The algorithms for simple and quick calculation of blocking probabilities have been used on office PC's for preliminary estimation in communication architecture designs for the Defense Communications Agencies 1995 and 2005 worldwide C^3 systems.

REFERENCES

Ackoff, R.L. and M.W. Sasieni. 1968. "Fundamentals of Operational Research." New York: John Wiley & Sons.

Akimaru, H. and T. Nishimura. 1963. "The Derivatives of Erlang's B-Formula." *Review of the Electrical Communication Laboratory*. 428-444.

Barnes, D.H. 1976. "Extreme Value Engineering of Small Switching Offices." *Eighth ITC*, Paper 242.

Bear, D. 1958. "The Use of 'Pure Chance' and 'Smoothed' Traffic Tables in Telephone Engineering." *Proceedings of the 2nd International Teletraffic Congress (The Hague)*.

Bear, D. 1973. "Some Theories of Telephone Traffic Distribution: A Critical Survey." *Seventh ITC*, Paper 531.

Bear, D. and Seymour, C.A. 1973. "A Traffic Prediction Model for a Telephone Exchange Network." *Proceedings of the 7th International Teletraffic Congress (Stockholm)*. 536/1-5.

Beckmann, P. 1968. "An Introduction to Elementary Queuing Theory and Telephone Traffic." Boulder, CO: The Golem Press.

Benes, V.E. 1965. *Mathematical Theory of Connecting Networks and Telephone Traffic*. Academic Press.

Berkeley, G.S. 1949. "Traffic and Trunking Principles in Automatic Telephony." Ernest Benn, 2nd revised ed.

Bininda, N. and G. Daisenberger. 1967. "Recursive and Iterative Formulae for the Calculation of Losses in Link Systems of any Description." Preprints of Technical Papers, *5th International Teletraffic Congress* (New York). 318-326.

Botsch, D. 1967. "International Standardising of Loss Formulae?" *5th International Teletraffic Congress*. (New York). 90-95.

Bridgford, J.N. 1964. "The Geometric Group Concept and its Application to the Dimensioning of Link Access Systems." *Proceedings of the 4th International Teletraffic Congress, (London)*. Paper 13.

Broadhurst, S.W. and A.T. Harmston. 1953. "Studies of Telephone Traffic With the Aid of a Machine." *Proceedings of the IEE*. 259-274.

Brockmeyer, E.; H.L. Halstrom; and A. Jensen. 1948. *The Life and Works of A.K. Erlang*. Copenhagen Telephone Company.

"Calculation of the Number of Circuits in a Group Carrying Overflow Traffic." CCITT Recommendation E.521, *Orange Book*. 2, No. 2: 218.

CCITT. 1964a. "Determination of the Number of Circuits Necessary to Carry a Given Traffic Flow," Recommendation E95, *Blue Book* II: 203 and Q84. *Blue Book* VI: 125.

CCITT. 1964b. "Measurements of Traffic Flow." Recommendation E90, *Blue Book* II: 143 and Q80. *Blue Book* VI: 119.

CCITT. 1976. "Determination of the Number of Circuits in Automatic and Semi-Automatic Operation." CCITT Recommendation E. 520, *Orange Book*. II.2: 211.

Clos, C. and R.I. Wilkinson. 1952. "Dialing Habits of Telephone Subscribers." *Bell System Technical Journal*. 32-67.

Dartois, J.P. 1970. "Lost Call Cleared Systems With Unbalanced Traffic Sources." *Proceedings of the 6th International Teletraffic Congress (Munich)*. 215/1-7.

Dayem R. 1979. "Alternate Routing in High Blocking Communications Networks." *NTC*. 28.4.1-28.4.6.

Duffy, F. and R.A. Mercer. 1978. "A Study of Network Performance and Customer Behavior During Direct Distance Dialing Call Attempts in the U.S.A." *Bell Systems Technical Journal* 57, No. 1.

Elsner, W.B. 1979. "Dimensioning Trunk Groups for Digital Networks." *Ninth ITC*, Paper 421.

Engset, T. 1918. "Die Wahrscheinlichkeitsrechnung zur Bestimmung der Wahleranzahl in Automatischen Fernsprechamtern." *Electrotech. Z*. 304-305.

Erlang, A.K. 1918. "Solution of Some Problems in the Theory of Probabilities of Significance in Automatic Telephone Exchanges." *Post Office Electrical Engineering Journal*. 189-197.

Feller, W. 1968. *An Introduction to Probability Theory and its Applications*. New York: John Wiley & Sons.

Furness, K.P. 1965. "Time Function Iteration." *Traffic Eng. & Control*. 458-460.

Goleworth, H.M.G.; R.C. Kyme; and J.A.T. Rowe. 1972. "The Measurement of Telephone Traffic." *Post Office Electrical Engineering Journal*. 227-233.

Gosztony, G. 1973. "Full Availability One-Way and Both-Way Trunk Groups With Delay and Loss Type Traffic, Finite Number of Traffic Sources and Limited Queue Length." *Proceedings of the 7th International Teletraffic Congress (Stockholm)*. 341/1-8.

Grinsted, W.H. 1915. "A Study of Telephone Traffic Problems with the Aid of the Principles of Probability." *Post Office Electrical Engineering Journal*. 33-45.

Hayward, W.S. 1958. "Traffic Engineering and Administration of Line Concentrators." *Proceedings of the 2nd International Teletraffic Congress (The Hague)*. Paper No. 23.

Hayward, W.S. Jr. and R.I. Wilkinson. 1970. "Human Factors in Telephone Systems and Their Influence on Traffic Theory, Especially with Regard to Future Facilities." *Sixth International Teletraffic Congress (ITC)*, Paper 431.

Hayward, W.S. and R.I. Wilkinson. 1970. "Human Factors in Telephone Systems and Their Influence on Traffic Theory Especially With Regard to Future Facilities." *Proceedings of the 6th International Teletraffic Congress (Munich)*. 431/1-10.

Iverson, V.B. 1973. "Analysis of Real Teletraffic Process Based on Computerized Measurements." *Review of the Electrical Communication Laboratory*. 3-64.

Jacobaeus, C. 1950. "A Study on Congestion in Link Systems." *Ericsson Tech*. 1-70.

Katz, S.S. 1979. "Improved Network Administration Process Utilizing End-to-End Service Considerations." *International Teletraffic Conference*.

Kleinrock, L. 1975. *Queueing Systems Volume 1: Theory*. New York: John Wiley & Sons.

Kosten, L. 1948. "On the Validity of the Erlang and Engset Loss Formulae." *PTT-Bedr*. 42-45.

Kosten, L.; J.R. Manning; and R. Garwood. 1949. *On the Accuracy of Measurements of Probabilities of Loss in Telephone Systems*. *J. R. Statistical Society*. 54-67.

Laue, R.V. and R.K. Even. 1977. "Traffic Consideration for Line Concentrators." *National Telecommunication Conference*.

LeGall, P. 1970. "Sur L'Influence des Repititions d'Appels dans l'Ecoulement du Traffic Telephonique." *Sixth ITC*, Paper 432.

Kosten, L. 1957. "Application of Artificial Traffic Methods to Telephone Problems." *Teleteknik (Engl. Ed.)*. 107-110.

Marrows, B. 1959. "Circuit Provision for Small Quantities of Traffic." *Telecommunications Journal, Aust*. 208-211.

Martin, N.H. 1923. "A Note on the Theory of Probability Applied to Telephone Traffic Problems." *Post Office Electrical Engineering Journal*. 237-241.

Members of Technical Staff, Bell Telephone Laboratories. 1977. *Engineering and Operations in the Bell System*. Western Electric.

Mina, R.R. 1974. *Introduction to Teletraffic Engineering*. Chicago: Telephony Publishing Corporation.

Molina, E.C. 1922. "The Theory of Probabilities Applied to Telephone Trunking Problems." *Bell System Technical Journal*. 69-81.

Morrison, J.A. October 1980. "Analysis of Some Overflow Problems with Queueing." *Bell System Technical Journal*. 1427-1462.

Myskja, A. and O.O. Walmann. 1973. "A Statistical Study of Telephone Traffic Data with Emphasis on Subscriber Behaviour." *Seventh ITC*, Paper 132.

Nivert, K. and C. Von Schantz. 1973. "Some Methods for Improving the Efficiency of Simulation." *Proceedings of the 7th International Teletraffic Congress (Stockholm)*. 214/1-5.

Palm, C. 1954. *Table of the Erlang Loss Formula*. Stockholm: L. M. Ericsson.

Parviala, A. 1973. "Calculation of the Optimum Number of Trunk Lines Based on Moe's Principle." *Proceedings of the 7th International Teletraffic Congress (Stockholm)*. 422/1-5.

Povey, J.A. and A.C. Cole. 1965. "The Use of Electronic Digital Computers for Telephone Traffic Engineering." *Post Office Electrical Engineering Journal*. 203-209.

O'Dell, G.F. 1927. "An Outline of the Trunking Aspect of Automatic Telephony." *Journal of the IEE*. 185-222.

Rahko, K. 1970. "A Study of the Traffic Process Based on Measurements." *Sixth ITC*, Paper 537.

Rapp, Y. 1968. "Some Economic Aspects on the Long-Term Planning of Telephone Networks." *Ericsson Rev*. Pt. 1: 61-71, 122-136.

Reference Tables Based on A. K. Erlang's Interconnection Formula. 1961. Siemens & Halske Aktiengesellschaft.

"Report of the 1st International Congress on the Application of the Theory of Probability in Telephone Engineering and Administration, Copenhagen." 1957 *Teleteknik (English Ed.)*. 1-130.

"Report of the 2nd International Congress on the Application of the Theory of Probability in Telephone Engineering and Administration, (The Hague, 1958). 1960. *PTT-Bedr*. 159-209.

"Report on the Proceedings of the 4th International Teletraffic Congress, London, 1964." *Post. Office Telecommunications Journal*. Special Issue. 1-66.

Smith, N.M.H. "Erlang Loss Tables and Other Parameters for Normally Distributed Offered Traffics."

Proceedings of the 4th International Teletraffic Congress, Paper No. 100.

Syski, R. 1965. *Introduction to Congestion Theory in Telephone Systems*. London: Oliver and Boyd.

Telephone Traffic Theory, Tables, and Charts. 1970. Munich: Siemens Aktiengesellschaft.

Teletraffic Engineering Manual. 1966. Stuttgart: Standard Elektrik Lorenz AG.

Wilkinson, R.I. March 1956. "Theories for Toll Traffic Engineering in U.S.A." *Bell System Technical Journal*.

Wilkinson, R.I. 1970. "Non Random Traffic Curves and Tables for Engineering and Administrative Purposes." Traffic Studies Center, Bell Telephone Laboratories.

Wilson, A.G., and I.G. Heggie. 1969. Discussion article in *Operations Research Quarterly*. 489-496.

Simulation and AI, 1989
©1989 by the Society for Computer
Simulation International
ISBN 0-911801-44-8

The essential components of an intelligent simulation training system

John E. Biegel
Intelligent Simulation Laboratory
University of Central Florida
Orlando, Florida 32816

ABSTRACT

The University of Central Florida, Embry-Riddle Aeronautical University and the General Electric Co.'s Simulation and Control Systems Department are building an Intelligent Simulation Training System (ISTS). The project has now been funded by the State of Florida for the third year of a five year proposed project duration.

This presentation defines and describes the required components (elements) of an ISTS. The components are the simulation, the expert domain knowledge base and the expert domain instructor knowledge base, and the control and instructional components. The control and instructional components include the translator, the input filter, the intelligent pre-processor, the author, the discourse module, the interpreter, the control module, the evaluator, the student model, the tutor and the inference engine. Lines of communication and the types of information to be passed and stored are also discussed.

INTRODUCTION

During the 1986/87 fiscal year, the Florida High Technology and Industry Council provided funding for the University of Central Florida, Embry-Riddle Aeronautical University and the General Electric Co.'s Simulation and Control Systems Department to build an Intelligent Simulation Training System (ISTS). The project is currently being funded on an annual basis by the State of Florida through State University System appropriations. Work on the project was started in January 1987.

The first and most important task was to define the system. The decision had been made to do the first demonstration in air traffic control training. The simulation for this domain is somewhat unique. At the start of a training session, the simulation "drives" the student. The student responds by giving an instruction to the simulator. This instruction "drives" the simulator. The process continues alternately throughout the training session.

It was also decided that system should be generic wherever possible. The rationale was that: 1) we wanted to be able to readily use the system in other domains, and 2) "management" of a simulation requires control of objects in time and space.

ISTS Model

The ISTS model has evolved into several identifiable modules or components. There is extensive interaction between modules and particularly between those within what we have called functional groups.
Those functional groups and their component modules are:

- .Interface Group
  - ..Author
  - ..Discourse

- .Input Group
  - ..Translator
  - ..Input Filter
  - ..Intelligent Pre-processor

- .Control Group
  - ..Interpreter
  - ..Control
  - ..Inference Engine

- .Instruction Group
  - ..Evaluator
  - ..Student Model
  - ..Tutor

- .Domain Expertise Group
  - ..Domain Expert
  - ..Domain Expert Instructor

- .Simulation
  - ..Simulator

Interface Group

The Interface Group provides the mechanisms for the student, instructor and the system analyst to interact with the Simulation/Tutoring process.

The Author provides a user-friendly interface to allow the necessary domain knowledge to be input off-line in an organized fashion. The Author prompts the system analyst for the information, analyzes this knowledge and sends it to the pertinent modules. Domain specific knowledge about instructional strategies, skills to be taught and graded, and methods on how to grade the skills is sent to the Domain Expert Instructor module. The author will also send knowledge on when and how to correctly apply the skills for the specified domain to the Domain Expert module. The keywords and attributes necessary to parse students' input to the system will be sent to the Translator. This domain specific information is now "known" by the system and may be used as required to perform the specified tutoring. The canned messages and menu option specifications are sent to the Discourse.

In the early models, the Author will also load Discourse with its windows, menus, messages, etc. Later, we plan to construct a Machine-Learning Author that will replace the human author.

The Discourse will provide the system communication dialog between the student, instructor, and Tutor. In early models, this will be done through windows, menus, messages, etc.

Discourse is a menu driven communication module between the system and the users. The inputs from the student directed to the Tutor or to the system and the inputs from the instructor are handled in separate menus.

The types of student inputs to Discourse are questions, comments, and tutoring mode requests. The questions reflect the student's need to understand the system or a lesson. A question typically takes one of the following forms, specified as menu options (The list is not exhaustive.):

   a)   What is the action recommended in a specific situation?

   b)   Why is an action recommended in a specific situation?

   c)   What are the alternative actions to handle a specific situation?

The Discourse requests the Tutor to respond to student queries. The Tutor sends the responses to the Discourse. These responses are displayed to the student. The student can also input comments during a lesson. Comments are saved in the Student Model for later review by the instructor. It represents a means of communication between the student and the instructor and vice versa. The student also has the option of requesting a particular tutoring mode.

Before the start of a session, the instructor can access the system through a menu. The instructor may ask for a review of the student records. The student records are read from the Student Model. The details are then displayed for the instructor.

Currently, the instructor can input the objective of the lesson, the level of difficulty, etc., (through a menu). This is based on the student's progress. Eventually, the entire responsibility for these decisions will be incorporated into the Tutor.

The Author supplies the canned messages and menu option specifications for the Discourse.

The Input Group

The Input Group provides the mechanisms by which the student's response to the simulation or the student's desire to modify the simulation are entered into the system.

Within the group, the Translator accepts or rejects student input on the basis of understandable spelling. Incorrectly spelled words are not understandable by the system and must be re-entered. For understandable input, the Translator parses the input. It then checks and accepts or rejects the input on the basis of syntax only. Accepted inputs are passed to the Input Filter.

The Input Filter accepts or rejects the parsed and syntactically correct input on the basis of the constraints of the operational domain. For "dumb" simulations, the Input Filter accepts or rejects the parsed and syntactically correct input on the

basis of the constraints of the object being addressed. Otherwise, inputs accepted by the Input Filter are passed to the object within the Simulator.

If the input is unacceptable to the object, it is rejected. Inputs acceptable to the object are then considered by the object's 'controller'. The 'controller' (pilot, in the case of the ATC system) either accepts or rejects the input. If the input is accepted, the instruction is passed to the object and the simulation is updated.

When an input is rejected, a message may be sent to the student (depending upon the mode in which the system is tutoring). Messages will be sent to the Evaluator when an input is rejected for syntax, for violation of the domain restrictions or for violation of domain rules. The student is not being graded for typing skills nor is the student presumed to know the object's detailed constraints nor the controller's preferences.

The role of the Input Filter is to provide for any filtering not implemented in the simulation objects or in the Translator. The Input Filter is the interface between a domain dependent simulation and a domain independent ISTS.

The form of the output from the Input Filter is an executable message addressed to a simulation object. The inputs that fail the object-related test are reported to the Evaluator with classification parameters. The student receives a simple message, possibly prior to a tutorial intervention. The message is representative of the error caught at the first or the second filtering activity.

Control Group

After the processing of a new input is completed, the Intelligent Pre-Processor communicates the updated event-list to the Interpreter.

The Interpreter keeps a record of the list of pre-input, Intelligent Pre-Processor events. It compares this list to the updated one. It determines if new events are introduced by the input and/or if some pre-input events were eliminated. Otherwise, it notes that there is no change.

The results of this incremental analysis are passed to the Evaluator and to the Control (this is referred to as "Delta-list" in implementation documents). The format of these outputs will be very similar to that of the Intelligent Pre-Processor events, augmented with "side-effect", or "eliminated", or "critical" labels. Another typical output is "no-significant-change-detected-after-the-input".

The Interpreter also checks for critical events. This activity is initiated periodically by the Control module to monitor the Simulation. An event will be considered critical if it is not eliminated before the time indicated on its time-tag or if any priority labels exceed typical threshold values.

The Control is responsible for activating the other modules at the proper time.

The Control follows the outputs of the Interpreter to monitor the critical student-simulation interactions. These outputs specify the changes introduced by a student input. Control uses them to activate the modules that monitor the student's current activity.

The major events in a session, such as student-inputs, situations that require tutor intervention, tutor requests to consult other modules, re-initializations of the simulation, help requests, etc. prompt the Control to activate the related module groupings.

The Control will call the Intelligent Pre-Processor and the Domain Expert for the global analysis of the simulation after a re-initialization, or for all the events related to a single object in the simulation after a student input.

The Interpreter is called to determine the effects of the student input on the Simulation. The Control assures proper Domain Expert/Evaluator communication for matching the student's and the expert's solutions. The Student Model is then activated to update recorded data. Finally, the Tutor is called to make decisions on the course of the session. In addition to the major control loops, the Control also initializes the Evaluator, the Student Model or the Domain Expert individually and directs them to answer consultation requests from the Tutor.

The Inference Engine works with the rules to make inferences based on the current facts in the working memory. The rules from different modules are entered through an editor. When the file containing these rules is compiled by the rule compiler, the rules are converted into an internal representation. The internal representation is a Rete net.

The state of the system is represented by the knowledge in the form of frames/facts in the knowledge base or working memory. Whenever the facts in the working memory satisfy the right hand side of a rule, the Rete net activates that rule. An activated rule is placed into the conflict set. The conflict resolution mechanism selects a rule for firing based on priority criteria specified by the user.

The actions on the right hand side of a rule being fired may cause a change in the knowledge base through assert/retract functions. The actions also could result in calls to other functions; such as prompting, graphic display, etc. Any change in the knowledge base is immediately reflected in the Rete net. This change may trigger some rules to be activated and placed in the conflict set. This process continues until there are no more rules to be fired in the conflict set.

The interface provides facilities for entering into and debugging the rules in the system. The user may watch the rule firing step by step to confirm the correctness of the rules during the debugging phase.

Instruction Group

The Evaluator accesses data from the Domain Expert Instructor to establish a method of scoring. This includes weighting factors and particular scoring criteria for specific lessons. During the course of the lesson, the Domain Expert provides the expert action to which the student's input is compared. The Domain Expert may suggest one or more solutions to related events in the simulation (snapshot-facts).

The syntax errors of the student's response are passed to the Evaluator through the Translator. the Tutor sends the lesson plan to the Evaluator. The Evaluator can identify information needed from the Domain Expert Instructor. This information details scoring mechanisms. The outputs of the Evaluator include raw scores which are provided to the Student Model.

The Input Filter provides the Evaluator with error messages associated with the refusal of student inputs. These messages are representative of contradictions with an object's physical attributes and/or with simulation constraints. The control action errors and other space management logic errors will be deducted from the inputs from the Interpreter. The inputs from the Interpreter allow for complete evaluation of the student's performance. It provides the effects of the student's response on the Simulation. The Evaluator also provides the Tutor with the logic errors associated with objects and traffic management. The Tutor then dynamically restructures the lesson plan so that the student can work on these particular problem areas.

Knowledge concerning how to teach a specific domain will be provided by the Domain Expert Instructor. This will be provided prior to run time; ie, during the authoring stage. The Tutor behaves differently according to the mode in which the system is set to operate for a given session. The demo mode may be requested by the student, in which the system will run through a demonstration. In the coach mode, the Tutor will interact with the student during a lesson to give feedback such as hints or remediation. This mode may be requested by an instructor or may be set by the system itself, if the system is aware that the student must cover certain lessons. Help from the Tutor may be requested by the student during the coach mode. The testing mode is provided to allow for examination and is requested by the instructor. Both student and instructor requests are handled by the Discourse module and this information is then passed to the Tutor.

Data concerning what the student knows about the domain and current student status is provided by the Student Model. Information on the performance skills to be measured and objectives of a lesson are sent to the Evaluator prior to each lesson. Evaluations of student's performance during a lesson are received from the Student Model from which the Tutor can determine if the lesson should be modified or if remediation is necessary.

The decision on the type and level of remediation is based on data about the student within the Student Model. The topics and level of instruction are then given to the Discourse to inform the student. Information about the remediation conducted is then sent to the Student Model for updating the student's record.

The Evaluator provides information about the student performance in handling a specific situation. The Tutor will be able to inquire from the Domain Expert as to how or why a solution was generated. The Tutor will decide when a lesson is complete based on the objectives of the lesson. The final scores and comments on amount of remediation or help given is retrieved from the Student Model, organized for presentation, and sent to the Discourse.

The requests of the Tutor to activate other modules or to re-initialize the Simulation are communicated to the Control. If necessary, the Control reactivates the Tutor after the completion of its request.

The Student Model maintains current knowledge about the student. It receives raw data about the student's performance within the domain from the Evaluator. It also receives remedial information about the student from the Tutor. It uses this current performance data along with the student's previous performance data to generate the student status. The student status is a measurement of overall student performance which is available to the Tutor. The Student Model also produces domain statuses. These statuses are determined from the raw score data of the Evaluator. The domain statuses inform the Tutor of student performance and understanding on specific domain topics.

Information within the Student Model can be requested by the student or the instructor through Discourse. The requested information is provided by the Student Model. Background information about the student is entered off-line by the instructor through Discourse. The student can enter comments about the system as a feedback to the instructor. These comments are entered through the Discourse and can be made both on-line and off-line. They are stored in the student's record for later reference. The system makes no attempts to parse these statements.

Domain Expertise Group

The Domain Expert gets rules and facts for the domain through the Author interface. This is an off-line procedure used to load the Domain Expert with the expertise necessary to generate problem solutions.

The Intelligent Pre-Processor maintains a list of events extracted from the Simulation. The Intelligent Pre-Processor calls the Domain Expert to update its list of current expert actions that deal with this list of events. The Control may pass a selected set of these events to the Domain Expert and read back the related actions.

The Domain Expert reads object data from the Simulation to generate solutions for each selected event. In addition, the Domain Expert is able to justify its solutions upon request. The information leading to the generation of each action (solution, suggested-action) is stored. Each action generated by the Domain Expert has time tags associated with it, defining its valid time period, generation time, etc...

On the Evaluator's request, the Control isolates a subset of actions for comparison with the student response to the Simulation.

The Domain Expert Instructor receives tutoring knowledge for the domain from the Author (lesson plans, guidelines, etc.) This is an off-line procedure initially used to supply the Domain Expert Instructor with the teaching expertise in the application domain. The Domain Expert gives solutions to a problem under a particular set of circumstances. It does not have knowledge on how to teach the domain. The Domain Expert Instructor is needed to fill this gap.

Upon system initialization, the Domain Expert Instructor makes the domain dependent teaching methods, lesson plans, guidelines, scenarios etc., available to the Tutor, and evaluation principles to the Evaluator.

Simulation

The Simulation is a pseudo-real-time process running in parallel with the tutoring system. An object-oriented approach is used in its implementation.

A number of objects with pre-assigned behaviors represent a scenario presented to the student. The scenario can be stopped, then restarted from some past point in time, or modified. These requests are initiated by the Tutor. Significant data is periodically saved for this purpose.

The Domain Expert and the Intelligent Pre-Processor are allowed to access any or all of the object data that is needed.

The student input is received from the Input Filter. If it is accepted by the intelligent object to which it is addressed, this input is allowed to be directly implemented in the current simulation.

The intelligence of the object represents its natural knowledge of its physical status, its physical capabilities and its behavior (such as object requests, input refusals...). In other words, the object has the responsibility for analyzing an input that concerns its own private data. (The Simulation can also do this for the object.) If the objects are "dumb", the Input Filter performs this activity.

Additional roles are available passively in each object. The active capability level of each object in a particular scenario is determined by the Tutor. The objects use this capability to initiate pre-determined situations, generate action requests, arbitrary input refusals, etc.).

An accepted input will update the Simulation. The input time and number will be recorded. If the input is refused, formatted outputs will be sent to the Input Filter. These outputs are comprised of the received input and a list of parameters classifying the error.

ACKNOWLEDGMENT

This research was performed in conjunction with the Intelligent Simulation Training System (ISTS) project, Department of Industrial Engineering and Management Systems, University of Central Florida. ISTS team members included Dr. John E. Biegel, Dr. George H. Brooks, Dr. Avelino J. Gonzalez, Dr. Jose A. Sepulveda, Dr. Chin H. Lee, Murat Draman, Leslie Interrante, Gajanana Nadoli, Cheryl Bagshaw, Jenifer Sargeant and Taha Sidani.

Simulation International
ISBN 0-911801-44-8

A generator of specification models for flexible manufacturing systems: simulation, expert systems and program engineering tools

PECQUET Pascal
Laboratoire d'Informatique
Université Blaise Pascal
B.P. 45 63170 AUBIERE FRANCE

and

ATAYA Ali
Laboratoire d'Informatique et de Productique
Université François RABELAIS Parc de Grandmont
37200 TOURS FRANCE

ABSTRACT

The first objective of this paper is to present the software engineering tools which comprise the simulators SIMAF and PRODUCTICS. In this regard, the principles of each system are introduced. Secondly, we examine the compatibility of the two approaches and the necessity of integration between them. By using a recent application concerning the study of manufacturing workshops, we show the relationship between SIMAF and PRODUCTICS. During the simulation process, a "master-slave" relationship is established. Lastly, we discuss the conditions necessary for optimization of capacity or operation in the job shop.

KEY-WORDS

Simulation, Flexible manufacturing system, Expert Automatic programming, Decision support systems.

INTRODUCTION

The simulation of manufacturing systems covers the domains of capacity and of operations testing. G. Bel mentions application generators in his works (Bel 1987; Steffen 1986), in which workshop models are developed based on capacity studies or on operations testing of restricted class configurations. It follows that the issuing simulation results are limited; the respective models favor either the system or the machine control system. Whereas a future-oriented study of concrete cases shows us that a satifactory analysis of capacity must take into consideration a wide class of production policies. Inversely, improvement of workshop functioning presupposes a fine analysis of the physical system.

Our approach consists in considering these two tendencies by showing the advantages of a common simulation process. This presupposes that, from the start, a data design model be defined, that the nucleus of the simulation be "transparent" to the user, and that the process environment be provided with generation modules and data processing.

THE SIMULATION PROCESS

The simulation process will be presented in two parts. In the first part, we will envisage the SIMAF system dedicated to job shop capacity determination, followed by the PRODUCTICS system, which we have adapted to operations testing.

The SIMAF System (1)

The SLAM (Pritsker 1986) language enables simulation of production systems; however, it is accessible only to specialists. Using the descriptive elements of a job shop (ROUTES, MACHINES, PRODUCTS,

PARTS LIST...), SIMAF generates SLAM, a model ready to be simulated. This software is divided into three parts (Fig. 1) :

- the composition of the job shop's data base,
- the generation of the SLAM model and preparation of the elements for animation,
- the parallel simulation and animation.

In our system, a job shop is defined as a set of convergent routes; each route corresponds to the fabrication of an individual product resulting from one or more assembly operations. Products can undergo either machining or assembly operations.

From a screen display (rolling menus and multiwindows) the generated SLAM file corresponds to the description of routes and their chain of operations.

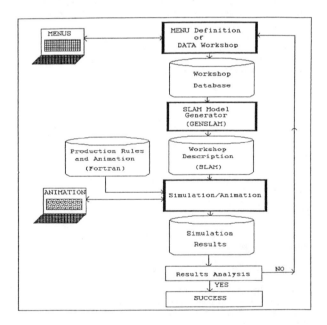

Fig.1 : The simulation processes with SIMAF

Operation rules are programmed in Fortran, made possible through SLAM's compatability with this language.

As defined in (Mellichamp 1987), these rules concern :

- dispatching of parts (erratic or backlog of orders),
- rules governing a machine's choices according to given criteria,

- assignment and release of resources,
- breakdown laws.

The animation parallels the simulation. It depicts the evolution of the job shop through time on three screens. These screens were designed with the PC ANIMATION software package contained in SLAM.

The first screen shows the movement of parts and bottlenecks, the state of the machines (free, occupied or brokendown); the second screen is an animated histogram showing rates of machine occupation, in time; and the third represents a simplified GANTT diagram, showing the state of the factory.

SIMAF is thus a system which adapts itself well to a capacity study of any production system. It is a competitive tool for its ease in defining such a system (Ataya 1988). The animation backup represents an additional advantage for decision making and for choosing a given configuration. On the other hand, operation rules remain rather limited as long as it is necessary to program each rule by a Fortran subroutine.

The PRODUCTICS system (2)

PRODUCTICS is a simulation tool designed to assist in production decisions. Its last version (Pecquet 1988) incorporates a production deadline. It is thus designed to facilitate the study of job operations when one or more production policies have been retained by the designer (Froment 1988). But even more, PRODUCTICS covers the entire simulation process, since it integrates a generator for management rules. The system revolves around three classic steps : modeling, simulation, and processing of results. For a critical approach, see (Guinet 1988, Roubellat 1987).

Modeling is actualized, in backward interface, by the generator (GENSNARK) which produces the expert system's initial base of knowledge, outputting in the syntax of the artificial language.

The simulation process proper is composed of an expert system, rendered totally transparent for the user by a pre-process. The inference engine integrated into the declarative language SNARK (3) (Lauriere 1986) produces a base of final facts and a log file of the simulation requested by the user.

The post-process, or forward interface, is made up of two result processing modules. One of them gives statistical details of the job shop performance studied, by requesting (STATIS). The other, (ANIMA), offers a detailed visualization of the functioning of the management rule tested.

The integration of a deadline into the simulation system henceforth permits us to set up a discrete simulation, step by step, and to analyze the results of "real" functioning, if the proposed model is sufficiently detailed. As seen in the figure (Fig. 2), the operation principle is based on implementing an expert system and its environment. This is so that requests from a backlog of orders may be satisfied, according to a horizon of scheduled production. In activating the rules base, the engine SNARK simulates several production cycles in sequence (Erschler 1988). Making use of meta-knowledge, it dynamically activates algorithms of sequence planning and proposes a leveling of the production according to the latest dates of dispatching as (Ranky 1988). Dispatching is then effected under the user's control, who observes the running of operations testing on the screen. For

the reasons above, and because of its compatibility with SIMAF, PRODUCTICS was designed for exploring a large number of planning algorithms, and for reproducing complex production policies, acceptable within the dimensions of a given job shop (Proth 1988). The base of knowledge, presently implanted, is composed of approximately one hundred rules and more than three hundred facts destined to reproduce about thirty possible combinations of hierarchical machine control rules.

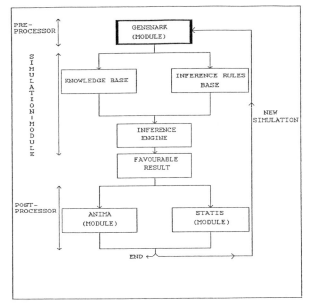

Fig.2 : PRODUCTICS : the expert system and its environment.

Up until now, we have presented the process such as it was developed for the needs of the research. Our study out in the field has shown that these processes should cooperate in the analysis of flexible manufacturing systems. In the second part of this paper, we shall discuss some data exchanges we have achieved.

COOPERATION BETWEEN PROCESSES

From the user's point of view, the simulation must end in a design or in an improvement of the system. In both cases, capacity determination and test operations must be foreseen. Changes in the job shop's operation rules could call into question existing performance capabilities. An increase in performance capability could, as well, reveal the command system's limits. For our part, we have foreseen cooperation between the processes described above. As seen in the figure (Fig. 3), these processes maintain a "Master-Slave" relationship. Our discussion will therefore begin with data exchange and continue through +implementation. These data concern the principal objects manipulated by the two nuclei of simulation. This includes both the objects relative to the physical model, as well as "predicate" objects, proper to the machine control system. Data must then be considered as knowns, available in a data base and able to be manipulated by the processes which are both producers and consumers.

In the case of job shop capacity determination, SIMAF provides results from a given configuration of machines. These results can be analyzed by PRODUCTICS, which provides a performance analysis. The rules from the base of knowledge are then evaluated in order to test the retained capacity measurement. PRODUCTICS plays the role of the consumer, and SIMAF that of the producer in a Master-Slave relationship, which is run by the expert system. The latter takes the role of the designer, measuring entering or exiting loads. Cooperation between the processes thus ends up in testing several management rules for a park of machines.

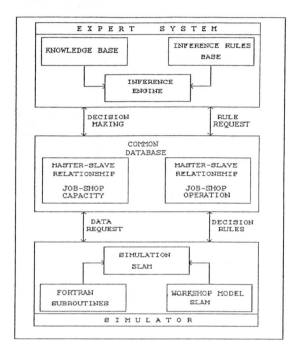

Fig.3 : The cooperation between processes.

During an operations study, PRODUCTICS furnishes the decision rules, proper to the job shop's functioning. By producing the state of the job shop, SIMAF is able to consult the expert system to learn which sequence to follow. In return, it receives a rule of behavior to be applied, which it translates into a new assignment (for example, MACHINE attributes which are able to be interpreted by SLAM). The expert system produces the data indispensable for running the new simulation, and SIMAF consumes them.

According to our aspired objective, the "Master-Slave" relationship evolves to the advantage of one or the other. In the present state of our research, cooperation between processes was studied in the case of simulation with discrete events. The two processes make parallel analyses of the backlog of orders. The operator then analyzes the results and decides whether or not to consult one of the processes again. In our case, the "Master-Slave" relationship is initiated by the operator who, for example, can propose that the expert system choose a rule of machine operation that SIMAF would call as needed for a new situation.

In the near future, cooperation may be partially automated, especially concerning job shop capacity. SIMAF will consume the assignment rules and will execute a simulation of a pre-specified system as long as the expert system has not obtained satisfactory results. As an example, it will be possible to isolate a class of production policies that assures an average rate of engagement superior to 50%.

INTEGRATION BETWEEN PROCESSES

Integration of processes refers to the different modules processed : the pre-process modules which refer to an identical data model (Bel 1988), the process proper, which cooperates and finally, the post-process which displays the results.

The pre-process

Two object generators produce the SLAM source (GENSLAM) and the SNARK source (GENSNARK). These modules are developed in turbo-pascal and produce two ASCII files which can be directly exploited by the simulators. Fusion of the modules is thus easy as long as the process relies on the same data design model of the type entity-association. Moreover, a common screen manager, developed from toolbox, assures a homogeneous preparation of text files, generated in the syntax of SLAM and SNARK.

The process

In the extent that the roles attributed to the expert system and to the simulator are complementary and different, preservation of the two nuclei of simulation is essential. Automatic cooperation will take the following form : it should ensure an exchange of data which can be interpreted by the two processes. This exchange will be made through intermediate entrance/exit files which are comparable to a represented by pointers which designate the type of relationship between files. A solution from a data base system is thus imposed.

The post-process

SIMAF and PRODUCTICS presently propose two distinct modules for statistical processing and for animated graphics. The analysis of results justifies a recasting of these modules into a single post-process. In particular, the animation module should simultaneously process a job shop's performance capability and machine control. In the case of capacity determination, for example, a complete and realistic view is imperative. In the same way, in the case of machine control testing, validation of a chosen performance policy is more convincing when viewing an animation. A common module inspired from the present versions will thus lead to filtering the same objects, outlining a specific process at the user's request, and outputting graphic results.

CONCLUSION

In this paper, we have shown the advantage of having processes cooperate in the idea of reproducing the various steps for simulating a flexible job shop. Beyond the usual steps, it concerns reproducing the analyst's behavior in its procedures for capacity determination or machine control testing. By their cooperation, the processes described above reproduce the various scenarios to simulate. In order to lighten the anylyst's load, it is necessary to assist him in kpthe modeling phase, and, which is new, in making a decision. This research points to the fusion of environment modules and the partial automation of cooperating systems.

(1) SIMAF is the french name of Flexible Manufacturing Simulator "SIMulation des Ateliers Flexibles".

(2) PRODUCTICS is the translation of the concept of PRODUCTIQUE in the respect of the creator Ch. N. SEN. (Philips France Inc.).

(3) SNARK is a Symbolic Normalized Acquisition and Representation of Knowledge (Laurière 1986).

BIBLIOGRAPHY

Ataya, A. 1988. "SIMAF, un outil d'aide à la conception et au pilotage des systèmes de production". Génie Industriel, Nancy(FRANCE).

Bel, G.; Cavaille, J.B.; Leveque, D. 1988. "Simulation and object-oriented languages for manufacturing systems : description and control", EURO IX / TIMS XXVIII, Joint International Conference, July 1988, Paris.

Bel, G.; Bensana, E.; Dubois, D. 1987. "Construction d'ordonnancements prévisionnels : un compromis entre approche classique et système expert", 2ème Conférence Internationale "Systèmes de production", Paris, Avril 1987.

Erschler, J.; Fontan, J.; Merce, C. 1988. "Agrégation et désagrégation en planification hiérarchisée", TEC 88, Congrés A.F.C.E.T, Grenoble, Octobre 88.

Froment, B. 1988. "Gestion en temps réel d'atelier flexible: analyse et contribution à l'optimisation, application au pilotage des services logistiques", Thèse de doctorat en productique, Cachan, Avril 1988.

Guinet, A. 1988. "Knowledge acquisition and assessment about production management systems", EURO IX / TIMS XXVIII, Joint International Conference, July 1988, Paris.

Lauriere, J.L. 1986. "Un langage déclaratif : SNARK". In T.S.I, March, 141-151.

Mellichamp, J.M.; Wahab, A.F. 1987. "Process planning simulation : an FMS modeling tool for engineers", Simulation, Vol. 48, N°5, Mai 1987.

Pecquet, P. 1988. "PRODUCTICS, an expert decision support system for production control". SESC'88, Orlando(USA).

Pritsker, A.Alan B. 1986. "Introduction to simulation and SLAM II-Third edition". Halsted (New York).

Proth, J.M. and Hillion, H.P. 1988. "Systèmes de gestion de production hiérarchisée : conception et utilisation", TEC 88, Congrés A.F.C.E.T, Grenoble, Octobre 88.

Ranky, P.J. 1988. "A real-time, rule-based FMS operation control strategy in CIM environment", International Journal of CIM, Vol. 1, N°1, Taylor and Francis Ed., Londres, Mars 88.

Roubellat, F. and Thomas, V. 1987. "Une méthode et un logiciel pour l'ordonnancement temps réel d'un atelier", 2ème conférence Internationale - "Système de production", Paris, Avril 1987.

Steffen, M.S. 1986. "A survey of AI based scheduling systems", Fall Industrial Engineering Conference, Boston, Décembre 1986.

Knowledge-based environment for modelling and simulation (KEMS)

S Bennett, M T Rahbar, D A Linkens, E Tanyi, M Smith
Department of Control Engineering
University of Sheffield
Mappin Street, Sheffield S1 3JD

ABSTRACT

The Knowledge-based Environment for Modelling and Simulation (KEMS) consists of three subsystems; a Graphical user-interface, an Expert System, and a Simulation Language linked together by a manager. A 'high-level' simulation environment has been created in which the user defines the connectivity of the components in the model and instantiates each component by entering its parameters. KEMS then generates the appropriate model and the simulation code, which can then be run. No knowledge of programming is needed. Based on the experience gained using a prototype version of KEMS some improvements are suggested.

INTRODUCTION

The Knowledge-based Environment for Modelling and Simulation (KEMS) was developed as a result of a study done at the Control Engineering Department to find an ideal simulation language for simulating large systems. Several languages such as ACSL, SIMNON, PSI, etc were evaluated. The study showed that existing simulation languages not only lack the facilities for simulating such systems but also require skilled personnel to develop and drive a simulation study. It was also found that the improvements in hardware technology, the emergence of Artificial Intelligence (AI), and maturity in database systems and widespread use of them in recent years could play an important role in future modelling and simulation software (Linkens et al 1988).

The traditional approach of simulating a system has been to satisfy a given set of technical requirements, using either a simulation language or a general purpose programming language. Simulation was mainly performed to aid understanding of the system dynamics. This was usually performed by a small number of people who had the expertise to develop models, write programs and run the simulation. A more modern approach in simulation calls for a broader perspective. This approach is characterised by the need to satisfy the demands of both technical management and of the engineering designers, who will be working in an interactive manner using a personal workstation. In turn, this calls for a knowledge-based environment for modelling and simulation. The concept of the 'environment' is appealing as it supports the whole range of activities involved in a simulation study (Cellier, 1983). A more comprehensive discussion on the functional requirements of Knowledge-based simulation is given in (Rahbar et al, 1987, Rahbar et al, 1988).

KEMS is an integrated system for modelling and simulating large systems. It provides a graphical user-interface, supports data and model management, and uses AI techniques (e.g. Expert Systems and Object-Oriented Programming) to automate, and therefore simplify, the process of simulating a system.

This paper describes the design and implementation of a prototype KEMS. Progress is also reported on current attempts to design simulation and database interfaces which will provide additional facilities for model experimentation, validation, archiving and documentation. These aspects include further AI techniques to simplify and give advice on the total methodology for personnel unskilled in the art of simulation.

DESIGN STRATEGIES

A fundamental aim is to create an open system which can easily be modified to use different simulation languages and to allow for a different graphical user interfaces. The basic strategy has been to use unmodified commercially available packages as much as possible and use a specially written manager to establish links between the packages. The prototype uses two commercial packages; EASE+ (Expert-EASE Systems, 1987) for the user-interface and PSI (Bosch, 1982) as the simulator. No suitable package has yet been found for the database and after investigating several expert system shells it was decided that the Frame based Environment for Modelling and Simulation (FEMS) would have to be constructed in house (Tanyi and Linkens, 1987). The system is based on the assumption that many simulation users will for the majority of the time be working with a limited set of components from which various models can be constructed. The system is thus designed to make it easy to re-configure existing models and to create new models based on an existing set of components or submodels. The creation of models for new components is considered to be a specialist task which will be carried out infrequently.

A simulation database management system that would support version control, librarian, file protection, and program security is useful in developing different versions and alternative models, collecting several versions of experimental runs and supporting documentation concerning; who developed a model, how a model is run, when a model was changed, why the change was made etc. Although the current version of KEMS does not support such extensive management facilities, research is currently under way to design a suitable librarian for a modelling and simulation environment. We aim to incorporate this in the next version of KEMS.

IMPLEMENTATION OF KEMS

Once the components of the environment were specified, the implementation was divided into two phases. Phase one was to develop separately the user interface, the modeller (FEMS), and the interface modules between PSI, modeller, and Ease+; and phase two was to integrate them and test the environment as a whole. Figure 1 shows the major components in

KEMS. A brief description of each component is given below.

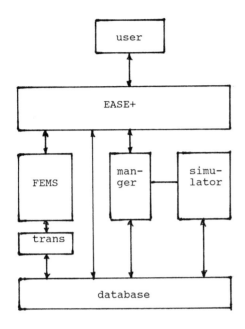

Figure 1. Major Components in KEMS

Ease+

Ease+ is a graphics tool box for simulation. It provides:

1. graphic tools to create icons, templates, menus

2. tools to execute external programs

3. limited database facilities for data management

4. plotting facilities for result processing

5. security facilities to give access priority to users.

Ease+ is customised for KEMS such that the topology of a system is drawn on the screen by selecting the required icons. A form associated to each icon is then presented to the user containing information such as the icon's name, its parameters and their valid range. Each form has default information stored in it. The pictorial representation of a model (i.e. icons and their associated connectors) is then translated automatically into a textual program which lists the components with upstream and downstream nodes. This is written into a file which is saved on the disk and which can be accessed by FEMS. At this level EASE+ is used to define the topology of the model.

After FEMS has constructed the model - by instantiating each component and creating the appropriate simulation code - the user is returned to EASE+ environment and can enter information to control the simulation for example length of run, variables to be plotted and can modify run-time settings made by FEMS (e.g. integration interval). Subsequent experimental runs can be made without re-entering FEMS. The simu-

lation is started by calling the manager (done by selecting the appropriate option in the command menu). At the end of the simulation run a return is made to EASE+ and a plot of up to four selected variables is displayed. The user can then choose to enter the result processing mode of EASE+ with extensive facilities for drawing graphs and manipulating results; or can carry out further simulation runs either saving the current results for later processing or abandoning the results.

Frame-based Environment for Modelling and Simulation (FEMS)

FEMS is a modelling environment (Tanyi, 1987), and is written in Turbo Prolog. FEMS uses Frame-based knowledge representation to integrate heuristics and deep knowledge into a single structure - the Frame. A Frame is a collection of knowledge elements describing a single entity as prototype. A prototype can be a class of objects or an individual object in a class. Frames can be linked into a network structure to allow for the sharing of information. The advantages of the frame based approach over the use of rules are: (i) inheritance - information can be shared between frames thus allowing complex models to be constructed from simple components; (ii) conceptual compatibility - conceptual frames are compatible with the engineers use of idealised models to describe processes and systems; (iii) structure - entities are structured in a way which facilitates database design. In addition to addressing the knowledge representation problem, there are other desirable features such as: (i) an in-built model base of components frames; (ii) a simulation interface for code generation; (iii) an interface to the Ease+ graphical front-end; (iv) limited simulation interface for model validation, and sensitivity analysis.

FEMS contains a library of generic objects: the prototype contains objects of type valve, pipe, pump, controller. Each generic object may be instantiated by specifying the kind of object and filling the appropriate slots of that object frame. An example of frame for a Valve is shown in Figure 2.

The connectors between objects are specified by defining the upstream and downstream nodes. The model is constructed by instantiation of the required objects and definition of their associated connectors. The list of components and their upstream and downstream nodes which are generated by Ease+ is read into FEMS which then generates either the mathematical equations for that model or the simulation code for input to the simulator.

The generation of the model by FEMS is a two-stage process. Using the graphical interface the modeller defines component interconnections and provides a subset of the parameters - the so-called engineering data e.g. valve type and size, fluid data, length of pipe. From this information FEMS begins to instantiate the model by filling in the slots in the frames. At the lowest level, the slots contain the simulation parameters and although FEMS uses default values and/or calculated values to fill in as many slots as possible, further information is required from the modeller in order to complete the instantiation.

Simulator and its Manager

A major problem with existing commercial simulation languages is that they have been developed as 'packages' rather than 'tools', where software is produced as small general purpose modules which con-

63

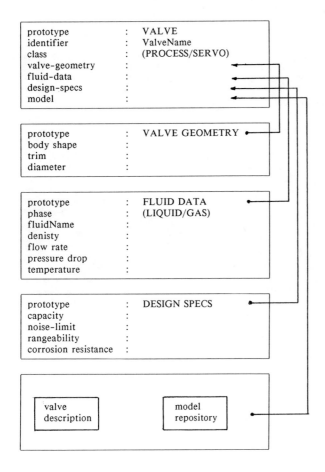

prototype	:	VALVE
identifier	:	ValveName
class	:	(PROCESS/SERVO)
valve-geometry	:	
fluid-data	:	
design-specs	:	
model	:	

prototype	:	VALVE GEOMETRY
body shape	:	
trim	:	
diameter	:	

prototype	:	FLUID DATA
phase	:	(LIQUID/GAS)
fluidName	:	
denisty	:	
flow rate	:	
pressure drop	:	
temperature	:	

prototype	:	DESIGN SPECS
capacity	:	
noise-limit	:	
rangeability	:	
corrosion resistance	:	

| valve description | model repository |

Figure 2. A Valve Frame

stitute a 'tool kit' and which can be used together to accomplish a wide variety of tasks (Maciejowski, 1984). Different packages don't 'talk' to each other and are very difficult to change or customise them to suit a particular user. Therefore, to integrate commercial packages without changing their code requires a good understanding of the operating system and the hardware on which these packages run. This also means that a long time is spent to develop the 'hooks' to a particular package. For example PSI has an internal file system and does not allow input from external ACSII files. This makes it difficult to link to other packages via disk files.

PSI Manager consists of three modules, two of which are memory resident programs and a main module which coordinates the information flow between PSI and the data files and supports a primitive database. There are, also, interface programs which filter the data between PSI, Ease+ and FEMS to produce the correct format required by each program.

CONCLUSION

The prototype system has been tested by considering the modelling of a gas supply pressure reduction station. Thus components representing valves, two (PI) and three (PID) term controllers, actuators and pipes have been constructed within FEMS. Models have been constructed using the system and the results

validated through comparing with the results obtained by building a model in PSI and SIMNON (Astrom, 1985) by standard means. The system has been demonstrated to several industrial organizations in order to obtain an assessment of the methodology. The prototype system has been on an extended trial with one user since September 1988.

Experience in using the prototype has led us to conclude that the system should support three levels of uses:

1. Basic: the user will have available a fixed model structure (or structures) appropriate to the application. The user will be able to choose specific components e.g. a specific type of valve and will be able to choose parameter values. Depending on the simulation language used the user may have restrictions on some run-time choices e.g. integration routines and step length.

2. Intermediate: the facilities available at basic level plus the ability to build simple models based on a library of component templates and standard function elements. Access to larger sets of run-time facilities.

3. Application developer: access to full facilities of the system with the ability to construct new components templates, modify existing templates, insertion of validation data, etc.

In KEMS a modelling program, a simulation language and a graphics program have been successfully integrated. The graphical user-interface provides mechanism to run each program, therefore, removing the necessity to learn how to model, write simulation program and run a simulation. However, KEMS can be further improved by: tighter coupling of components, applying Expert System techniques to other stages of a simulation study such as result interpretation, and adding database facilities to cope with the large amount of data involved in large-scale simulation. Work is in progress in all of these areas.

ACKNOWLEDGEMENT

One of the authors (M T Rahbar) gratefully acknowledges financial support via a Research Scholarship from British Gas plc.

REFERENCES

Astrom, K.J. 1985. "Computer Aided Tools for Control System Design". Computer-Aided Control Systems Engineering, M. Jamshidi and C.J. Herget, eds. North-Holland, Amsterdam: 3-40.

Bosch, P.P.J. van der. 1982. "PSI-Interactive Simulation Program". IEEE Control System Magazine, 2, no.4: 42-47.

Cellier, F.E. 1983. "Simulation Software: Today and Tomorrow". In Simulation in Engineering Science, Burger, J. et al, eds, North-Holland, Amsterdam: 3-19.

EASE+ Tools User Manual. 1987. Expert-EASE Systems Inc.

Linkens, D.A., E. Tanyi, M.T. Rahbar, S. Bennett. 1988. "Artificial Intelligence Techniques Applied to Simulation". In Proceedings Control '88 (Oxford, April 13-16) IEE.

Maciejowski, J.M. 1984. "Data Structures for Control System Design". In Proceedings EUROCON 84, Brighton, UK.

Rahbar, M.T., S. Bennett, D.A. Linkens. 1987. "Functional Specifications for an Intelligent Simulation Environment". In Proceedings of UKSC Conference on Computer Simulation, Bangor, (September 9-11), UKSC: 182-197.

Rahbar, M.T., E. Tanyi, S. Bennett and D.A. Linkens. 1988. "A Framework for a Knowledge-based Modelling and Simulation Environment (KBMSE)". In Proceedings of IMACS 1988 12th World Congress on Scientific Computation, Paris, July 18-22, vol.4: 255-257.

Tanyi, E. and D.A. Linkens. 1987. "A Frame-based Modelling and Simulation Environment". In Proceedings UKSC Conference on Computer Simulation (Bangor, September 9-11) UKSC: 215-219.

ISBN 0-911801-44-6

The application of AI techniques to model maintenance

Norman R. Nielsen
Information Industries Division
SRI International
Menlo Park, California 94025

ABSTRACT

The use of a simulation model frequently involves making a variety of program changes. But commonly used change procedures often introduce undetected errors into the model, reducing if not destroying the model's value. Various techniques derived from the discipline of artificial intelligence (AI) offer the prospect both for speeding the model modification process and introducing fewer errors by focusing the user's attention on the concept of the modification and letting an intelligent support program carry out the detailed program adjustments. SRI conducted an experiment to evaluate the potential of this approach using a previously developed network simulator as a framework.

Ten classes of model changes were established, and the knowledge requirements of each class were assessed to estimate the ability of AI-based techniques to support them. The assessment revealed that modifications within 60% of those classes could be assisted by generic modification capabilities built into a model-development tool. Although the system could not make all of the necessary changes in a number of cases, it could still control the completeness and consistency of the modification by querying the user with respect to each derivative change. Modification support for a smaller set of changes could also be provided, but at the model level rather than at the tool level. That is, the support capability would have to be built into the model at the time of its development. The remaining two types of modifications require capabilities that the technology can not yet support.

INTRODUCTION

Both traditional simulation and artificial intelligence have been concerned with the representation and use of knowledge to model systems, be these physical systems, logical systems, or thought processes. These two disciplines have developed fairly independently, although there have been some notable exceptions (e.g., object-oriented programming capabilities that were introduced in SIMULA [Dahl and Nygaard 1966] were later popularized in the AI domain). Considerable interest is now developing in cross-fertilization between these two disciplines.

AI researchers are actively considering the use of simulation techniques to improve the reasoning capabilities of expert systems (Nielsen 1986a). Further, interest in these approaches is growing. At the recent AI and Simulation Workshop held at the National Conference of the American Association of Artificial Intelligence in August 1988, a number of papers discussed the use of a simulation model as part of the knowledge-based reasoning process. Tentative conclusions from the reasoning process could be applied to the model to confirm their effectiveness and to match modeled outputs with the state of the real world. Model outputs could also be used to support further reasoning.

Similarly, simulation researchers are actively considering the use of AI techniques to improve the development and application of simulation models (Nielsen 1986b). Functional roles that AI techniques can play in the simulation process include:

- Representation of model knowledge

- Decision making within a simulation

- Rapid prototyping of models

- Analysis of simulator output data

- Modification of models.

The first four roles are discussed in a study by Nielsen (Nielsen 1987) in which object-oriented programming and knowledge-based reasoning were used to develop a generic factory control system simulator. The fifth functional role, providing support for the maintenance and modification process, is the subject of this paper. The issue to be addressed, however, is not whether AI techniques can be used for this purpose, for they demonstrably can. What is of interest is the value of the results. Unless these techniques offer advantages such as faster maintenance or more reliable modification, they will be of little value to model developers and users.

THE MODELING PROCESS

The process of simulating a system can be viewed as involving a set of five activities:

1. Conceptualize and design the model

2. Implement the model on an appropriate computer

3. Test and debug the resulting program

4. Validate the model

5. Use the model.

This process is iterative rather than sequential, for there will likely be considerable repetition of the first three activities. Once the development process has been completed, the model is put to use (Activity 5). This use comprises three classes of activities that are combined iteratively to form a series of circular patterns, as illustrated in Figure 1.

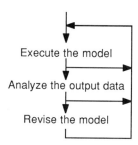

Figure 1
Model Usage Activity Sequence

The process of revising a model can be quite dangerous, for the testing and validation activities performed during development are frequently not repeated. All too often model changes are made "on the fly" following the analysis of one simulation run and prior to the making of the next run. This type of change process is generally supported by arguments to the effect that these changes are often "small," so there is no "need" to retest. Further, conducting a series of test runs just so that the next simulation can be run is uneconomic.

Yet, there are accuracy and reliability issues that must not be ignored. It is well known that "small" changes tend to be error prone. In too many instances simulated results may be reflecting the behavior of a system other than the one intended. Sometimes the resultant behavior is counter-intuitive, and the user becomes suspicious, leading to an investigation (i.e., debugging); at other times, however, the intuition is wrong, and what is accepted as appropriate behavior is actually erroneous. Because of the pressures not to retest and revalidate the model after small changes, it is unrealistic to expect significant changes in user behavior to occur. Therefore, a different approach must be taken in an effort to reduce the impact of modification errors. What are needed are mechanisms for reducing the frequency of error introduction during the model modification process rather than mechanisms detecting errors once they have been introduced.

ERROR REDUCTION TECHNIQUES

Two mechanisms for reducing the introduction of logical errors during program maintenance are:

1. Graphical representations

2. Intelligent modification.

Both of these approaches involve techniques that have been developed or enhanced by AI researchers.

The first approach, representing the system graphically, enables the user to employ a graphical editor to make modifications. People are far more capable of detecting errors in a system diagram than in columns of words or numbers. In fact, many people tend to think in visual terms. A network specified in numerical form would most likely be converted into a mental image before the user could reason or answer questions about it. Because the graphical representation is closer to the mental model, the user can better "see" mistakes of omission or commission from such representations. Although this approach doesn't prevent human errors, it makes them more obvious, leading to their detection and elimination as part of the modification process, rather than later on.

The second approach, applying intelligence (e.g., knowledge-based reasoning) to the modification process, enables users to propose changes at higher levels than would otherwise be possible. Ideally the user would indicate changes at a conceptual level, leaving the system to make the more detailed or derivative changes required to implement the concept. Of course, it is not always possible for the system to make every change that might be needed to install a conceptual change, but the system could point out needed changes that it couldn't make, soliciting advice or guidance from the user. In this way the system could control completeness and consistency while accepting inputs as needed from the user.

Why will these two approaches reduce modification errors? First, they focus the user's attention on higher-level considerations, where humans excel. Feedback is provided to the user in a form in which the implications of changes can be more readily assessed. Second, the computer's "attention" is focused at a more detailed level, carrying out the steps necessary to implement a change strategy and thus performing those functions at which the computer excels. This division of responsibilities makes it possible to accomplish changes that are more nearly complete and consistent.

The techniques necessary to support these approaches are available. Graphical routines, objected-oriented programming languages, and process representations for entities exist. Intelligent routines can be (and have been) developed. The critical issue is whether such capabilities can be routinely developed to handle meaningful fractions of the types of changes that are commonly made by simulation users. Definitive data do not yet exist, but some insights are becoming available. A small experiment recently conducted at SRI contributes one such insight.

THE EXPERIMENT

An existing simulation model was taken as the basis for an experiment to assess the generality of intelligent maintenance techniques and the degree to which such techniques might be applicable to a model that had been designed previously without any consideration of supporting intelligent maintenance. This model characterized the behavior of a small telecommunications network consisting of a set of links and nodes with messages being transferred between pairs of designated nodes. Many nodes were not directly connected by a common link, so the network utilized a store-and-forward mechanism to transfer messages from their origin to their ultimate destination. The simulation made extensive use of object-oriented programming and had been designed to help technicians detect, isolate, and correct network faults.

Ten representative modifications were selected to serve as the framework within which intelligent support might be provided. Each of these ten changes represents a class of changes of the type a user of the simulation might wish to make. There is no implication, however, that these changes proportionally represent the population of changes made in the course of using a simulation model. That is, they have not been weighted by expected frequency of occurrence.

Modifications

The ten types or classes of modifications selected for consideration were:

1. Change the bandwidth or transmission rate of a link between two specified nodes. This type of change might be viewed simply as modifying a program parameter or adjusting a value in a table.

2. Delete an existing link from the network. This change involves not only deleting the link but also updating all routing tables or mechanisms to reflect the absence of the connection previously provided by the deleted link.

3. Define a new link and connect it between two existing nodes in the network. This change involves not only creating the link and connecting it to the network but also updating all routing tables to reflect the availability of the new connection. This type of change also illustrates a cooperative modification. The system can create a link and update routing tables in response to the user's request to link

nodes **x** and **y**. However, the system will need to solicit guidance from the user as to what priorities should be assigned to each route that includes the new link.

4. Delete an existing node from the network. This change involves not only removing of the node but also removing all attached links and updating all routing tables to reflect the absence of both the node and its links to the network.

5. Define a new node and connect it to the network at a specified point (i.e., node). This change involves not only creating the node but creating and attaching a link and updating all routing tables as well.

6. Modify the queuing algorithm for message forwarding at the nodes to favor messages having such characteristics as high priority, old age, or small size (i.e., length). This change differs from the previous changes in that it may involve a programming change rather than just the update of a table value.

7. Change the message routing procedure (e.g., from a fixed one to a dynamic one). This change involves the assignment of a route from node **x** to node **y** on the basis of congestion (or other dynamically varying information) along the route rather than on the basis of a predetermined, fixed sequence of nodes for each route. This change does not modify the character (centralized versus decentralized) that had been established for the routing procedure. Both the fixed and dynamic approaches can be applied on a centralized basis (complete path assigned at the time of message creation) or on a decentralized basis (path assigned incrementally, a node at a time, at each node along the route).

8. Develop and install a mechanism to collect data concerning message transit time using a new metric. This change can be expected to involve a cooperative man-machine effort. The system can develop data collection and summarization routines, but the user will have to provide guidance as to the points at which transit time is to begin and end (e.g., from time of creation at the originating node until receipt at the destination node, but excluding the actual node-to-node transmission times, so as to provide a measure of the overhead and queuing delay added to the absolute minimum transmission time).

9. Change the measure of network congestion (e.g., from a "link queuing delay" metric to a "time to receipt of acknowledgement" metric). This change involves an algorithmic change, so that a different procedure will be used to compute the congestion measure. No change will be required, however, in any routine making use of that metric.

10. Develop and insert into the network an algorithm for routing messages that will avoid congested links whenever possible. This change involves both creating a new algorithm and installing that algorithm in the system, connecting it to existing code at appropriate places. Such an algorithm might cover the congestion threshold that would trigger the algorithm, the congestion level on alternate routes that would suppress the algorithm's execution, as well as the alternate routing procedure itself.

The reasoning sophistication needed to make a given change will depend in part on the structure of the model. In addition, two levels of intelligence may be involved in the change process--a higher level to determine the modification *strategy* and a lower level to *make* the indicated changes.

Consider, for example, making a change in the bandwidth of a link. A model having an object-oriented structure would require only that the "transmission rate" parameter of the specified link be changed. Other models having different structures would require different changes. If link characteristics were associated with the message generation process rather than with the link in question (providing each message with a transit-time parameter that combined message size and link performance), the intelligent maintenance assistant would need to be able to determine how link performance parameters were incorporated in other parameters. Once this had been determined, it would be a fairly straightforward procedure to make the necessary change(s).

Consider, as another example, the definition and connection of a new link. The connectivity pointers between the link and its end-point nodes (and between those nodes and the link) can readily be constructed and stored. A modification strategy will be needed, however, to determine the routing adjustments. Changes will be needed at the nodes attached to each end of the new link at a minimum and potentially at every node, depending on the design structure (e.g., centralized routing). Although the same routes might be assigned to messages, regardless of structure, the route characterizations to be stored at each node could be quite different.

Thus, even simple changes can require sophisticated capabilities to determine how the changes should be made. This example does, however, illustrate the likely error reduction that might be obtained by removing from the user the responsibility for implementing the detailed changes.

Measures of Applicability

The applicability of intelligent maintenance procedures to the model modification process was measured by classifying each type of change according to its degree of independence:

- Model independent

- Model dependent

- Modification dependent.

Model-independent changes are those that do not depend on the characteristics of a particular model. Capabilities for making such changes can thus be built into the modeling tool or system rather than into the model. Note that the system-provided maintenance support is not achieved in a vacuum. It is assumed that the system was involved in building the model initially (e.g., graphical assembly of object-oriented modules for a library), thereby providing it with the means to understand various facets of the model's operation. The fact that a change is model independent does not imply that the modeling tool could make that change in an arbitrary program, relying only on the source code to provide information about the model's embedded structure and function (e.g., pointer protocol and location). It is unrealistic to expect the system to be able to assist with the maintenance activity without structural knowledge of the model.

Model-dependent changes are those that depend on specific characteristics of a particular model. Capabilities for making such changes must therefore be built into the model by the developer (as opposed to being provided generically by the model development tool). This requires that the model developer anticipate the possibility of users seeking to make a variety of model-dependent changes.

Modification-dependent changes are those that depend on specific ideas of the user (e.g., modifications to a procedural algorithm). The details of such changes cannot be anticipated by either the tool developer or the model builder. Further, the state of the technology is such that it would not be appropriate to specify syntax and semantics sufficient to permit the system to understand such an unanticipated user-described change. Hence, much greater reliance must be placed on the correctness of user actions with respect to these types of changes. This does not imply, however, that no assistance can be provided to a user seeking to make such changes. On the contrary, the system can provide information, such as pointing out locations of all dependencies on existing variables; but the responsibility for making the changes must lie with the user, as only the user will understand the implications of the desired change.

The extent of the opportunities for applying intelligent maintenance procedures can be estimated by examining the characteristics of the various types of changes. This estimation procedure provides some insight into the possible benefits. It is not, of course, as satisfactory an approach as measuring the actual impact of intelligent maintenance procedures on a particular simulation program (rather than the opportunity to apply them) Two direct measures are available:

1. Reduction in the elapsed time required by the user to make modifications

2. Reduction in the number of errors introduced by the user in the course of making modifications.

These measures, however, can only be calculated by actually conducting a set of controlled model modifications. Such experimentation is beyond the scope of this study and remains a topic for future research.

RESULTS

The ten classes of model modifications previously described were examined to determine their degree of dependency and hence to estimate the ability of AI-based techniques to support each of them. Of the ten classes of changes, the system could take responsibility for 1-6. These are generic types of modifications that could be foreseen by the designer of the modeling tool used to develop the model initially. Although the system could accept responsibility for making the changes and hence cover such matters as completeness, it could not make all the changes independently. Consultation with the user would be necessary to clarify data associated with system-proposed changes.

Changes 7 and 8 represent modifications for which the simulation model could take responsibility if the model's developer had foreseen the need for such modifications at the time the model was constructed. Again, the making of these changes would require a user dialog to clarify data associated with system-proposed changes.

Changes 9 and 10 involve modifications that could not be anticipated by either the tool developer or the model developer and that could not be described in a fashion the system could understand. Without a rich natural language capability, it would be difficult for the system to understand the conceptual details of the changes proposed by the user. Further, without having constructed the part of the program to be changed, the system would have great difficulty understanding the structure of what would appear to be an arbitrary selection of code. An intelligent maintenance assistant would contribute relatively little toward improving the reliability of model maintenance in such cases.

CONCLUSIONS

The study reported herein is quite limited in scope. The results represent but a single data point, so the reader must take care in generalizing the findings. Nevertheless, the fact that six of the ten identified classes of modifications can be assisted by generic intelligent support capabilities built into a model development tool is encouraging. Such breadth of applicability may not only indicate the extent to which errors introduced during the maintenance process can be reduced through model-independent mechanisms, but it may also encourage vendors of simulation tools to include intelligent modification support capabilities in their products. Thus, some of the benefits described in this paper may be realized by practitioners in the field in the coming months.

REFERENCES

Dahl, O. J. and K. Nygaard. 1966. "SIMULA - An Algol-Based Simulation Language," *Communications of the ACM*, Vol. 9, No. 9.

Nielsen, N. R. 1986a. "Expert Systems and Simulation," in *Computer Networks and Simulation III*, S. Schoemaker (Editor), Elsevier Science Publishers B. V., The Netherlands

Nielsen, N. R. 1986b "Knowledge-Based Simulation Programming," *Proceedings of the 1986 National Computer Conference*, Vol. 55, AFIPS Press, Reston, Virginia

Nielsen, N. R. 1987. "The Impact of Using AI-Based Techniques in a Control System Simulator," in *Simulation and AI*, edited by P. A. Luker and G. Birtwistle, The Society for Computer Simulation, Simulation Series, Volume 18, Number 3 (July)

Simulation and AI, 1989
©1989 by the Society for Computer
Simulation International
ISBN 0-911801-44-8

AUDITION - an intelligent simulation environment

Iain M. Begg and R. Chris P. Worsley
Synaptec Software
1718 Commercial Drive, Suite 103
Vancouver, B.C. V7L 3C8

ABSTRACT

The paper will discuss the importance of closely integrating knowledge representation with the simulation environment in the production of user-customizable simulations. A specific simulation example will be presented using AUDITION, an intelligent simulation and visual programming environment. These simulations are rich micro-worlds incorporating both discrete and continuous evaluation. Once constructed, simulations can be reused whole, or in part, in different situations. All simulations are capable of being customized by end-users. Thus, generic components are simply reconfigured to fit into the users' environments.

Knowledge representation in **AUDITION** is based on a Stage/Performer paradigm. The Stage/performer paradigm combines the classification networks of object-oriented representation (Performers) with the orthogonal concept of 'worlds' (Stages). This permits a versatile knowledge representation scheme to be developed. Since knowledge can be built into the Performers and Stages which are the basic components of the simulations, the use, maintenance and extension of the knowledge-based component of the simulation is greatly facilitated. Further, AUDITION provides a rich symbolic environment in combination with automatic access to an object databases. This encourages the development of reusable generic stages which can then be readily incorporated into new simulations.

INTRODUCTION

Simulations cover a wide range of computational mechanisms designed to offer the user the ability to experiment with a model. The user can then vary conditions, equations, constraints and parameters to explore the solution space of that model. Crucial to the validity of these results is the extent to which the model accurately represents the situation being modelled; the central issue being how close the structural and behavioural representations map to the structures and behaviours being represented.

This paper will discuss and demonstrate the importance of closely integrating knowledge representation into the simulation environment. By so doing, the user of the simulation is presented with a truer model of the complex situation he/she intends to examine. An equally important issue is the incorporation of visual components and interactions into the simulation. When existing simulations are coupled with accurate, interactive display graphics, the resulting Visual Interactive Simulator has been shown to have a much higher impact (Bell and O'Keefe 1987). VIS offer more than a tool for gathering statistics; they allow users to examine the model solution space quickly, providing a powerful tool for the validation of ideas, for teaching and for diagnostics. Finally, instead of adding graphics and interactive capabilities after the model has been run (TESS, Standbridge 1985; CINEMA,

Pegden et al. 1985), *the display in VIS is the model*. Bell and O'Keefe point to object-oriented systems as an excellent implementation mechanism.

The application of object-oriented techniques to simulation offers some real advantages to the simulation arena (Kreutzer 1986). In object-oriented programs, (and simulations), related information is strongly localised (**data abstraction**), objects guard themselves against invalid requests (**data encapsulation**), properties and behaviour can be inherited (**inheritance**) and many objects may respond to the same message through their own implementations (**polymorphism**).

Support is provided for object-oriented simulations in Smalltalk (Goldberg and Robson 1983; Kreutzer 1988). Stairmand and Kreutzer have implemented POSE, a process-oriented discrete-event simulation environment. From the knowledge representation side, KEE implement simulations through the use of SIMKIT (Intellicorp, 1987), although it is significant that the simulation occurs after the problem has been solved. Object-oriented techniques were coupled with intuitive modelling in the ARIA project (Shrager et al, 1987). ARIA attempted to simulate a range of photocopying machines but succeeded only in either modelling one type exactly or several types very inexactly. The two major reasons for this were the difficulty in mapping qualitative values onto a quantitative scale for evaluation and the fact that their object model did not enforce strict encapsulation. A major point, mentioned by many but summarised by Kreutzer (Kreutzer, 1988), is the merit of computer-based simulations with animation. We would go further than animation to embrace a complete integration of interactive graphics with simulation, as can be expected with Visual Interactive Simulators. When such a system can also offer component reusability and an interaction and programming mechanism to treat these components as visible objects, the simulation user has a tool of tremendous flexibility, accessiblity and usability. We believe AUDITION is such a system.

OVERVIEW OF AUDITION

AUDITION, figure 1, is a PC-based environment well suited to programming and simulation needs. It was designed to allow users to program their solutions without need of expert programming knowledge, to provide reusable components and to be customizable and intuitive. A key requirement was the need to provide an environment which was efficient in user terms. To this end, the interface is non-modal, allowing the user, and the system, to do several things at the one time.

AUDITION supports an efficient class hierarchy of 120 classes. This can be grouped into basic data types (Buffer, Set, Dictionary, Integer Float, Point, etc), graphic primitives (such as Arc, Ellipse, Polyline; based on the GKS standard) and interaction entities (such as gauges, graphs, text and other Performers). It provides an intrinsic Knowledge Representation

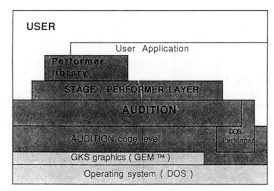

Structure of AUDITION

Figure 1: AUDITION structure

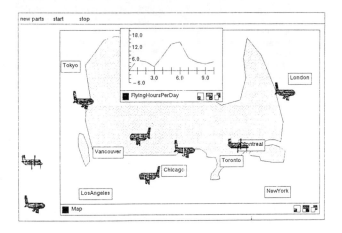

Figure 2: Air Traffic simulation

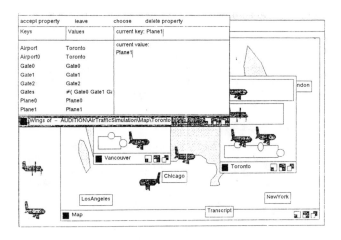

Figure 3: Interrogation during Air Traffic simulation

```
Class newClass: 'Plane' supers: Turtle
        instanceVariables: '( capacity:Float
                            range:Float
                            taxiSpeed:Float
                            flyingSpeed:Float
                            passengers:Float
                            flightSchedule:Buffer )'

Plane new name= Boeing767
Boeing767 addProperties:
#( #UnloadingTime
        ProbabilityDistribution newNormalMean: 2.0 sigma: 0.5 #Times
    #LoadingTime
        ProbabilityDistribution newNormalMean: 4.0 sigma: 1.0  #Times
    #MaintainanceTime
        ProbabilityDistribution newExponentialMean: 60.0  #Times
    #LandingSeparation 2.5 #Times )#

Boeing767 taxiSpeed: 20.0
Boeing767 flyingSpeed: 550.0
Boeing767 enterStage

Plane methods category= PROCESSES
:m  travelAlong:inTime:steps:
    { logicalPath:PointBuffer totalTime:Float steps:Integer }
    | stepTime:Float stepPath:PointBuffer step:Integer stepCount:Integer |
    logicalPath getPathSteps: steps -> stepPath
    totalTime / ( steps asFloat ) -> stepTime
    self moveTo: ( stepPath at: 1 )
    2 -> step
    stepPath getCount -> stepCount
    begin
        [ ] scheduleWait: stepTime in: AirTrafficEvents
        self moveTo: ( stepPath at: step )
        1 +> step
    until( step > stepCount )
    AirTrafficEvents resumeCue: #all for: self  ;
:m taxiFrom:to: { a b }
    | taxiRoute:PointBuffer |
    Airport getRouteFrom: a to: b -> taxiRoute
    self travelAlong: taxiRoute
            inTime: ( self getTaxiTimeFor: taxiRoute )
            steps: 3 ;

:m flyFrom:to: { depart destination  }
    | aRoute:PointBuffer possibleRoutes:Buffer flightTime:Float |
    Map getRoutesFrom: depart to: destination -> possibleRoutes
    self selectRouteFrom: possibleRoutes -> aRoute
    self getFlightTimeFor: aRoute -> flightTime
    destination getReadyFor: self  in: flightTime
    self travelAlong: aRoute inTime: flightTime steps: 5 ;
:m flyRoutes
    | nextGate aRunway aMonitor:EventMonitor nextAirport newPassengers:Float |
    AirTrafficEvents -> aMonitor
    self startFlyingDay
    begin
    while( self inService? )
        self enter: Airport
        Tower getGateFor: self -> nextGate
        [ self taxiFrom: self to: nextGate ] transferIn: aMonitor
        self getNextAirport -> nextAirport
        [ ] scheduleWait: ( self getPassengers * ( UnloadingTime getNext ) )
            in: aMonitor  " unload passengers "
        self passengers: 0.0
        nextGate getPassengersCapacity: self -> newPassengers
        [ ] scheduleWait: ( newPassengers * ( LoadingTime getNext ))
            in: aMonitor  " load passengers "
        self passengers: newPassengers
        Tower getTakeOffRunwayFor: self  -> aRunway
        [ self taxiFrom: nextGate to: aRunway ] transferIn; aMonitor
        [ self hasTakeOffClearanceFor?: aRunway ]  waitUntil scheduleIn: aMonitor
        self enter: aRunway
        self takeOff
        [ self flyFrom: Airport to: nextAirport ] transferIn: aMonitor
        nextAirport getLandingRunwayFor: self -> aRunway
        [ self canLandOn?: aRunway ] waitUntil scheduleIn: aMonitor
        self landOn: aRunway
    repeat
    self undergoMaintainance ;
```

Figure 4: Selected Code for Air Traffic simulation

72

scheme based upon its object-oriented classification hierarchy. Like other object-oriented systems, AUDITION supports strong encapsulation, inheritance, polymorphism and message passing. Unlike other object-oriented systems, AUDITION extends these concepts in three areas: efficiency, representation, and reusability. Efficiency is provided to the user both through its implementation and through the provision of a high-level modelling layer, the Stage/Performer paradigm. Representational advantages come about through its instance-based inheritance, mediated by Performer usage. To enable reusability of function (not just source code as in mosts systems), AUDITION can create relocatable binary images of complete objects. These images contain **both** structure **and** behaviour. Importantly, these images can be reloaded into an arbitrary AUDITION environment, thus allowing true reusability at the user's level.

AUDITION is a weakly-typed object-oriented system offering early- and late-binding of messages to classes and allowing both class- and instance-based specialization. AUDITION code is compiled into a token-threaded format for run-time interpretation. An assembler provides machine access and a solution for time-critical operations. All code whether native or threaded is encapsulated as objects and treated equivalently by AUDITION through its stack-based operation. Audition is also capable of high-performance numerical operations supporting both stack- and object-based treatment of integers and reals.

Stage/Performer paradigm

The Performer layer is built on top of the basic object-oriented body. Performers, having properties in addition to their instance structure, are the fundamental mechanism for mediation between user and computer, a fact which is as true in design as it is in implementation. Performers are a natural way through which to implement entities. They provide the structural and behavioural characteristics with which to map implementation entities to the components being represented. This mapping can be 1::1, so that the user can actually model with true representations of the components themselves. Indeed, Stages and Performers already perform the same roles for AUDITION as do Encapsulators, Managers, Rovers, Mimics and Teammates for Smalltalk-80 (Conrad et al. 1987). Thus, AUDITION's Performer layer provides the built-in power and leverage which the XSIS workers had to create in order to aid the design and manage the implementation of their system, ANALYST.

The Performer part of the Class hierarchy consists of the classes (TextPerformer, Spreadsheet), Stage, (CircleGauge, BarGauge, LineGraph, BarChart), (DisplayPerformer, Turtle) and (List, Menu). They offer a basic capacity for controlling user interaction, participating in a visual hierarchy and displaying data models (e.g. text would be the model of a TextPerformer, or a picture the model of a Turtle) Stages are specialised Performers which extend the repertoire by providing a visible platform for Performers, a local symbol table and a local named object dictionary. This gives Stages a dual role:- as a sort of "superPerformer" containing other Performers in their own visual hierarchy and as a local partition of the symbol and name space.

The Stage/Performer paradigm enhances AUDITION's Knowledge Representation as provided in two ways:- through the use of a classification hierarchy and through the use of "worlds". The former is represented by the object hierarchy, which includes both the class-based hierarchy and the instance-based hierarchy formed through Performer instance inheritance. Since each Performer has its own set of properties (structure and behaviour), the ability to inherit properties from **other** Performers is a strong organising principle. What distinguishes this from other knowledge representation methods is the encapsulation of these elements into functional objects directly accessible to users. It is easy to see the object instance structure and Performer properties map to 'frames', whereas the inheritance links map to 'ISA' relationships. However, a further classification is possible: delineation into **type**. Because AUDITION supports instance specialisation, any Performer instance can act as a 'class' type, an 'instance' type or just an instance. The implications of type inheritance are described below.

Stages enhance this knowledge representation through the provision of "worlds". Worlds have been introduced in several areas (Filman 1988; Wile and Allard 1987; Doman 1988; Karam, 1988). While the uses vary, they offer a mechansim for name scoping and the cloning of groups of objects in a particular state. Stages provide both a local dictionary for objects and a local symbol table. Thus, on the one hand, Stages are used to group Performers onto a visible platform, e.g. all tools in AUDITION are collections of individual, specialised Performers on a Stage. On the other hand, Stages can hold identical, named Performers and retain their own identity. This mechanism allows the user to explore complex hypothetical scenarios from within the same model. This is an important explorartory and reasoning mechanism.

Stage networks

Key to the provision of accurate Knowledge Representation and simulation, AUDITION provides the capabilities to connect and disconnect networks of Performers and Stages. In a consistent fashion with AUDITION's aim of providing user accessibility, these connections can be examined and altered interactively by the user. Particularly important is the ability to link Stages into networks. This provides a clear mechanism for localizing interaction and attention through the simulation. This point is especially pertinent in the Visual Interactive Simulations (Bell and O'Keefe, 1988). For instance, consider the airport simulation shown in Figures 2 and 3. By representing the airports as Stages, we can view the operation of the whole simulation by collapsing the airports to visible titles (a default Performer action) or concentrate on particular airports, such as Toronto, by bringing them back to full size. During all this activity the simulation is continuing to run, accumulating statistics. Individual airports (or Stages) can be queried at any time.

Stages, Performers and the ability to interconnect them, provides the user with a powerful tool to model real problems both quantitatively and qualitatively. Crucially important is the way in which attention can be focussed on parts of the problem, allowing users to examine the whole solution space in a much shorter time than is normally expected.

KNOWLEDGE TRANSFER IN AUDITION

The networks of Stages, Performers and Objects described above constitute a distributed knowledge representation scheme, where any portion of the network can obtain knowledge from other portions through *message sending, type inheritance, stage inheritance* or *process communication*.

Message Sending

This is essentially the late-binding mechanism which allows objects to communicate dynamically, exchanging information and effecting changes to the states of the system. In the ACTOR languages (Agha and Hewit 1987), designed for fine-grained concurrent computation, this is the only way that information is shared or states are created (there is no concept of assignment). As detailed below in the discussion of the simulation example, message sending is generally safer and more reliable than direct access to non-local knowledge. One of the problems presented by encapsulating state as behaviour in this way is the difficulty of reasoning about such knowledge since most expert systems, such as ARIA, expect to reason about the actual variables in a system.

Type Inheritance

Object-oriented systems have evolved along many paths and each significantly different implementation has tended to develop its own understanding of such key concepts as *type* and *inheritance*. Wegner provides a good summary of the present state of object-oriented systems and their use of these concepts (Wegner, 1987). Although the situation is actually more complex, for the present purposes we can state that, in AUDITION, if an object A can inherit behaviour or structure from object B, then A is a kind of B and instances of A may be used in situations calling for instances of type B.

AUDITION combines the Class-based inheritance structure of Smalltalk with instance-based inheritance for Performers along similar lines to the exemplar-based system Actra (Lalonde, Thomas and Pugh, 1987). Instance-based extensions to structure and behaviour can be inherited independently of Class-based values, allowing a much more intuitive separation of the fundamental type of an object (its Class) from its assumed type or role as represented by its instance-based relationships. In particular, the instance-based extensions to a Performer can be dynamically altered without changing the Class, providing for sophisticated modelling techniques such as adaptive behaviour.

In the **AirTrafficSimulation** example, the instance **Boeing767** will always retain the class **Plane**, but it is expected that different instances will be formed from the prototypical **Boeing767**. These new instances may in turn combine features from other instances, for example certain common policies and strategies of an air carrier may be applicable to any aircraft in their fleet and an easy way to incorporate this knowledge is to provide an abstract prototype of a plane whose behaviour will be shared by all fleet instances. The role of an abstract "Policy Plane" would be similar to that of *mixins* found in Lisp-based Flavors implementations.

Properties and behaviour can be dynamically resolved across the entire type-network for an instance, instance variables are transmitted only along the Class heirarchy. The principal reason for retaining instance variables in AUDITION is efficiency, since access to instance variables is similar to field access in record-based systems, whereas properties must be found by searching a network of dictionaries. We feel the strategy of combining static and dynamic structure gives the programmer more control over the resulting performance of their solution. In the prototyping stages, for example, the structure of the types required tends to vary as much as the behaviour, which suggests the use of Performer instances to represent the types. When a satisfactory solution has been found, various instances may be reconstructed as Classes, with properties transformed to instance variables.

Stage Inheritance

As discussed above, AUDITION provides an orthogonal environment for resolving names, that provided by Stages. In particular, all Performers, including Stages, own a *superStage* which determines the context within which named objects are resolved. Other objects resolve names from the scope of their Classes. Behaviour which makes use of named entities (such as the **flyRoutes** method for Planes) is therefore dynamically re-

interpretable by altering the scope of the receiver. This may be contrasted with the situation in Smalltalk, where there exists a single global environment (called Smalltalk) for such name resolution.

Like the instance-based inheritance discussed above, Stage environments can be linked in arbitrary networks (in fact the same objects, instances of **LinkedDictionary** are used) and abstract environments can be added to existing stages. This linking of environments forms an alternative inheritance scheme for named entities and as discussed above forms a basis for "world-based" hypothetical reasoning.

Process Communication

This is discussed in more detail below, but in essence AUDITION supports method-based process creation which are co-ordinated by instances of **EventMonitor**. A number of dynamic paradigms, such as *broadcasting, send/wait* and *demons* , can be supported by this mechanism. Direct inter-process communication is supported by both semaphores and identification (instances of a process in an EventMonitor are identifiable through their receiver and source method).

SIMULATION MECHANISMS IN AUDITION

In process-oriented simulation environments such as SIMSCRIPT II.5 (Law and Larmey 1984), the processes of the simulation are often also the entities of the simulation. Although provision exists for the specification of other permanent or temporary entities, their usefulness is limited by restrictions on naming, structure and behaviour. Object-oriented simulation environments such as Smalltalk-80 (Goldberg and Robson 1983) and POSE (Stairmand and Kreutzer 1988) have typically followed the process-oriented paradigm in their discrete-event simulation mechanisms, making use of objects to manage the entity component of processes. The management of the temporal state of processes (local variables and other transient bindings) is supported by some equivalent to a closure in the underlying language. The importance of closures to the ease of specification and implementation of discrete-event simulations has been recognised (Kreutzer 1986). However, while support for multiple independent processes is often included in object-oriented environments, the relationship between the temporal objects (instances of an event/process), the objects comprising the simulation model and the scheduling classes and objects is highly variable across different environments.

In Smalltalk-80, all processes are expected to be a kind of **SimulationObject** and to implement the methods **startUp**, **tasks** and **finishUp**. Event monitoring and scheduling is handled by instances of the class **Simulation** (or subclasses), but there is provision for only one active simulation at any time. POSE implements processes as "flavors" of the flavor *Process* and permits the user to nominate individual monitors for scheduling of events. The ability to combine flavors gives the POSE solution greater flexibility than the Class-based Smalltalk system. However, the close indentification of entities and processes in a simulation assumes that the primary function of the entities is to participate in a discrete-event simulation. If deeper models of a problem are required to be constructed, then there may be significant other structure and behaviour that must be attached to entities. Since processes are more intuitively related to the behaviour of entities rather than the entities themselves, a strategy that separates a process as a "script" from the entity following the script leads to a more natural modelling style.

For example, in an airport simulation one can choose representional forms for entities like "Plane" which primarily consider the static requirements of modelling a plane and separately define one or more behaviours for planes such as "flyRoutes" or "undergoMaintainance". In this way the plane entities can be enriched or simplified for the purposes of modelling independently of any modifications to the dynamic requirements of the simulation.

Processes involving a number of interacting entities are easier to manage if there is a supportive environment for mutual communication and inspection. As described above, the Stage/Performer contructs in AUDITION supply a rich naming and scoping environment to aid the communications between entities in a simulation. Further, the application of object-oriented principles of design encourages a more robust and modular simulation. For instance, one could model the plane-gate problem above by attaching a state variable **IsFree?** to each gate and allowing incoming planes to directly inspect this variable. The object-oriented solution would be to define a behaviour of gates **isFree?**, which may do nothing more than consult the local state **IsFree?**, but which may also perform considerably more sophisticated analyses, such as searching for a closer plane which would reach the gate before the requestor. Equally important to the development and maintainance of simulations, the transition from a simple to complex understanding of the state of an entity can be undertaken without having to modify the behaviour or structure of any other entity in the simulation and that this modification can be made at any time, including *while the simulation is running!* This last consideration is particularly important for the support of Visual Interactive Simulations.

AUDITION processes

One of the expectations of a process-oriented model of simulation is the automatic maintainance of local state information across re-invocations of the process. This preservation of local state creates the illusion that the script for a process is being continuously followed; whereas, in fact, the execution of the process is actually interleaved with the execution of other processes and subject to suspension and resumption according to internal calls to the scheduler or in response to external events.

AUDITION provides three components to support the process-oriented model - process-derived events (instances of class **Closure**), entities (objects) and schedulers (instances of class **EventMonitor**). The relationship between these concepts is illustrated by the **AirTrafficSimulation** example.

An AUDITION example - modelling aircraft movements

The example, illustrated in figures 2 and 3, models an abstract air traffic system of airports located on a map and simulates the movement and activities of planes in each airport (unloading and loading passengers, undergoing maintainance and taxiing to and from runways) and between airports (flying along air routes). Any particular network of airports and population of planes can be constructed graphically or specified textually by the user. When reading the portions of code presented in Figure 4, we should note that the *identities* such as **Airport**, **Terminal** and **AirTrafficEvents** are dynamically resolved within the context of the receiver. Part of this context is the *superStage* of the receiver and for planes this is set either to an airport, a runway or to the map if the plane is in transit between airports.

For this example, we could make the following mappings:

ENTITY-CLASS-TYPE
      Plane, Airport, Tower, Gate, Runway.

ENTITY-INSTANCE-TYPE
      Boeing767, DeHavilland-Dash-7 (Plane)

ENTITIES   AirCanada001, AirCanada002 (Boeing767)
      AirBC01 (DeHavilland-Dash-7)
      Vancouver, Toronto (Airports)
      VancouverTower (Tower)
      Runway210 on Vancouver (Runways)
      Gate16 on Vancouver (Gates)

PROCESSES   flyRoutes, undergoMaintainance,
      travelAlong:speed:steps:.

EVENTS   advance step (in travelAlong:speed:steps:)
      taxi to gate, unload passengers, load passengers,
      taxi to runway, fly to next airport,
      wait to land. (in flyRoutes), do maintainance,
      wait overnight (in undergoMaintainance)

Each event in the model corresponds to an instance of a Closure. Each closure created from a method obtains a copy of the local state at activation and maintains any changes to this local state for the lifetime of the closure. When a process is resumed, a subsequent statement may create another closure, which will be generated from the current local state of the process. In this way, the notion of a process as a sequence of events sharing a common temporal state can be realised in AUDITION by writing a single method containing, among other statements, the events of the process.

Since closure creation terminates only the immediate context, there must be a provision for one process (method) to call another (method), suspending the caller and allowing resumption at some indeterminate future point. This type of inter-process communication can be mediated by semaphores, but this would complicate generic sub-processes like the **travelAlong:atSpeed:inSteps:** method. An alternative approach in AUDITION is to use the **transferIn:** activation method, in which the suspended process may be resumed by identification.

Combining shallow and deep modelling

One of the principal disadvantages of current-generation expert systems is the absence of adequate mechanisms for incorporating causal reasoning (Sykes, Cochran and Young 1988), which significantly limits their ability to handle problems at the periphery of their knowledge, or to provide pedagogically satisfying explanations of behaviour. Similarly, simulations which rely heavily on stochastic processes are capable of only shallow reasoning about the model. While shallow reasoning provides distinct advantages in computational efficiency and model simplification, it would be desirable to develop models that can progress from shallow to deep representations, or vice versa, with minimum impact on the structure and behaviour of the model.

Using the airport example, we see that when a plane begins its flight in **flyFrom:to:** it requests the destination airport to get ready for its arrival. The method **getReadyFor:in:** is dynamically resolved against the destination airport. This allows the destination **Tower** to reserve a gate for the requesting plane using anything from a simple first-available strategy to a more complex strategy which takes into consideration topology and other aircraft schedules. The strategy employed and supporting structures such as rules, can be specified at the Class (**Tower**) or instance (**VancouverTower**) level. Further, each **Tower** evaluates its strategy within the scope of its airport, allowing the simulation designer great flexibility in designing generic strategies that are locally appropriate.

Equally, the designer could choose to simplify the model by reducing various behaviours or structures to simpler, more stochastic forms. For example the method **flyFrom:to:** may be effectively reduced from a process to an event by using a probability distribution to modify the flight time, rather than the more detailed evaluation of the original. The plane would then advance in a single jump to the destination airport.

The precision of a simulation will be linked to the level of abstraction. As Fishwick points out in his discussion of Qualitative Simulation (Fishwick 1988), different users will tend to interact most strongly with a model at different abstractive levels (a sort of "abstractive resonance" between the user and model). If understanding and intuition are more desirable outcomes of a simulation than rigorous accuracy, then a simplified, more understandable model is preferable. The significant advantage of object-oriented simulation environments is that they permit complex models to be constructed so that the user interface (the "stages" with their "cast" of objects and "cues" to use the AUDITION metaphor) can appear to be very simple and abstract, while the true complexity of the model is well "hidden" in the structure and behaviour of the model entities.

REVIEW AND FUTURE DEVELOPMENTS

Object-oriented programming has its origins in simulation (the language SIMULA introduced the such concepts as "Class"), so it is not surprising that object-oriented systems are good platforms for discrete-event simulation. Object-oriented systems are well suited to managing complex structures and their behaviour, process-oriented discrete event simulation systems help manage complex temporal models. Our experience with AUDITION suggests that a close integration of these concepts yields significant benefits in terms of model credibility, validation and complexity. Further, interactive, graphical programming environments significantly aid the development and acceptance of models.

"Intelligent" simulation systems are typically expected to be able to reason about the state of a simulation. Such reasoning is necessarily predicated on the quality of information about the system. AUDITION is designed to support complex models with many layers of abstraction. A future project will be to develop a reasoning mechanism and language for AUDITION which can adequately reason about these abstractive states and thus permit more robust, generic intelligent simulation to be developed.

REFERENCES

Agha, G. and C. Hewitt. 1987. "Actors: A Conceptual Foundation for Concurrent Object-Oriented Programming" in *Research Directions in Object-Oriented Programming* (eds. B. Shriver and P. Wegner) MIT Press Cambridge, MA: 49-74.

Bell, P.C. and R.M. O'Keefe. 1987. "Visual Interactive SImulation - History, recent developments and major issues" SIMULATION 49, no. 3: 109-116.

Conrad, R.; K. Piersol; E. Van Orden. 1987 "Tutorial: The ANALYST project: A Smalltalk-80 application case study" *Object-oriented programming systems, languages and apllications conference (OOPSLA'87)* (Orlando, FLA) ACM Press, New York, NY.

Doman, A. 1988 "Object-PROLOG: Dynamic object-oriented representation of knowledge" *Artificial Intelligence and Simulation: The Diversity of Applications* (ed. T. Henson) SCS, San Diego, CA: 83-88.

Filman, R.E. 1988 "Reasoning with worlds and truth maintenance in Knowledge-based programming environment" *Communications of the ACM*, no. 4: 382-401.

Fishwick, P.A. 1988. "Qualitative Simulation: Fundamental concepts and issues" *Artificial Intelligence and Simulation: The Diversity of Applications* (ed. T. Henson) SCS, San Diego, CA: 25-31

Goldberg, A. and D. Robson. 1983. *Smalltalk-80: The Language and its Implementation* Addison Wesley reading MA.

Intellicorp 1984 *The Knowledge Engineering Environment* Menlo Park CA.

Karam, G.M. 1988 "An ICON-based Design Method for PROLOG". IEEE Software July: 51-65.

Kreutzer, W. 1986. *System Simulation: Programming Styles and Languages* Addison Wesley London UK.

Kreutzer, W. 1988. "A modeller's workbench - Simulation based on the desktop metaphor" *Artificial Intelligence and Simulation: The Diversity of Applications* (ed. T. Henson) SCS, San Diego, CA: 43-48.

Lalonde, W.R.; D.A. Thomas; J.R. Pugh. 1986. "An Exemplar-based Smalltalk" *Proceedings of Object-oriented programming systems, languages and apllications conference (OOPSLA'86)* (Portland, OR) ACM Press, New York, NY.

Law, A.M. and C.S. Larney. 1984. An Introduction to Simulation using SIMSCRIPT II.5 CACI Los Angeles, CA.

Pegden, L.A.; T.I. Miles; and G.A. Diaz. 1985. "Graphical interpretation of output illustrated by a SIMAN manufacturing simulation model" *Proceedings of the 1985 Winter Sim. Conference*, SCS, San Diego, CA, 244-251.

Shrager, J.; D.S. Jordan; T.P. Moran; G. Kiczales; D.M. Russel. 1987 "Issues in the pragmatic of qualitative modelling: Lessons learnt from the Xerographics project" *Communications of the ACM*, no. 12: 1036-1047.

Stairmand, M.C. and W. Kreutzer. 1988. :POSE: a Process-Oriented Simulation Environment embedded in SCHEME" *SIMULATION* 50, no. 4: 143-153.

Standbridge, C.R. 1985. "Performing *simulationprojects with The Extended Simulation System (TESS)" *SIMULATION* 45, no. 6: 283-291.

Sykes, D.J.; J.K. Cochran; H.H. Young. 1988 *Artificial Intelligence and Simulation: The Diversity of Applications* (ed. T. Henson) SCS, San Diego, CA: 32-38.

Wegner, p. 1987 "The Object-Oriented Classification Paradigm" in *Research Directions in Object-Oriented Programming* (eds. B. Shriver and P. Wegner) MIT Press Cambridge, MA: 479-560.

Wile, D.S. and D.G. Allard. 1986. "Worlds: an Organising Principle for Object-Bases" SIGPLAN Notices 22, no. 1: 16-26.

Simulation and AI, 1989
©1989 by the Society for Computer
Simulation International
ISBN 0-911801-44-8

Specification of an architecture for intelligent simulation environments

Suck-Chul Hong, Jeffery K. Cochran, and Gerald T. Mackulak
Systems Simulation Laboratory
Industrial and Management Systems Engineering
Arizona State University
Tempe, Arizona 85287

ABSTRACT

Considerable discussion has appeared in the literature lately concerning intelligent simulation environments. Such environments are computer programs with both knowledge and computation components. Development of such software involves the combination of concepts and computer programming techniques from disparate sources. In addition, new methodologies for model creation, manipulation, and execution have been proposed. In this paper, we present our views based on lessons from a previous intelligent simulation environment for the semiconductor industry. The critical new thrusts include generic models, user design goal knowledge bases, and many supporting data bases. These new ideas are presented in a unified format which we call a "specification". The implementation aspects in terms of hardware and software are also presented. This approach to preliminary specification appears to be a promising area for future research.

BACKGROUND

The current race for manufacturing productivity has had a major impact on the development of automated factories characterized by the presence of hundreds or even thousands of programmable devices. The amount of software necessary to control these devices is quite formidable. Producing enormous software systems has been a major roadblock to the successful development of discrete manufacturing systems. The critical need for generic software has been repeatedly echoed, but the only results achieved so far are unsubstantiated claims and resounding failures.

Modeling complex factories through simulation is much more complicated because of the nature of its intricacy. Shannon (Shannon 1975), Law (Law and Kelton 1982), Banks (Banks and Carson II 1984), Pritsker (Pritsker 1986) indicated difficulties in modeling as well as in analyzing results. Reducing computer simulation's complexities has been another problem in the successful development of discrete manufacturing systems through simulation.

Since the advent of the artificial intelligence concept through fifth-generation languages such as Prolog, researchers have tried to embed expert systems into simulation to create intelligent simulation systems/environments to solve these problems. Haddock (Haddock 1987) has developed simulation generators which assist analysts in developing and updating models, as well as in analyzing alternative scenarios. Wichmann (Wichmann 1986) has described a user-friendly simulation environment, and Cochran, et. al. (Cochran et al. 1987) has presented system requirements for configuring software into an AI/ES environment for automated manufacturing simulation design on the PC. These systems can be categorized as Intelligent Front Ends (IFEs), as described by O'Keefe. IFEs are expert systems that interface the user with the package, generate the necessary code by following a dialogue with the user, and interpret and explain outputs generated.

INTRODUCTION

Among the current trends in simulation, most of the existing systems have problems in modeling the system and in providing an intelligent system environment. The primary problem is that modelers view all simulation models as unique, and generate a new system only with different parameters from the previously developed models. Another problem is that the current systems do not provide user design goals. Providing user design goals is very important, because experimental design selection and specific model structure are affected by these goals. Thus, output results with certain user design goals are meaningless to the user who has different user design goals.

In this paper, we present a specification of an architecture for intelligent simulation environments for discrete manufacturing systems. In addition, we propose a new methodological approach for the simulation process, and compare a traditional simulation process with our research approach. Finally, we discuss specification implementation in terms of hardware and software configuration and language needed.

PROPOSED METHODOLOGICAL APPROACH

Simulation is an iterative process in which modelers design the model, decide upon a scenario (inputs), run the experiment, analyze the results, decide upon another scenario, run the experiment, etc. The traditional simulation process is divided into 10 to 12 steps, depending on the researchers, that provide a typical, sound simulation study to guide a model builder.

However, the traditional simulation process does not aid modelers in deciding upon an appropriate model, nor in determining how to exercise it to find an answer to a given problem. Our new approach presented here combines many of the steps of the traditional simulation process with several knowledge bases and data bases, so that modelers' responsibilities are altered. Our approach is divided into 6 steps: design goal formulation, generic model selection, specific model generation, execution of experiments, output interpretation and validation, and documentation and implementation. The traditional simulation process is compared with our new approach in Table 1.

ARCHITECTURE SPECIFICATION

A user-friendly intelligent simulation environment automatically selects the appropriate generic model from related knowledge bases which contain the group technology (GT) meta-code for user goals and the GT code for the physical system. User input generates a specific model by providing data, selecting experimental designs, running the executable model, and providing standard outputs. Plots, histograms, confidence intervals of performance measures, etc. are also provided when appropriate. This not only allows the user to model an appropriate system, but also decreases users' fallacies in modeling the system and in analyzing output results.

NEW APPROACH	OLD APPROACH
Design Goal Formulation Formulate user goals GT code to identify specific user design goals through related knowledge base, based on information provided by the user (computer controlled).	**Problem Formulation** Define the problem to be studied including a statement of the problem-solving objectives (manual effort).
Generic Model Selection Generate GT code for physical system in accordance with the abstraction of the system to serve as a basis to select particular generic system to be simulated (computer controlled).	**Model Building** Abstract the system into mathematical-logical relationships in accordance with the problem formulation (manual effort).
Specific Model Generation Instantiate components in the system and then connect them with data provided by permanent factory database. Hands-on data for specific nature might be collected. All the components are provided based on the generic model so that this step depends highly on the type of generic model (computer controlled).	**Data Acquisition** Identify, specify, and collect data (manual effort). **Model Translation** Prepare the model for computer processing (manual effort). **Verification & Validation** Establish that the computer program executes as intended and that a desired accuracy or correspondence exists between the simulation model and the real system (manual effort).
Execution of Experiments Select experimental design through statistics knowledge base or knowledge base for past simulation results which assists the experimental design selection and also prevents duplicating the same simulation runs. After selecting the experimental design, the executable model will be run to produce output results (computer controlled).	**Strategic & Tactical Planning** Establish the experimental conditions for using the model (manual effort). **Experimentation** Execute the simulation model to obtain output values (computer controlled).
Output Interpretation & Validation Output results are interpreted and validated by the related knowledge bases. The statistics knowledge base provides several statistical system performances, and the knowledge base with historical data compares the historical data concerning the actual system behavior with the simulation results for output validation. In addition, error codes knowledge base contains possible error codes and knowledge regarding how to diagnose and correct run time errors (computer controlled).	**Analysis of Results** Analyze the simulation outputs to draw inferences and make recommendations for problem resolution (manual effort).
Documentation & Implementation Report generator provides knowledge for generating reports in various forms based on simulation activities and results as well as on documenting the model for later use.	**Documentation & Implementation** Implement decisions resulting from the simulation and document the model and its use.

Table 1. Comparison of New Approach and Old Approach
to Discrete Simulation of Manufacturing Process

Figure 1 shows a specification of an architecture for an intelligent simulation environment. This environment is divided into a preprocessor and postprocessor environment. The preprocessor environment consists of design goal formulation, generic model selection, and specific model generation steps, and explains how the specific model is built once the problem is defined. The postprocessor environment consists of execution of experiments, output interpretation and validation, and documentation and implementation steps, and explains how experimental design is selected and output results are interpreted and validated. Each step is discussed in detail in the following subsections. In addition, Table 2 shows the contents of the knowledge bases and data bases which were used in these environments.

Design Goal Formulation

The GT meta-code knowledge base for user goals provides group technology classification and a coding scheme for possibly using simulation in a discrete manufacturing system which will, in turn, be used to identify specific user goals based on user input. Providing user goal alternatives is very important, because the user might have different design goals within the same physical system. This step constitutes a basis for specific model generation and experimental design selection.

Generic Model Selection

In this step, the GT code for the physical system is generated. The physical system GT code knowledge base provides group technology classification and a coding scheme for the physical manufacturing system characteristics which will serve as a basis to select the particular generic system to be simulated. The end goal of this step is to avoid generating variations of previously developed models. After creating a GT code for the user design goals and the physical system, a type of generic model is selected.

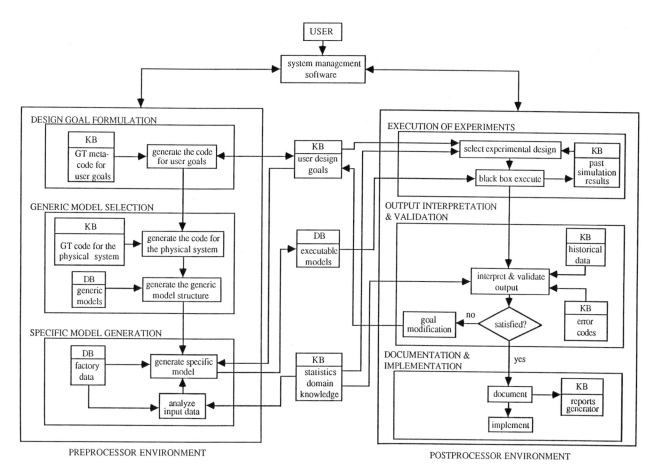

Figure 1. Specification of an Architecture for Intelligent Simulation Environments

Specific Model Generation

Once a generic model is created, the model is completely structured by simply instantiating components (or elements) in the system and then connecting them with data provided by permanent factory database. This data includes operation routings, processing times, resource availabilities, manufacturing orders, cost data, reliability data, and manufacturing scheduling, from which data required for a simulation run will be extracted.

Input data is analyzed by a statistics domain knowledge base which contains statistical methods for input data analysis such as probability distribution fitting. The user-friendly intelligent simulation environment provides the user with options for configuring the components in the system based on the generic model. Therefore, this step depends highly on the type of generic model used. Next, the models are interpreted by the SIMAN simulation program processor, and then linked to produce the executable models. These executable models are stored in an executable models data base, and can be modified later if the user is not satisfied with output results.

Execution of Experiments

Before running the executable model, experimental design is selected based on the user design goals through the statistics domain knowledge base. This knowledge base provides methods for selecting the number of runs, and for the starting conditions of simulation runs. At this point, knowledge base for past simulation results provides assistance in the experimental design selection, and in preventing duplication of the same simulation runs, particularly for real time studies. After selecting the experimental design, the executable model is run to produce output results.

Output Interpretation and Validation

Running the executable model generates output results which are interpreted and validated in this step. At this time, the error codes knowledge base provides possible error codes and knowledge regarding how to diagnose and correct run time errors. For instance, execution will be interrupted if server utilization is always 1.0 in a single queueing system, or if a queue is growing exponentially. The knowledge base with historical data compares the historical data concerning the actual system behavior with the simulation results for output validation. If the output results are not satisfied by the user, the model goes through the user design goals knowledge base to either modify the specific model or change the user goals. Otherwise, it generates output results. The statistics knowledge base contains methods for constructing confidence intervals as well as plots and histograms for the measures of system performance supported by the SIMAN output processor.

Documentation and Implementation

This step contains the report generator which provides knowledge for generating reports in various forms (tabular or graphical) based on simulation activities and results, as well as for documenting the model for later use.

SPECIFICATION IMPLEMENTATION

Hardware and Software Configuration

We propose to use existing commercially available software products in a micro-computer-based configuration to support our system, instead of using specialized hardware products and customized softwares. There are many advantages to implementing our system on a micro-computer base. The primary advantage is cost. The total cost of our proposed hardware and software is less than $15,000, which is much less in contrast to hardware and software costs for a main-frame-based approach. Another advantage is that the user is usually more familiar with microcomputer usage than with mainframe usage.

Table 3 lists hardware and software configurations including itemized costs for a micro-computer-based approach for constructing the intelligent simulation system. We selected the Sun386i workstation, but there is no reason not to use other workstations, if desired. Sun386i combines the UNIX operating system and disk operating system (DOS) into one powerful, fully integrated package. In this way, our configuration will be compatible with all mainstream DOS applications, and we will be able to take advantage of the UNIX environment at the same time. We use a 32-bit processor to speed up simulation runs which sometimes require considerable number-crunching.

Languages Needed

Next, we will explain how we configured the software shown on Table 3, and how those languages are used to develop an architecture specification. There are a number of languages that can be use for our research purpose. Each language has its own characteristics in terms of language structure. We selected Turbo-

Name of KB or DB	Contents of KB or DB
GT META CODE FOR USER GOALS (KB)	GT classification and coding scheme for the possible objectives of using simulation in manufacturing system design which will be used to identify specific user design goals.
GT CODE FOR THE PHYSICAL SYSTEM (KB)	GT classification and coding scheme for the physical manufacturing system characteristics which will serve as a basis to select particular generic system to be simulated.
USER DESIGN GOALS (KB)	The specific GT code of user design goals which is generated by interrogating the user and will constitute a basis for specific model generation and experimental design selection.
STATISTICS DOMAIN KNOWLEDGE (KB)	Statistical methods (hypothesis testing, curve fitting, correlation analysis, etc.) for input and output data analysis as well as validation.
PAST SIMULATION RESULTS (KB)	Knowledge of past simulation results to assist in the experimental design selection and prevent duplication of the same simulation runs (particularly for real-time studies).
HISTORICAL DATA (KB)	Knowledge to compare the historical data concerning the actual system behavior with the simulation results for output validation.
ERROR CODES (KB)	Possible error codes and knowledge regarding how to diagnose and correct run time errors.
REPORTS GENERATORS (KB)	Knowledge for generating reports in various forms (tabular or graphical) based on the simulation results.
GENERIC MODELS (DB)	Generic models/submodels from which specific user models will be generated based on the GT codes for the user goals and the physical system.
FACTORY DATA (DB)	Permanent factory database including operation routings, cost data, processing times, reliability data, and resource availabilities from which data required for a simulation run will be extracted.
EXECUTABLE MODELS (DB)	Ready-for-execution models generated by modifying and configuring the generic model structures.

Table 2. Contents of Knowledge Base and Data Base in
Intelligent Simulation Environment Architecture

Hardware:	Software:		
Sun386i workstation with	Turbo-Prolog	$	99.00
25MHz Intel 80386 CPU	Microsoft FORTRAN	$	350.00
25MHz Intel 80387 math coprocessor	Lattice C compiler	$	272.00
8 Mbytes main memory	SIMAN	$	1,500.00
91 Mbytes hard disk			
1.44 Mbytes 3.5" diskette drive			
Owners documentation set			
SunOS/DOS right-to-use-license			
16" color monitor			
Total Hardware Cost : $ 11,693.50	Total Software Cost : $ 2,221.00		
Total System Cost : $ 13,914.50			

Table 3. Proposed System Hardware and Software
Configuration (with Costs)

Prolog to handle logic-based computations; however, this does not mean that we cannot use other languages such as LISP products. The primary reason we chose Prolog is that we are more familiar with Prolog products than with other declarative languages. Turbo-Prolog also allows us to access other languages such as C, FORTRAN.

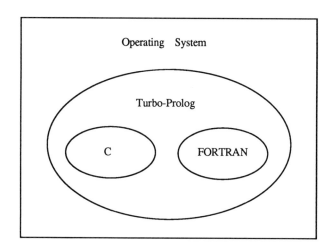

Figure 2. Computer Language Topology for
the Specified System Configuration

Table 4 shows an appropriate language selection for each step in Figure 1. Figure 2 represents the language topology for our system configuration. We have decided to use C language, which handles string manipulation and generates a type of generic model and specific model structure. It is also used to manipulate files such as storing data. FORTRAN language will be used to analyze input and output data. In addition, SIMAN has been programmed by FORTRAN. Finally, we used Turbo-Prolog to handle logic-based computation, including multiple windows, interactive input/output, and word processing facilities. All the knowledge bases are programmed by Turbo-Prolog.

Module and Language Interface

GT code generation for both user goals and the physical system are done with Turbo-Prolog. Knowledge about the GT scheme is already kept in tree structures, an Prolog provides the user with the necessary questions by following the tree structure and determining specific GT codes.

All the data and generic models/submodels are stored in "flat" data files and manipulated by C language to generate the GT code. Each model has its own file, and each file contains several types of logic records which are linked by pointers. At the beginning of a file, a pointer list maintains the locations (file positions) of the first record of each type. Each type of record maintains certain information and data such as resources, queues, and processing information. Data are stored and retrieved according to the record's pointer. Among the languages we have chosen, C offers the most sophisticated file processing capabilities and potentially fewer interface problems.

Language	Steps in which the language is used
FORTRAN	Analysis of input & output data. Black box execution. Interpreting & validating output.
C	Generating the generic model structure. Generating the specific model structure.
Turbo-Prolog	Generating the code for user goals Generating the code for physical system. Selecting experimental design. Interpreting & validating output. Goal modification. Documentation. Implementation.

Table 4. Preliminary Computer Language Selection
for Each Step in New Approach

CONCLUSION

In this paper, we combined the artificial intelligence concept and simulation techniques to produce intelligent simulation environments. We presented a specification of a proposed architecture for intelligent simulation environments, and we applied the new simulation process for building the architecture to aid in modeling the system as well as in analyzing results. Finally, we discussed the implementation aspects of the specification.

ACKNOWLEDGEMENTS

The authors thank Nur Ozdemirel, Jordan Snyder, and Eric Du, graduate student members of the System Simulation Laboratory, for their active participation in this research.

REFERENCES

Banks, Jerry and Carson II, John S. 1984, *Discrete-Event System Simulation,* Prentice-Hall, Inc.

Cochran, J. K., Mackulak, G. T., Castillo, D., and Du, E. 1987, "Configuring Available Software Into an AI/ES Environment for Automated Manufacturing Simulation Design on the PC," *SCS Conference on Simulation of Computer Integrated Manufacturing System and Robotics,* pp. 1-7, San Diego, CA.

Ford, D. R. and Schroer, B. J. 1987, "An Expert Manufacturing Simulation System," *Simulation,* Vol. 48, No. 5, pp. 193-200.

Haddock, J. 1987, "An Expert System Framework Based on a Simulation Generator," *Simulation,* Vol.48, No. 2, pp. 45-53.

Law, A. M. and Kelton W. D. 1982, *Simulation Modeling and Analysis,* MacGraw-Hill Book Company.

Mackulak, G. T. and Cochran, J. K. 1987, "MASCOT: A Prolog-Based Simulation Modeling and Training Environment," *Proceedings of Intl Symposium on Modeling and Simulation Methodology - Intelligent Environments and Goal-Directed Models,* pp. 18-21.

O'Keefe, R. 1985, "Simulation and Expert Systems - A Taxonomy and Some Examples," *Simulation,* Vol. 46, No. 1, pp. 10-16.

Pegden, C. D. 1987, *Introduction to SIMAN,* Systems Modeling Corporation.

Pritsker, A. A. B. 1986, *Introduction to Simulation and SLAMII,* Systems Publishing Corporation, 3rd Edition.

Reddy, R. 1987, "Epistemology of Knowledge Based Simulation," *Simulation,* Vol. 48, No. 6, pp. 162-166.

Shannon, R. E., Mayer, R., and Adelskerger, H. H. 1985, "Expert Systems and Simulation," *Simulation,* Vol. 44, No. 6, pp. 275-284.

Shannon, R. E. 1975, *Systems Simulation - The Art and Science,* Prentice-Hall, Inc.

Wichmann, K. E. 1986, "An Intelligent Simulation Environment for the Design and Operation of FMS," *Proceedings of European Conference on Artificial Intelligence and Simulation,* pp. 1-11.

Selection of projects under uncertain conditions: a SDSS approach

D.S. Kira
DS&MIS Department
Concordia University
Montreal, Quebec

D.H. Murray
CN Rail
Montreal, Quebec

ABSTRACT

It has become devastatingly obvious to many firms that they can no longer conduct "business as usual" in order to remain competitive in the market. While rapid and continuous improvements in the underlying technology of information systems have encouraged the use of information as a competitive weapon, only a few advancements have been made in the development of management techniques in this area. In this paper, a specific decision support system (SDSS) is developed, using well known management science techniques, to provide IS managers with an effective planning and decision-making tool. This SDSS provides them with an optimal mix of IS projects based on profit maximization criteria. The system determines when to begin the project development, which systems development language to use, and the number of systems development staff to assign to each project. A typical use of SDSS in an uncertain environment is described.

INTRODUCTION

Modern corporations, faced with an increasingly volatile environment and fierce competition, often demand more from their IS development department than their existing staff can manage. The resulting backlog must be prioritized and scarce resources allocated to IS projects in such a way that the choices maximize "value" for the corporation (see Porter and Millar 1983). These decisions will ultimately determine the nature and timing of the firm's information system, which is frequently a key factor in their ability to respond quickly to opportunities or competitive threats in the market place. A portfolio of new projects must be selected from the development backlog and resources assigned in such a manner that maximizes value under the constraints imposed by a limited staff. At present, IS planning lags behind most other corporate-level planning systems, despite the strategic importance of these systems for corporate survival and potential growth. Existing studies have found that effective IS planning systems are still relatively rare in contemporary computer centres (Cash et al. 1983, Kanter 1982, 1984; Long 1982, McFarlan 1981).

The need for an effective framework in which a firm's IS project portfolio can be selected in an uncertain environment is readily apparent. Efficient use of IS resources can be achieved through the integration of systems, the minimization of system changes, and the effective prioritization and scheduling of competing IS projects. These projects should be evaluated in the same critical manner as any other major corporate investment such as plant equipment or the introduction of a new product line. In fact, IS planning can utilize techniques used for capital budgeting allocation decisions, where scarce or limited resources and the presence of uncertainty are also major issues (Clark, et al 1984, Gordon et al 1984). In this paper, we propose a specific decision support system (SDSS) which utilizes a typical resource allocation model framework as a modelling component of the system (Sprague et al 1982).

Finding the optimal mix of development projects over some defined planning interval is a formidable task. Furthermore, the changing nature of IS systems introduces considerable uncertainty to many of the factors involved in the portfolio decision. These uncertainties can affect the estimation of project benefits, development time and hardware requirements. A need for a comprehensive set of tools to improve decision making process of IS portfolio management appears to be imminent (see Porter and Millar 1983, Pyburn 1983, Robinson 1984). The proposed SDSS, detail description to be given in section 3, hopes to fill this gap.

IS PROJECT PLANNING TOOLS

The most common forum for IS portfolio management decision making is the IS Steering Committee, according to the survey of 127 companies performed by Nolan (1982). A distinct majority (85%) of those companies claimed to use this approach to select projects and allocate staff, although most of the committees (73%) met no more frequently than every three months for a few hours. We can therefore assume that the formulation of the proposed IS portfolio is relegated to lower-level committees and the IS executive support staff. In these lower-level forums, decision making by consensus is typical, with only limited recourse to analytical tools (Nolan 1982). There is very little explicit evaluation, therefore, of the trade-offs between the risk and return of various projects. However, see (Boehm 81, Putnam 78, 80) for the risk and return trade-off among individual projects and Figenbaum and Thomas (1986) for the discussions on risk-return.

A number of models have been suggested to improve this process. Among them is one suggested by Buss (1983), in which the IS executive must form a composite ranking of potential projects based on financial costs and benefits, intangible benefits, technical importance, and conformity to the organization's objectives. Presumably by allowing intangible, technical, and strategic issues to enter into this ranking process, the uncertainty associated with profitability estimates can be avoided. Unfortunately, accountability for financial results and the ability to compare the financial benefits of different IS projects are lost in the process.

McFarlan (1981) takes an important step by including risk assessment in his model. He argues that the size and structure of a project and the firm's experience with the technology involved are the chief determinants of risk. He does not directly determine the relationship between risk and return, however, and the methodology relies on a number of somewhat arbitrary surrogates to link expected return with degree of risk. Kanter (1982, 1984) uses a rating system to prioritize projects. This also depends on an arbitrary, intuitive scale. Another approach, presented by Long (1982), uses a series of evaluators to form a consensus risk evaluation in a matrix format. Putnam (1978, 1980), and Rubin (1983) both used similar techniques on management of a software project. However, their main goal is to provide a methodology in managing a project rather than a portfolio of projects. Research and Development (R&D) portfolio selection models utilizing a myriad of ranking procedures or mathematical programming methods are described in (Clark 1974, Dean 1968, Gear et al 1971, Madey 1985).

In this paper, an SDSS system based on both integer linear programming and Monte Carlo simulation techniques is described. It incorporates the following features, which we believe to be essential for an IS portfolio management model in today's competitive environment:

1) multi-periodicity- Staff allotment, the time-value of money and the improvement of price-performance of computer hardware can all be included as a function of time.

2) effect of uncertainty- Sensitivity analysis is performed to examine the possible effects on expected return, cost, and project size.

3) development technology- Tradeoffs concerning development staff productivity and hardware costs are considered.

4) diminishing marginal productivity- The reduction in productivity of each additional person assigned to a project is also taken into account in this model.

5) value of additional information- The informational phase of the SDSS contains a technique for assessing the value of a further study to reduce uncertainty.

THE SDSS MODEL

The SDSS described in this paper, defined here as a computer system designed to aid management decision making (see, Sprague et al 1982 and Vazsonyi 1978) is conceptually divided into three distinct phases: deterministic, probabilistic, and informational. The second two phases use the output of the preceding phase as input. The initial, or deterministic phase, is generated using data determined by the IS manager according to his own environmental estimates and assessment of project characteristics. Although, the estimations of project characteristics such as size, complexity, effort, and benefit are a difficult task for IS managers there are some will known estimation models he/she can utilized. For example, COCOMO model estimates the man-month development effort as well as the software development time (Boehm 1981). SLIM (Putnam 1980) and ESTIMACS (Rubin, 1983) are softwares that can provide cost estimates of the projects. The proposed SDSS software package is written in Statistical Analysis System (SAS). Each phase will now be examined:

Deterministic Phase

The various inputs required for the integer linear program used during this phase can be categorized as follows: a performance measure (for the objective function), exogenous parameters, policies and constraints, decision variables, and intermediate variables.

The chosen performance measure consists of the total net benefit of all projects completed within the planning horizon, expressed in present value terms. This value is the sum of the differences between the value of actual benefits and the actual dollar investment in hardware for all projects selected.

Exogenous parameters, estimated by the IS manager, include the following:

1) Net Project Benefits, excluding hardware and systems development costs but including all other costs, are expressed in terms of equivalent monthly savings in current dollars which would result from an immediate implementation of the project.

2) The Price-Performance Improvement Factor (PPI), reflecting the declining cost-per-unit of computing power and the lower price of computer hardware with time, must be predicted for the planning horizon in question.

3) Program Language Efficiency is expressed in terms of a "language efficiency multiplier" for each type of language, given that high-level languages require considerably more computing hardware than lower-level languages.

4) The cost of additional computer hardware required for each project must be expressed in current dollars (as if purchased immediately), assuming that a conventional programming language has been used.

5) Development effort "size" is frequently measured in "function points" (see Boehm 1981, Kemerer 1985, Konsynski 1981, Rubin 1983) which are based on a number of factors related to size and complexity, i.e., number of user inputs, user outputs, inquiries, logical master files and logical interfaces to other systems.

6) Labour productivity estimates are based on two known factors related to project labour efficiency: the greater programming efficiency of higher level languages versus lower-level languages and the diminishing marginal productivity rate associated with each additional worker added to a project for each language type.

Policies and constraints, provided by the IS manager, are used as input parameters during this phase. Three such inputs are included in this model:

1) A fixed programming staff during the planning horizon is assumed and the cost of retaining this staff is considered to be a sunk cost in this analysis.

2) Prior to input, net present values must be established. Specifically, the firm's weighted average cost of capital (WACC) is used in this study as a discount rate.

3) A fixed planning horizon, which may consist of several planning periods, must be established by the IS manager.

Intermediate variables must be determined for each project. For the purpose of this exercise, three key variables are included:

1) The duration of development effort for each project, a function of language selected and staff assigned to the project, must be established.

2) Actual benefits for each project must be determined as a function of stated project benefits, starting time of the development, the duration of the development effort, and the discount rate employed.

3) Hardware costs required to support the implementation of each project are based on current hardware costs, the price-performance factor, a language efficiency multiplier, start and finish time for the development effort, and the discount rate.

Finally, the decision variables produced by the integer linear program will provide the IS manager with the following four optimal decisions, based on the inputs outlined above:

1) Which projects to develop.

2) When to begin the development of each chosen project.

3) The number of people to assign to each project.

4) The appropriate programming language for a given project.

A net benefit is computed for each combination of decision variables, and an integer linear program is constructed with these net benefits as objective function coefficients to maximize total net benefits subject to fixed staff constraints within a given horizon.

The relationships discussed previously provide the foundation for an integer linear programming model which enables the IS manager to make an optimal choice of projects, starting times, programming languages and staff levels. Each of the projects being considered can be thought of as a number of mutually exclusive sub-projects, one for each combination of programming language, staff assignment size and starting time. A net benefit can be computed for each such combination and an integer linear program (ILP) then constructed with these net benefits as objective function coefficients. This ILP is formulated to maximize total net benefits subject to fixed staff constraints within a given horizon.

Here, we are assuming that IS managers can provide appropriate subjective or objective assessments of various parameters. Estimation models such as COCOMO, SLIM and ESTIMACS can assist managers in developing quantitative estimates. If this is not feasible, then the subjective estimation procedures such as expert resolution (see Morris 1974, 1977) can be utilized in estimating the parameters.

We also note that ILP problem size increases rather quickly. For example, consider the following: 10 projects under consideration, three possible levels of programming language, 100 possible staff allotments corresponding to a total staff of 100, and 60 months in the planning interval, the problem will involve 360,000 variables and 183,070 constraints.

Suggested simplifications which will not significantly reduce the usefulness of the results include:

1) Reducing the number of time periods by introducing quarter periods (i.e., 3 months at a time) as well as limiting the total period considered (i.e., from 5 to 3 years) alters the number of periods considered from 60 to 12.

2) Reducing the number of possible staff sizes to be allocated to each project in a manner which favours small sizes to reduce the effect of diminishing marginal productivity of large groups will result in fewer group sizes used (see, Esterling 1980). For example, instead of considering every combination possible, only 8 staff sizes could be considered.

3) Depending on the firm, it is possible that only 2 levels of language may be realistically included, rather than 3.

The resulting example would now have only 3,840 variables and 2,102 constraints. Further reductions could be achieved through the exclusion of sub-projects which are found to have hardware costs which exceed their benefits or cannot be completed within the planning horizon established.

In summary, the deterministic phase of the SDSS generates an integer linear program customized by the specific values of the exogenous and policy parameters of the model user. An IP solution is then generated to obtain that combination of projects, start times, and language levels which optimizes the net present value of the project mix.

The next phase of the SDSS addresses the important issue of uncertainty. It appears that the main reason associated with the managerial difficulties in software development can be traced to the uncertainty that pervades software development (Boehm 1981, Putnam and Wolverton 1977, Zmud 1980).

Probabilistic Phase

We will now introduce uncertainty to the modelling component of the SDSS, and observe how the profitability of the optimal decision found by the integer linear program in the deterministic phase is affected. In this manner, uncertainty can be considered explicitly in terms of its impact on profits. This is accomplished by allowing some of the exogenous parameters, which so far have been considered fixed, to become random variables. Values for these will be generated using a Monte Carlo simulation. The pioneering work of utilizing the Monte Carlo method in project selection problems is largely due to Hertz (1964). Spetzler (1968) provides a similar method of dealing with risk where a corporate capital investment decision must be made. Three parameters have been chosen to become stochastic in our example on the basis that they are most frequently the source of serious estimation errors in IS planning: project benefits, hardware costs and project size. We assume that their probability distributions, which may be developed from historical data or subjective assessment, are known to the IS managers. Realizations are then generated according to their respective distributions. A new optimal solution and its benefits are computed for each of the realizations generated for these parameters, which we had assumed to be fixed in the deterministic phase. When this process is repeated many times, a cumulative probability distribution function of the total net benefits under these conditions of uncertainty can be developed.

In our example, the distribution of benefits is assumed to be normal and that of the project size and hardware investment to be Erlang variates. The IS manager must specify the mean, standard deviation, and the distribution form of each random variable. SAS has the ability to generate random variates from a large number of distributions, should other distributions prove more appropriate than those chosen for this example. As stated in Putnam (1978), the estimators developed for the particular company cannot be used as a "standard" estimator for the industry since each company has its own characteristics that need to be determined.

Certain infeasible situations must be dealt with when trying out each of these new possibilities. In the case where a staff shortfall is introduced through the changing variables, the simulation assumes that temporary programmers will be obtained from an outside source at double the gross salary for the period in question. It is also assumed that a temporary group will be employed to complete any work beyond the planning horizon, under the same salary conditions.

The SDSS allows the random variables to be considered individually as well as in combination. The final output for each selection of variables to be analyzed is a cumulative probability distribution of total net benefits which can be used to assess the sensitivity of this value to random changes in the selected parameter(s).

Informational Phase

Having made a posterior analysis to determine the degree of variability of profitability of the optimal solution under uncertainty, the IS manager may wish to reduce this uncertainty in specific parameters if the variability is at unacceptable levels. Various measures, such as work studies to establish project benefits more firmly, or a more detailed system design to establish project size and hardware requirements, can be performed for certain projects at this stage. However, the delays associated with further studies and the costs incurred by these studies may exceed potential benefits. An estimate of the value of this additional information would be beneficial before commissioning extra design work or studies. The procedure by which this value is obtained is generally referred to as preposterior analysis.

In order to establish this value, that is, the value of perfect information, the integer linear programming of the first phase and the Monte Carlo simulation techniques of the second phase must be combined. The original optimal solution of the deterministic phase is evaluated under each of the random 'realizations' generated during the probabilistic phase, using the same assumptions concerning infeasibility as were used earlier. These benefits will then be compared with those of the new solutions generated under the same realizations during the probabilistic phase. The new optimal solution, by definition, will yield higher benefits than the deterministic solution which was generated under different conditions. The difference represents the increase in total benefits that would have been obtained if the realizations generated on a random basis had been forecast, and the new optimal solution had been implemented instead of the original solution generated during the deterministic phase. This process is repeated until a cumulative frequency distribution emerges for all of these differences. This cumulative distribution function represents the value of perfect information for the chosen variables. It provides the frequency that a minimum amount of money can be saved if the IS manager can foresee the future and make an optimal decision accordingly.

SDSS RESULTS

It is not within the scope of this

paper to detail all the results that can be obtained by the SDSS model. We will use an example which illustrates those analyses deemed of general interest and the type of results which are considered most useful. In this example, we assume that the IS manager of a medium-sized installation has a total programming staff of 50 people. Five possible projects were identified, in conjunction with the user departments. Initial feasibility studies and external designs have been conducted, resulting in the following information:

PROJECT NUMBER	EXPECTED BENEFITS (/month)	STANDARD DEVIATION	EXPECTED INVESTMENT (Hardware)	FUNCTION POINTS
1	$ 25,000	$ 5,000	$ 500,000	3,800
2	$ 35,000	$ 5,000	$ 500,000	7,000
3	$ 40,000	$ 4,000	$ 60,000	7,600
4	$ 75,000	$ 30,000	$ 900,000	7,500
5	$ 100,000	$ 50,000	$ 200,000	9,500

The "standard deviation" figures in this table refer to the project benefits. It has been determined through discussions with users that the project benefits are normally distributed. The distributions of project size and hardware investment, on the other hand, have been found to be Erlang variates. Of course, these distributions differs for various projects and need to be determined empirically. In this example, we have set T = 50, Q = 12, P = 5, L = 2, S = 8, WACC = .16, and PPI = 0.1. The deterministic phase of this problem required 5,542 iterations, and consumed 114 minutes of computer time on an IBM-compatible processor with an execution speed of approximately 6.5 million instructions per second. SDSS initially creates an input file with project information, and constructs and then executes the integer program to select an optimal solution. The optimal solution is as follows: begin project 3 immediately, use an upper-level language, and assign 19 people. The project will require 9 months to complete. Begin project 5 immediately, also using an upper level language, and assign 31 people. It will be completed in 9 months. When projects 3 and 5 are complete, assign all 50 people to project 4 using a lower-level development language. This project will then require two years to complete. Following this plan will result in net benefits with a present value of $11,300,300.

The probabilistic phase of SDSS was performed allowing the following parameters to vary: benefits, hardware investment and size estimates. Each one was allowed to vary on an individual basis and then all three exogenous variables were made to vary simultaneously. In each case, 500 iterations of the Monte Carlo simulation process were performed. The resulting cumulative distribution functions are reproduced in figure 2. We note that the project size estimate appears to be the most critical parameter among the 3 parameters we chose, since it has the highest variation. We also note the relative insensitivity of benefit and hardware parameters.

The final (informational) phase of the SDSS can provide some assistance in determining the amount of effort the IS manager should spend in obtaining better estimates of these parameters. Although, an additional information can provide decision makers with the ability to improve their decision status through reducing the uncertainty they face before committing to a decision, the "value" obtained due to reduction in uncertainty, does not always add any "value" to the decision making process. This follows since no amount of additional information can alter the "optimal" decision. In such a case, the information is valueless and any cost incurred in gathering additional information is a sunk cost. The numerical value of an additional information, the expected value of sample information (EVSI), is the difference between the expected value of the optimal decision with sample information and the expected value of the optimal decision without any additional information (EV). This value range from zero to an upper bound of the expected value of perfect information (EVPI), depending upon the reliability of the estimates. The SDSS was run allowing benefits, hardware investment, and project size to vary simultaneously.

In total, 100 iterations of the Monte Carlo simulation in the informational phase were performed, each involving the construction and solution of a large integer linear program. 1,398 minutes of computer time on a 6.5 million-instructions-per-second processor were required to conduct this analysis.

The cumulative frequency distribution of differences between the net present value of the optimal solution for each random state-of-nature and those of the original deterministic phase solution evaluated under the conditions represented by the random state-of-nature is presented in figure 1.

On the basis of this information, the IS manager would be justified in spending up to $2 million on activities that provide better estimates of the three parameters allowed to vary in this example. This follows from the cumulative graph of figure 1, since there is a very good chance (greater than 90%) that EVPI exceeds 2 million dollars.

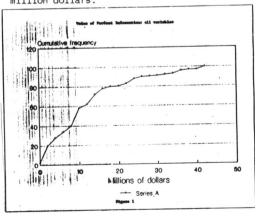

REFERENCES

Boehm, B. 1981. Software Engineering Economics, Englewood Cliffs, N.J.

Buss, D.J. 1983. "How to rank computer projects." Harvard Business Review, (Jan-Feb.): 118-125.

Cash, J.I., F.W. McFarlan and J.L. McKenney. 1983. Corporate Information Systems Management: Text and Cases. Richard D. Irwin Inc., Homewood Illinois.

Clark, J.J.; T.J. Hindelang and R.E. Pritchard. 1984. Capital Budgeting: Planning and Control of Capital Expenditures. Prentice-Hall, 2nd ed. Englewood Cliffs, New Jersey.

Dean, B.V. 1968. "Evaluating selection, and controlling R&D projects." AMA Res. Study, Vol. 89.

Esterling, B. 1980. "Software Manpower Costs: A Model." Datamation, (March):164-170.

Figenbaum, A., and H. Thomas. 1986. "Dynamic and risk measurement perspectives on Bowman's risk-return paradox for strategic management: An empirical study." Strategic Management Journal, (Vol. 7): 395-407.

Gear, A.E., A.G. Lockett, and A.W. Pearson. 1971. "Analysis of some portfolio selection models for R&D." IEEE Trans. Eng. Manag., (Vol. EM-18): 66-87.

Gordon, L.A. and G.E. Pinches. 1984. Improving Capital Budgeting: A Decision Support System Approach. Addison-Wesley, Reading.

Hertz, D. B.. 1964. "Risk analysis in capital investment." Harvard Business Review, Vol. 42, (No. 2): 95-106.

Kanter, J. 1984. Management Information Systems. Prentice-Hall Inc., Englewood Cliffs, New Jersey.

_____ 1982. "MIS Long Range Planning: Why Don't More Companies Do It?" Infosystems, (1982).

Kemerer, C.F.. "An Empirical Validation of Software Cost Estimation Models." Communications of the ACM, Vol. 30 (No. 2): 414-429.

Konsynski, B. and J. Kotternann. 1981. "Complexity Measures in System Development," in Preceedings of Conference on Information Systems, Cambridge Mass., pp. 173-199,

Long, E.L. 1982. Design and Strategy for Corporate Information Services. Prentice-Hall Inc., Englewood Cliffs, New Jersey.

Madey, G.R. and B. V. Dean. 1985. "Strategic Planning for Investment in R&D Using Decision Analysis and Mathematical Programming," IEEE Trans. on Eng. Manag., Vol. EM-32, (No. 2): 84-90.

McFarlan, F.W.. 1981. "Portfolio approach to information systems." Harvard Business Review. (Sept-Oct.): 142-150.

Morris, P.A..1974. "Decision Analysis Expert Use." Management Science. Vol. 20, (9): 1233-1241.

_____ 1977. "Combining Bayesian Approach." Management Science. Vol. 23, (7): 679-693.

Nolan, R.L.. 1982. "Managing information systems by committee." Harvard Business Review. (July-Aug.): 72-79.

_____ and C.F. Gibson. 1974. "Managing the Four Stages of EDP Growth." Harvard Business Review. (Jan.-Feb.): 76-85.

Porter, M.E., and V.E. Millar. 1985. "How information gives you competitive advantage." Harvard Business Review. (July-Aug.): 149-160.

Putnam, L.H.. 1978. "A General Empirical Solution to the Macro Software Sizing and Estimation Problem." IEEE Transactions on Software Engineering, Vol. 4, (No. 4): 345-361.

_____ .1980. Software Cost Estimation and Life Cycle Control. IEEE Computer Society Press.

Putnam, L.H. and R.W. Wolverton. 1977. "Quantitative management: Software cost estimating." COMPSAC 77, IEEE Computer Soc. Conference, Chicago, IL, (Nov).

Pyburn, P.J. .1983. "Linking the MIS Plan with Corporate Strategy, An Exploratory Study." MIS Quarterly.

Robinson, D.G.. 1984. "Synchronizing Systems With Business Values," Datamation, June.

Rubin, H.A. 1983. "Macro-estimation of Software Development Parameter: The Estimation System, Software Proceedings IEEE, (July): 109-118.

Spetzler, C.S..1968. "The development of a corporate risk policy for capital investment decisions." IEEE Transactions On Systems Science and Cybernetics. 279-300, Sept..

Sprague, Jr. R.H. and E.D. Carlson. 1982. Building Effective Decision Support Systems. Prentice-Hall, Englewood Cliffs, 1982.

Vazsonyi, A.. 1978. "Decision Support Systems: The New Technology of Decision Making?" Interfaces, (Nov.):.

Zmud, R. W.. 1980. "Management of large software development efforts," MIS Quarterly, June.

Computer simulation modeling in the hands of decision-makers

Onur M. Ülgen   Timothy Thomasma

Industrial and Systems Engineering Department
School of Engineering
University of Michigan - Dearborn
4901 Evergreen Rd., Dearborn
Michigan 48128 U.S.A.

ABSTRACT:

In this paper we investigate the computer simulation model building tools that can be directly used by decision-makers. Such computer simulation programs are generally known as Simulation Program Generators (SPGs). The main characteristics of the SPGs are that (1) they can be used directly by people that are not experts in the field of simulation but knowledgable about the system to be investigated, (2) once the user has enough information about the system to be modeled, model building and analysis of model results are done in a very short amount of time, (3) the application areas of the industrial-strength SPGs are generally limited to one type of system (e.g., assembly line systems, flexible manufacturing systems, automated guided vehicle systems, etc.).

We classify the SPGs into two main classes. The first class is the domain-independent SPGs. These SPGs can be used in modeling any type of a system but they require the description of the system in some intermediate form before using the SPG. Two examples of such intermediate forms are activity-cycle diagrams and causal diagrams. The rules for building these intermediate forms can easily be programmed and the user can be guided interactively by a computer program in constructing his/her system's activity-cycle or causal diagram. Once the intermediate forms are finalized, the program for the simulation model of the system is automatically generated by the SPG after some more input from the user.

The second class of SPGs are the domain-dependent SPGs. These SPGs can be used to model specific systems and they are the more popular ones used in industry. Their main advantage is that they don't require the representation of the system in some intermediate form. One can further classify the domain-dependent SPGs into three sublasses, namely; parameter-characterized models, event-characterized models, and icon-characterized models. As one goes from the parameterized to icon-based SPGs, the flexibility and the domain boundary of the systems that can be modeled increase while the initial development times taken by simulation experts to develop such models decrease.

In the paper, we investigate each class of SPG discussed above in some detail and give examples of some of them. We also list the advantages and disadvantages of each type of SPG and discuss the current and future research areas on SPGs.

INTRODUCTION:

A major challenge to the American industry in the 1980's and beyond is to reduce labor and material costs while increasing the productivity, quality, and flexibility of production systems. Automation in production and the application of new operational policies have helped managers to attain some of these goals. Automation in production is achieved mostly by the use of programmable numerical control machines, automated material handling devices, and robots. The new operational policies involve the computerization of information flow, just-in-time inventory, real-time inventory and scheduling control, statistical quality control, and integration of automated components. Automated production systems are built with high-cost capital equipment and, because of their complex and integrated nature, they require specialists in their design and control. These large investments must begin to pay off in the first days of operation. Therefore, detailed analysis of production systems should be made during the concept stage of planning and design. Such analysis can eliminate costly errors in design and inefficient operational policies before the system is installed.

Production systems can be analyzed by a number of modeling techniques including mathematical models, probability and statistical models, and computer simulation models. As the complexity of the production systems increases, computer simulation models start playing a major role among the different modeling approaches (Shannon, Long, and Buckles, 1980, Dunhan and Kochhar, 1983). In a recent article, Suri (Suri, 1988) discusses the use of a computerized rapid model building technique in analysis of production systems. Suri's approach is based on mathematical modeling (using recent advances in the theories of queuing and reliability) and makes an approximate model of the production system that can be used by decision-makers in early stages of decision-making. Suri claims that his rapid modeling technique takes a minimum amount of time in training and it can test the effects of different policies on a production system in minutes on a computer. Ulgen and Ulgen (Ulgen and Ulgen, 1988), in another recent article, point out the importance of computers in decision-making as perceived by managers. Their empirical study shows that managers expect an increase in the use of quantitative techniques as computerization increases at the work place. The important task is to make these computerized tools user-friendly enough such that a minimum or no training is required to use them.

The computer simulation programs that can be directly used by decision-makers and that require a minimum amount of training in computer programming and simulation are generally known as Simulation Program Generators (Mathewson, 1984). SPGs are also referred as Generic Models (Henriksen, 1983) and Interactive Program Generators (Pidd, 1984). SPGs accept the description of systems to be modeled using a natural language-like input format and produce an executable computer simulation program. In other words, an SPG is a user-oriented simulation-model-building software package.

In the following sections of the paper, we first suggest a classification of the SPGs and describe their main characteristics. In the next two sections, we give examples of domain-independent and domain-dependent SPGs, respectively. In the last section of the paper, we discuss the current and future research areas in the development and use of SPGs.

A CLASSIFICATION OF SPGS:

One way to classify SPGs is based on the types of systems that an SPG can successfully model. We define domain-independent SPGs as those that can model any type of a system. On the other hand, domain-dependent SPGs can be applied to only a few types of systems (mostly to only one). Table 1 gives summary information on the characteristics of five domain-independent SPGs. The user input to the first three (DRAFT, CAPS/ECSL, AUTOSIM) is based on activity cycle diagrams whereas the input to CASM is based on a causal diagram and Subrahmaniam & Cannon's SPG is based on an English-like metalanguage. All the SPGs in Table 1 have discrete-change variables except CASM which has continuous-change variables. The world-views of the target simulation language can be of all the possible kinds for discrete-event simulation (process orientation, activity-scanning, discrete-event scheduling, and the three-phase approach). The first three domain-independent SPGs are available as commercial products while the last two are prototypes used for academic purposes. In the next section we will give examples of activity-cycle and causal diagrams for two simple problems.

The domain-dependent SPGs generally have specific problem domains. Table 2 gives characteristics of six domain-dependent SPGs. Domain-dependent SPGs are also known as data-driven SPGs, since the appropriate model is automatically generated based on the data supplied by the user. Prior to the dialogue with the user, domain-dependent SPGs are primed with information about a single or multiple specific problem areas (e.g., assembly lines, transfer lines, job shops, flexible manufacturing systems, etc.). In the dialogue process, they obtain further information about specifics of the user's problem (customization of the program). The SPGs in Table 2 are designed to model production systems, which is the most popular application area for domain-dependent SPGs. This is because of the repeated use of the similar types of equipment (e.g., conveyors, machines, cranes, AGVs, transporters) in a variety of production systems. Almost all the SPGs in Table 2 have a user-friendly, English-language dialogue. Note that only one them, NLPQ, uses a natural language processor with limited vocabulary. NLPQ, as such, is much more flexible than the others and it generates programs "from scratch" while the others just customize pre-written programs. Most of the more recent domain-dependent SPGs have graphical capabilities for animation and icon-based model input (AUTOGRAM/AUTOMOD, Thomasma, et. al., 1986).

TABLE 1 : SUMMARY OF FIVE DOMAIN-INDEPENDENT SPGS
(Ulgen and Williams, 1988)

SPG NAME	DRAFT	CAPS/ECSL (Computer Aided Programming System/ Extended Control and Simulation Language)	AUTOSIM (Automatic Simulation Generator)	CASM (Computer-Aided Simulataion Methodology)	SUBRAHMANIAM & CANNON
TIME PERIOD	1975 -	1978 -	Early 1970's -	1978 -	1981 -
INPUT REQUIREMENTS	Activity cycle diagram. English-like problem description. Interactive.	Activity cycle diagram. English-like problem description. Interactive.	Activity cycle diagram. English-like problem description. Interactive.	Causal diagram. English-like problem description. Interactive.	Problem description in English-like meta-language.
TRAJECTORY OF DESCRIPTIVE VARIABLES	Discrete-change	Discrete-change	Discrete-change	Continuous-change, discrete-change	Discrete-change
FORMALISM USED TO DESCRIBE THE MODEL	Discrete-event, activity-scanning, process-interaction, three-phase.	Activity-scanning	Process-interaction	Differential equation, difference equation	Discrete-event
STATUS	Product	Product	Product	Prototype	Prototype
LANGUAGE USED	FORTRAN	FORTRAN	SIMULA	FORTRAN	Metalanguage, PL/1
TARGET LANGUAGE	GASP II, SIMON/FORTRAN, SIMSCRIPT II.5, SIMULA or 2900 ACSL	ECSL	SIMULA	FORTRAN	SIMSCRIPT
COMMENTS	Complex models require hand-coding.	Complex models require hand-coding.	Complex models requires hand-coding.	Based on system-theoretic concepts. Uses system dynamics terminology.	Based on system-theoretic concepts.
RELEVANT REFERENCES	Pidd, 1984 Mathewson, 1974, 1984 Mathewson, et. al., 1977 Davies, 1979	Pidd, 1984 Hutchinson, 1981 Davies, 1979	Warren, et.al., 1985	Burns, et. al., July 1978 Dec. 1978	Subrahmanian, et. al., 1981

PG NAME	JSSPG (Job Shop Simulation Program Generator)	NLPQ	GENTLE (Generalized Transfer Line Emulation)	MAST (Manufacturing System Design Tool)	MAP/1 (Modeling and Analysis Program/1)	AUTOGRAM/AUTOMOD
TIME PERIOD	1967 - ?	1968 - 1972	1975 -	1980 -	1983 -	1983 -
PROBLEM DOMAIN	Job shop production system	Queuing simulations	Transfer lines, assembly lines	Flexible manufacturing systems	Manufacturing and material handling systems	Manufacturing and material handling systems
LEVEL OF DETAIL	Variety of part types and mix (routing, processing times, etc.). Job dispatching rules, resource selection rules.	Simple queues with canonical structure.	Multiple machine operations. Repair loops. Assembly and splitting of parts. Tool changes. Pallets.	Variety of part types and mix. Conveyors carts, machine tools. Process control algorithms.	Variety of part types, fixtures. Workstation ranking. Conveyors or regular transporters. Operator types.	Conveyors, AGVS, and other transporters. Machining centers, transfer lines, FMS. Speeds, load and unload times.
INPUT REQUIREMENT	Multiple choice English language questionnaire.	English language problem description dialogue with limited vocabulary. Interactive.	Multiple choice English language queries. Interactive.	Free formatted input values.	Multiple choice English-like problem description. Interactive.	English-like problem description or graphical menu-driven description.
STATUS	Prototype	Prototype	Product	Product	Product	Product
LANGUAGE USED	SIMSCRIPT	FORTRAN, NLP	FORTRAN	FORTRAN	FORTRAN	AUTOMOD (C)
TARGET LANGUAGE	SIMSCRIPT	GPSS	GPSS	FORTRAN	FORTRAN	GPSSH, AUTOGRAM-Display (C)
TASK	Customize programs.	Generate programs.	Customize programs.	Customize programs.	Customize programs.	
COMMENTS		Uses a natural language processor (NLP)	Only one part type. Ford Motor Company, proprietary product.	Graphical animation of the process. CMS Research, Inc., proprietary product.	Output graphics available using TESS. Pritsker & Assoc., Inc., proprietary product.	Animated display. Requires special hardware. Auto Simulations, Inc., proprietary product.
RELEVANT REFERENCES	Oldfather, et. al., 1966, 1967	Heidorn, 1976	Ulgen, 1983	Lenz, 1983 Bevans, 1982	Miner, et. al., 1984	Farnsworth, et. al., 1987

Although not shown in Table 2, one can also classify SPGs as (i) parameter-characterized SPGs, (ii) event-characterized SPGs, and (iii) icon-characterized SPGs. Parameter-characterized SPGs are the SPGs that have the smallest amount of modeling flexibility in the problem domain area. For example, in a warehouse SPG that is parameter-characterized, the user may be able to change the speed of loader cranes, the speed of conveyors, the number of vertical and horizontal bins in an aisle, the number of aisles, store and retrieve rules, and the input and output levels of the total system. The parameters (attributes) of the temporary entities (transactions) will specify some of these characteristics (number of loader cranes) while some type of global variable (savevalues in GPSS, XX(I) in SLAM II, or X(I) in SIMAN) will specify other parameters (the speeds, physical dimensions). There will be different sections of code dedicated for the implementation of different operational policies (store and retrieve rules). Most of the parameter-characterized SPGs can be easily modeled using the process-orientation world-view of the simulation language (i.e., block orientation in GPSS and SIMAN, network orientation in SLAM II, and process orientation in SIMSCRIPT II.5). Parameter-characterized SPGs can be developed using other world-views of simulation languages too (i.e., event scheduling, activity scanning, or the three-phase approach). Generally, parameter-characterized SPGs are good for low and medium complexity models. For example, it is generally hard to

model interactions among permanent entities (i.e., cranes, servers, machines) in such SPGs (Ulgen, 1983). On the other hand, parameter-characterized SPGs have shorter development times than the event-characterized SPGs.

Event-characterized SPGs use the event-scheduling world-view of the simulation languages (e.g., event-scheduling approaches of SIMSCRIPT II.5, SIMAN, and SLAM II). For example, for a job-shop SPG using this approach, each machine will be represented by its start of machine cycle event, end of machine cycle event, start of machine downtime event, end of machine downtime event, start of machine tool change event, end of machine tool change event, and arrival of job to machine event. Although some of these events are secondary events (e.g., start of machine cycle event is secondary to arrival of job to machine event), it is generally desirable to separate these events for complex models to give much more flexibility to the SPG. Event-characterized SPGs generally execute much faster than the parameter- and icon-characterized models although they take much more time in development. They are also suitable for much more complex models and they provide the user with the most flexibility (Manufacturing Systems Group, 1988).

Icon-characterized SPGs use icons representing the real system elements in the model development phase (e.g., WITNESS, Thomasma, et. al., 1986, 1987). Icons are also used in the output display via animation. The

91

more common world-view of simulation used in such SPGs is event-scheduling approach. Programming languages that are natural to use are the object-oriented programming languages such as SMALLTALK and Objective-C. In a following section, we will describe an icon-characterized SPG developed using object-oriented programming. The icon-characterized SPGs appear to be more user-friendly than the parameter- and event-characterized SPGs. They can model complex systems and have the flexibility of event-characterized SPGs. The model development times are medium to short but they may require an expert in object-oriented programming.

DOMAIN-INDEPENDENT SPGS

In this section we will give two simple examples of domain-independent SPGs. As discussed before, domain-independent SPGs generally require the representation of the system in some intermediate form before generating the simulation model of the system. The first SPG to be considered is the CAPS/ECSL (Hutchinson, 1981, Pidd, 1984). The intermediate model representation for CAPS/ECSL is the activity-cycle diagram of the system. Figure 1 shows an activity-cycle diagram for a simple job-shop (see Pidd, 1984 for more detail). In Figure 1, the rectangles and circles represent the the active and dead states of an entity. The active states represent some type of service times that are generally scheduled. In Figure 1, the operative goes through three active states, AWAY, RETOOL, and RESET. The active states of the machines are RETOOL, RESET, RUNNING. Note that two of the active states, RETOOL and RESET, require cooperation between the two classes of entity. The dead state is a state where an entity waits for something to happen. Generally, there is no cooperation between entities of different classes in a dead state. In Figure 1, the operative is at the dead state WAITING when it is not at one of the active states. The machines' cycle diagram shows three dead states, namely; STOPPED, OK, and READY. In real life, the dead states OK and READY may not exist but they are placed here to make sure that each active state is followed by a dead state (see Pidd, 1984 for more information). CAPS/ECSL user needs to generate the system's activity cycle diagram before entering a dialogue to give specific information about the system to be modeled. During the dialogue, the user specifies the logical order of the active and dead states of each class of entity, the capacity of each type of entity, the data for service times and arrivals, the initial conditions of the system, etc. The result is the ECSL model of the system. One of the disadvantages of CAPS/ECSL is the complexity of the activity-cycle diagrams for complex systems. One has to be trained in building the activity-cycle diagrams to use CAPS/ECSL effectively.

The second domain-independent SPG to be discussed is CASM (Burns et. al., 1978a, 1978b) which is based on the system-theoretic concepts and uses the systems dynamics terminology. CASM identifies six types of variables in a model, namely; states (X), rates (R), auxiliaries (V), outputs (Y), parameters and inputs (PU). There are some well defined rules governing the relationships among these variables which can be used to specify an interaction matrix of the type shown in Figure 2. Figure 2 shows the interaction matrix of a two-sector system. In CASM, a sector is a sub-structure (consisting of quantities and couplings) that can be associated with one and only one flow. Flows may represent material flow (F) such as population, goods, housing, etc. The other type of flow is information flow (I) about the state of a certain entity. Figure 2 delineates five types of matrices (matrices A through E) in an interaction matrix. The CASM dialogue goes through a series of eight steps in filling up this interaction matrix in a systematic fashion. The steps of CASM is as follows (Burns et. al., 1978a, 1978b):

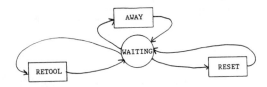

The operative's activity cycle

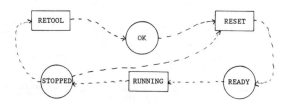

The machines' activity cycle

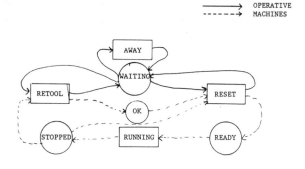

Figure 1. The job-shop activity cycle diagram (see Pidd, 1984)

1- Familiarization with the problem and approach.

2- Determination of the sectors that comprise the system.

3- Determination of the interaction among sectors.

4- Determination of state-rate interactions within sectors.

5- Determination of interacting state-rate pairs between sectors.

6- Determination of between-sector quantities.

7- Determination of within sector parameters, inputs, outputs, and auxiliaries.

8- Insertion of delays where appropriate.

A portion of the step 4 dialogue for a simple problem involving the interaction between population growth and available housing in a residential community is shown in Figure 3 (see Burns et. al., 1978b, for more detail). Figure 3 shows a portion of the interaction matrix of the housing sector (sector 1) as well as the corresponding causal diagram (Forrester-schematics, flow diagram). The remaining tasks in CASM are (1) the

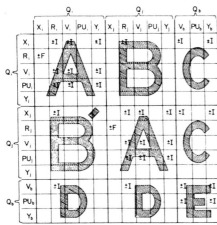

Figure 2. Interaction matrix for a two-sector system (Burns, et. al., 1978a)

composition of equations from the flow diagram and (2) execution of the simulation program. These tasks are completed with further information obtained from the user.

CASM is suitable for building continuous simulation models. The user of CASM has to be somewhat knowledgeable with the types of quantities (variables) used in system dynamics and the development of causal diagrams in system dynamics. CASM, just like CAPS/ECSL, is a domain-independent SPG and can model any type of a continuous system.

DOMAIN-DEPENDENT SPGS

In this section we will discuss a domain-dependent SPG that is icon-characterized. In Thomasma et. al., 1986, an icon-characterized, domain-dependent SPG was developed based on the object-oriented paradigm using SMALLTALK-80. The domain of the SPG was assembly line and transfer line type of manufacturing systems. Icons were used in model development as well as animation of model outputs. Figure 4 gives the icons and their states. There are five different permanent entity icons (workstation, storage facility, router, source, and sink) and an optional number of temporary entity (part) icons in the SPG. Each of the icons has a menu system

```
CONSIDER SECTOR 1: HOUSING          .
ENTER A NEW STATE NAME FOR SECTOR   1:HOUSING        .
housing
  ARE THERE ANY MORE STATES IN SECTOR  1:HOUSING      ?
  ENTER Y OR N.
n
  NAME A RATE (NOT PREVIOUSLY NAMED) WHICH AFFECTS STATE   1:HOUSING      .
home cons rte
  DOES   2:HOME CONS RT AFFECT    1:HOUSING        IN A POSITIVE
OR A NEGATIVE MANNER?  ENTER + OR -.
+
  LIST OF RATES PREVIOUSLY NAMED.
    2: HOME CONS RT
  DOES ANY OTHER RATE (NOT PREVIOUSLY NAMED) AFFECT STATE   1:HOUSING      ?
ENTER Y OR N.
y
  NAME A RATE (NOT PREVIOUSLY NAMED) WHICH AFFECTS STATE   1:HOUSING      .
home demo rt
  DOES  3:HOME DEMO RT AFFECT    1:HOUSING        IN A POSITIVE
OR A NEGATIVE MANNER?  ENTER + OR -.
-
  LIST OF RATES PREVIOUSLY NAMED.
    2: HOME CONS RT
    3: HOME DEMO RT
  DOES ANY OTHER RATE (NOT PREVIOUSLY NAMED) AFFECT STATE   1:HOUSING      ?
ENTER Y OR N.
n
```

Figure 3. A portion of Step 4 conversations of CASM and the corresponding segment of the interaction matrix and the respective Forrester-schematic diagram (Burns, et.al., Dec., 1978)

idle   busy   down

Graphical States of a WorkStation

empty 25% full 50% full 75% full 90% full 95% full 100% full

Graphical States of a StorageFacility

good part   bad part

Graphical States of a Part

Figure 4. Graphical states of an icon (Thomasma, et. al., 1986)

with a number of submenus. Figure 5 shows the main icon menus. Once the user defines the system with the icons using icon menus, animation of output is automatically obtained. Figure 6 shows a simple manufacturing system with two machines with limited capacity storages between them. The system can also detect wrong types of parts (rejects) and remove them from the system. The development of such a system takes a few minutes and the SPG is designed in such a way that the user can make copies of existing icons and update only those parameter values that need updating. Icon-characterized SPGs are very user-friendly since the user can identify an icon object for each real object in his/her system. Animation also gets the user much more involved with the model and helps to identify better operational policies for the system. The disadvantage of the icon-characterized SPGs is that they may require more expensive work stations to run on.

CONCLUSIONS AND RESEARCH AREAS:

One of the most frequent causes of simulation analysis failure is an inadequate level of user participation in the simulation project (Annino and Russell, 1979). SPGs help to alleviate this problem by involving the user directly in the model building process. We classified SPGs into two main categories; domain-independent and domain-dependent SPGs. We have seen that although the domain-independent SPGs may model any type of a system, they need to represent the system in some intermediate form first (activity-cycle diagram, flow diagram, or in metalanguage form). We have further classified the domain-dependent SPGs into parameter-characterized, event-characterized, and icon-characterized SPGs. As one goes from the parameter-

characterized SPGs to event- and icon-characterized SPGs, the complexity that one can represent in the model increases too. On the other hand, event-characterized models take more time to develop than the parameter-characterized models. Icon-characterized SPGs may take more time if they use event-scheduling world-view of a simulation language (e.g., WITNESS). Icon-characterized approaches that use object-oriented paradigm may take much less time to develop (e.g., Thomasma, et. al., 1986). In the paper, we have also given some simple examples of domain-dependent and domain-independent SPGs.

If one looks at the current research in the development of SPGs, one can identify different activities that can improve shape of future SPGs. One of these areas is the system-theoretic approaches suggested by different researchers (Oren, 1979, Zeigler, 1984). They promise a well-founded conceptual framework for simulation modeling. Applications of system-theoretic concepts will support, among other things, the specification of hierarchical model structures, checking of the consistency and completeness of model descriptions, and automated model documentation (Oren & Zeigler, 1979).

Other research areas that may significantly contribute to the development of SPGs is the artificial intelligence expertise in the simulation modeling approach including automatic selection of various abstraction levels of the model, the application of knowledge engineering (expert systems), automatic sensitivity analysis and experimental design features (Shannon et. al., 1985).

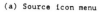
(a) Source icon menu

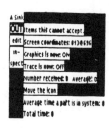
(b) Sink icon menu

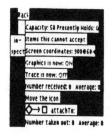
(c) StorageFacility icon menu

(d) Router icon menu

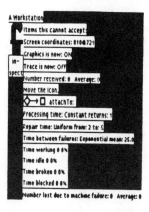
(e) Workstation icon menu

Figure 5. Icon menus (Thomasma, et. al., 1986)

94

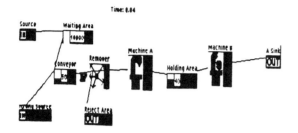

Time: 0.04

Source　Waiting Area

Conveyor　Remover　Machine A

Holding Area　Machine B　A Sink

Reject Area

Figure 6. The layout of a simple manufacturing
system (Thomasma, et. al., 1986)

REFERENCES:

Annino, J.S. and Russell, E.C., 1979, "The Ten Most
Frequent Causes of Simulation Analysis Failure - and How
to Avoid Them," Simulation, 32:6, June.

Beavens, J.P., 1982, "First, Choose an FMS Simulator,"
American Machinist, May, pp. 143-145.

Burns, J.R., et. al., 1978a, "A Sector Approach to the
Formulation of System Dynamic Models," Inter. Journal of
Systems Science, 4:6, July, pp. 649-680.

Burns, J.R., et. al., 1978b, "An Integrated Approach to
the Development of Continuous Simulations,"
Socio-Economic Planning Sciences, 12, December, pp.
313-327.

Davies, N.R., 1979, "Interactive Simulation Program
Generation," Methodology in Systems Modeling and
Simulation, Ziegler, B.P., et.al., (eds.), North-Holland
Publishing Co., pp. 179-200.

Dunhan, N.R., and Kochhar, A.K., 1983, "Approaches to
the Computer Simulation of Production Systems," Proc. of
the SCS Conf. on Simulation in Inventory and Production
Control, San Diego, January, pp. 19-24.

Farnsworth, K.D., Norman, Van B., and Norman, T.A.,
1987, "Integrated Software for Manufacturing
Simulation," Proc. of the 1987 Winter Simulation Conf.,
pp. 195-201.

Heidorn, G.E., 1976, "Automatic Programming Through
Natural Language Dialogue: A Survey," IBM Journal of
Research and Development, July, pp. 302-313.

Henriksen, J.O., 1983, "The Integrated Simulation
Environment (Simulation Software of the 1990s),"
Operations Journal, 31:6, pp. 1053-1073.

Hutchinson, G.K., 1981, "The Automation of Simulation,"
Proc. of the 1981 Simulation Conf., pp. 489-495.

Lenz, J.E., 1983, "MAST: A Simulation Tool for Designing
Computerized Metalworking Factories," Simulation, 40,
February, pp. 51-58.

Levy, M.R., 1983, "Automation Simulation: Utilizing
computer graphics in Industry," Simulation, 41:5,
November, pp. 194-195.

Manufacturing Systems Group, Ford Research Labs, 1988,
GPC Manual, April.

Mathewson, S.C., 1974, "Simulation Program Generators,"
Simulation, 23:6, pp. 181-189.

Mathewson, S.C., 1984, "The Application of Program
Generator Software and It's Extentions to Discrete Event
Simulation Modeling," IIE Transactions, 16:1, pp. 3-8.

Mathewson, S.C., and Allen, J.A., 1977, "DRAFT/GASP-A
Program Generator for GASP," Proc. of the Tenth Annual
Simulation Symposium, pp. 211-228.

Miner, R.J. and Rolston, L.J., 1984, "MAP/1 Tutorial,"
Proc. of the 1984 Winter Simulation Confer., November,
pp. 59-62.

Oldfather, P.M., et. al., 1966, Programming by
Questionnaire: How to Construct a Program Generator,
RAND Report RM-5129-PR, November.

Oldfather, P.M., et. al., 1967, Programming by
Questionnaire: The Job Shop Simulation Program
Generator, Rand Momerandum RM-5162-PR, July.

Oren, T.I., 1979, "Concepts for Advanced Computer
Assisted Modelling," Methodology in Systems Modeling and
Simulation, Ziegler, B.P., (eds.), North-Holland
Publishing Company, pp. 29-55.

Oren, T.I. and Ziegler, B.P., "Concepts for Advanced
Simulation Methodologies," Simulation, 32:3, March, pp.
69-82.

Pidd, M, 1984, Computer Simulation in Management
Science, John Wiley & Sons.

Shannon, R.E., Long, S.S., and Buckles, B.P., 1980,
"Operations Research Methodologies in Industrial
Engineering: A Survey," AIIE Transactions, 12:4,
December, pp.364-367.

Shannon, R.E., et. al., 1985, "Expert Systems and
Simulation," Simulation, 44:6, June, pp. 275-284.

Subrahmaniam, E. and Cannon, R.L., 1981, "A Generator
Program for Models of Discrete-Event Systems,"
Simulation, 36:3, March, pp. 93-101.

Suri, R., 1988, "RMT Puts Manufacturing at the Helm,"
Manufacturing Engineering, February, pp. 41-44.

Thomasma, T., et. al., 1986, "Simulation Modeling in an
Object-Oriented Environment Using Smalltalk-80," Proc.
of 1986 Winter Simulation Confer., December, pp.
474-484.

Ulgen, O.M. and Williams, E., 1988, "Simulation of
Production Systems," Handbook of Technology Management,
John Wiley, Inc. (in print).

Ulgen, H. and Ulgen, O.M., 1988, "An Empirical Study on
the Impact of Computers on Businesses in a Developing
Country," Inter. Business Schools Computer Users Group
(IBSCUG) Annual North American Confer., Oxford, Ohio,
July.

Ulgen, O.M., 1983, "GENTLE: GENeralized Transfer Line
Emulation," Proc. of the SCS Confer. on Simulation in
Inventory and Production Control, San Diego, January,
pp. 25-30.

Warren, H.J., et. al., 1985, "AUTOSIM: An Automatic
Simulation Program Generator," Mathematics and Computers
in Simulation, 27, pp. 107-114.

Ziegler, B.P., 1984, "System-Theoretic Representation of
Simulation Models," IIE Transactions, 16:1, March, pp.
19-34.

Simulation and AI, 1989
©1989 by the Society for Computer
Simulation International
ISBN 0-911801-44-8

Applying case technology to the development of expert systems in business

James A. Sena, D.B.A.
Department of Management
California Polytechnic State University
San Lius Obispo,California

L. Murphy Smith, D.B.A., C.P.A.
Accounting Department
Texas A&M University
College Station, Texas

ABSTRACT

Computer Aided Software Engineering (CASE) comprises a set of tools to support the front-end systems analysis and design phases for the construction of computer-based systems. Types of support provided by CASE tools includes specification production, analysis, and coordinated aids. Of special interest in the development of business expert systems are the functional and data modeling capabilities inherent in CASE.

Expert systems are computer programs that manipulate knowledge to solve problems in a narrow domain. In business an expert system would rely on a knowledge base consisting of corporate data and rules and facts applicable to a particular problem area of the organization. An inference engine facilitates the application of these rules, facts and data revolving about the corporate data base in order to assist the user in problem solution.

In previous research we developed an expert system for financial statement analysis using a data base consisting of the financial statements of the sixteen top oil and gas companies. The system, in its basic form, has been implemented using the Guru expert system package. As we made enhancements to the financial statement analysis expert components we experienced difficulty maintaining, augmenting, and documenting the system. Through the use of a CASE software package, Excelerator, we are better able to define the knowledge base, formulations and rules. In this way we can see the pattern of relationships to augment and understand the dynamics of financial analysis.

INTRODUCTION

Emergence of Expert Systems in Business

Expert systems are just beginning to be developed and used for business applications. Expert systems are computer programs that emulate the behavior of human expert in some specific area of knowledge (Leibowitz, 1987). They are useful in situations where expertise is expensive, scarce, or unavailable, and they serve as useful means of capturing the professional, experiental learning and knowledge of experts.

There are several areas in which expert systems have been applied in business. One fruitful area has been financial management. Expert systems have also been developed to help portfolio managers determine client investment goals and select portfolios that best meet these goals. Another area where expert systems have been used for business applications is in training managers and salespersons. Planning and Control are other areas where business expert systems are being developed and used.

Expert Systems Defined

Expert systems can be defined (Sena and Smith, 1987) as sophisticated computer programs that manipulate knowledge to solve problems efficiently and effectively in a narrow problem domain. They are composed of two basic components:

o An explicit and accessible body of knoqledge that is known as the knowedge base and includes the rules and facts applicable to a particular domain or range of acceptable values.

o An inference engine -- allows the applicaton of the rules and facts in the knowledge base to a problem. These two components combine to provide expertise, symbolic reasoning, and self-knowledge.

A database can be defined (Weiderhold, 1984) as a collection of data representing facts. The amount of data is typically large, and these facts change over time. A knowledge base, as opposed to a database, contains information at a higher level of abstraction. The knowledge in a knowledge based system is used mainly for data analysis and planning.

An expert database represents a combination of the knowledge base (expert system rules) and the database itself (that which the expert system will examine in performing an analysis). By placing the knowledge and the data together, the expert system becomes dynamic -- as the database changes, the expert system reasoning can change.

CASE Defined

Many software system developments have experienced problems with meeting development schedules, coorinating design efforts and maintaining their systems. Computer Aided Software Engineering (CASE) is a series of softwaretools and techniques designed to assist (Aranow, 1988) users in several aspects of system development as:

o a programmer/project productivity tool -- support back-end of system development life cycle ... includes tools for natural language programming, rapid prototyping, and document -ation;

o system development support tools -- support or supplement traditional tools at all stages of system life cycle ... includes diagramming tools data dictionary and analysis tools;

o system development methodology tools -- used to minimize redundant effort and maximize coordination between tasks ... includes the enforcement of methodological rules, providing 'expertise' to the user.

The first aspect, that of a productivity tool applies to the development of an expert system through the definition of standards. A consistent, systematic approach can insure a more thorough expert system definition. The traditional centralized information system has the greatest level of system development support.

For other types of managerial and processing systems (e.g. distributed systems, decision support and expert systems, etc.) the CASE approach needs to be tailored to work within these special environments.

For expert systems the system development methodology tools are not as important because of the availability of sexpert system shells and expert system development environments. CASE methodologies systematically assist the expert system developers in the pre-formulations of variables, rules and relationships.

Of special importance in the use of CASE is the concept of 'reverse engineering' (Bachman, 1988) where business rules can be extracted from existing information system applications and data bases. CASE can aid expert system developers through a reflective, cooperative mode of development. There is a duality in such an approach: data analysis focuses on data-oriented problems and systems analysis on process-oriented parts.

Design objects deal with requirements, specifications, implementation and operation. These objects relate to each other as progressions from conceptual to physical rules for the expert system.At the requirements level the expert system developer would identify and define the business requirements of the design objects. At the specification level, CASE supports the definition of the information required to use the expert system (e.g. knowledge and data bases), the flow of information, and the rules by which business decisions are made. Design objects include entities, relationships, messages, processes and procedures.

The implementation level identifies the explicit areas for source-level description of files, databases, rule hierarchies and networks including data sets, reports, screens, procedures and statments. Independent of an actual expert system shell or ES development package the expert system developer can 'paint' a picture of what they would like to see.

BACKGROUND

Financial statement analysis deals primarily with data reported in financial (external) reports as well as supplementary information from other sources. The primary objective is to identify major changes or turning points in trends, amounts, relationships, and investigations of the reasons underlying those changes.

Analysis involves an organized approach to glean selected data from the financial statements that are relevant to the decisions of statement users. Analysis of that data and interpretation of the results are important steps in the evaluation and interpretation of financial statements. The analytical steps are depicted in exhibit 1. These steps represent the focus of the expert system developments, both in the initial expert system and the expert data base implementations, as well as consideration of the CASE application.

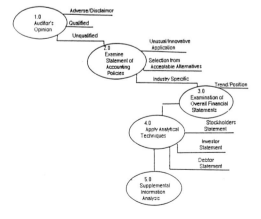

97

The intention of the expert system useage was to compare a company against an industry standard (averages and standard deviation of ratios). We focused on the analytical techniques which consisted of comparative statements, percentage analysis of financial statements, and ratio analysis.

The ability to dynamically change the data base and have that change reflected in the expert system does not exist in an expert system developed using an expert system shell. This process is feasible if the system is developed in an integrated system approach, such as that provided by Guru (Holsapple and Whinston, 1987). There, the data base can be dynamically referenced by the expert system rules.

The most important financial statement analysis tool is the comparison of the firm's ratios to industry averages. Ratio analysis involves measurement of the relationship between two amounts from one statement, such as the income statement, or from two statements, such as the income statement and balance sheet. The analysis used for the expert system and the expert data base implementations includes ratios that measure current position, equity position, and operating results. The specific ratios under each of these major positions are shown in Exhibit 2.

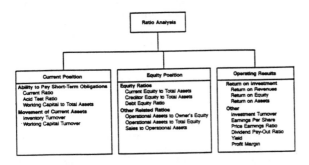

CONSTRUCTION OF THE INITIAL EXPERT SYSTEM

Creating the Initial Database

Financial statement information needed for ratio analysis was obtained from two sources. First, Standard and Poor's Industry Surveys provided a number of ratios already computed for individual firms. Second, the oil and gas firms' financial statements were used to obtain information for computing other ratios.

Sixteen major oil and gas companies were selected for inclusion in the database. The ratios were computed for a five year period 1980 - 1984. The computational results consisted of counts, averages, and standard deviations for the five-year period. Exhibit 2, presented earlier, depicts the various ratio groupings.

The initial database was constructed on on an IBM/PC using the Reflex analytical database software package. Individual fields can be added or deleted from the record definition and the data records in the file at the any time. Computational fields can be created using other fields and operators within the same record. In this initial implementation many of the ratios had to be computed from the data fields entered.

Constructing the Rules for the Expert System Shell

The ES 's rules were constructed according to the major groupings shown in Exhibit 2. If the ratio is one standard deviation below the industry average, the interpretation would be unfavorable for that category. For example, if a company's Current Ratio is more than one standard deviation below the industry average the company's Ability to Meet Current Obligations from current assets is questionable.

The system would function by combining the groups and subgroups (e.g. Ability to Pay Short Term Obligations and Movement of Current Assets into Current Position) as a weighted favorable, staisfactory, or unfavorable -- favorable being above one standard deviation, satisfactory being within one standard deviation, and unfavorable below one standard deviation from the industry average. In turn, the three measures would be consolidated to provide an overall indication of the company's financial position.

Thus, the financial statement analysis , to be employed by the expert system, would begin with the question "Is the financial status unsatisfactory?" (In a later implementation we added the 'satisfactory' and 'exceptional' cases.) With an expert system (ES), the user can determine whether the financial status of the company under review is unsatisfactory, The major query ("Is the financial status unsatisfactory?") is located at the top of the hierarchy. The evidence for that query becomes the the next level of inquiry, and the process continues until direct answers can be obtained to determine the answer to the major query.

The Expert System Shell

Initially the rules were entered onto Expert Edge, an ES shell used for developing interactive knowledge-based systems. The package accepts the expert's knowledge expressed as rules (see Exhibit 3), and creates an interactive dialogue that leads users through the same decision-making process that an expert would use. The rules included calculations, equations, logical reasoning, judgement, facts, and uncertainties.

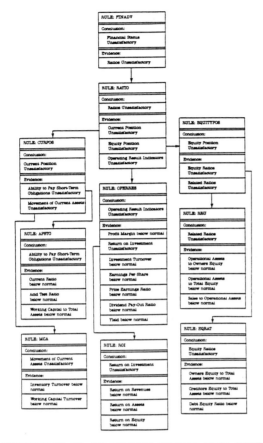

CONVERSION TO AN EXPERT SYSTEM DATA BASE

Conversion Basics

We abandoned the ES shell approach in order to create a dynamic and more flexible ES the data contained in the analytical Reflex database and the rules contained in the Expert Edge were entered into an expert database software package called Guru.

GURU Features and Capabilities

Guru was developed by Micro Data Base Systems (MDBS), Inc., From the application builder's point of view, the different parts of Guru are tightly integrated (seamless) (PC Magazine, 1987). Parts of databases can be moved into the spreadsheet easily, text files can extract information from spreadsheet or databases, and a spreadsheet cell can be defined by any collection of Guru commands, such as a database extraction or statistical function.

A rule premise can reference spreadsheet cells, fields in relational data tables, and data values downloaded from a host computer. The conclusion of rules can initiate consultation with other expert or knowledge systems, update table files, create or modify spreadsheets, call a preprogrammed procedure, write a report, or present a graph to a user.

There are four different interface: a command interface ; a natural-language interface; a menu interface; and user defined input and output screens. The unique aspect of Guru is the ability to build and use expert systems that are linked to the other parts of the software package. Unlike Expert Edge, which requires specification of rules in non-computational form (e.g. Current Ratio Below Normal .. requires a HELP access for the user to determine that "Below Normal" could be interpreted as being less than 1.22) Guru permits the use of a wide range of premises and conclusions.

In Guru a rule's premise , the IF clause, can be a logical expression that uses all of the standard Boolean operators. The clause can include database fields (CR, ROI, etc.) or spreadsheet cells. If preparatory actions are required after Guru has selected the rule for testing but before it has evaluated the premise, these can be specified in an optional READY clause.

If a rule's conclusion, its THEN clause, includes an assignment to a variable, then the rule itself can have a certainty factor (for instance, "If the current ratio (CR) is less than 1.22 and the Acid Test Ratio (ATR) is less than 0.49 and the Working Capital Turnover is less than 0.01 then it is 80 percent certain that the Ability to Pay Short Term Obligations is "Unsatisfactory").

Actual Conversion and Implementation

The menu approach primarily was used to create the database and to enter the rules. The conversion consisted of creating an output file from the Reflex database. The fields selected were those that came from the original data. The computed fields were not brought forward; instead they were computed in Guru using the virtual field feature.

The first step was to define the database, FINDAT, that was to contain the financial statement information to be referenced by the expert system. After verification, we transferred the data records from the Reflex output file. The records in the FINDAT table were then examined to insure that the file had been converted successfully.

The menu option would not allow the creation of virtual fields in the FINDAT table. (A virtual field allows the inclusion of computed data from other fields in a data record.) To modify the FINDAT table such that the virtual fields were included the Command Option was accessed.

After all of the fields were entered, the system automatically calculated all of the values for each record. If an error in definition was encountered the system would indicate that the computation could not be made. The results were compared to a printout of the computations from the initial ES effort using Reflex.

All of the statistics for the ratios used in the various rules were computed and stored in an array. All values for all years and all companies were used in the computations. If a particular ratio value did not have a result because of missing data a null value was assigned. The statistical computation automatically ignored the null values.

Creation of the Expert System

A rule set in Guru consists of five main parts. The parts include: an initialization section -- a procedure for opening any needed tables, resetting the value of variables, asking the user for information to start the consulting, etc.; definition of goals, windows, etc. -- makes it possible to specify a particular goal for the inference engine; a rule section -- contains the rules that the expert system is to process in finding the goal; a variable section -- defines how the value of variables will be found; and a completion section -- describes the action that the system is to take when a value for its goal has been found.

The main ingredients of the Rule are the IF - THEN parts. In Guru these can use formulas and numeric values as opposed to only logical expressions in Expert Edge. Other features provide for an explanation of the rule. The variables that the rules reference also needed to be entered. One of the most important aspects of a variable's definition in Guru is the "Find" window. This window controls just how the value is to be determined. It may contain the name of a program to run, a relational data base call, a query to the user, or some other method required to resolve the variable's value.

After the rule set was developed, the rule set compiler was invoked. The compiler checked for errors in the rule syntax, logical inconsistencies, and missing components. There were a number of situations where a variable was referenced in the premise of a certain rule but was not either defined, did not have a "Find" window, or its value could not be determined by another rule.

Following several compiler iterations the financial statement analysis was then ready to invoke the inference engine. The primary rule, FINADV, being the primary focus of the analysis was consulted using the Consult option on the rules menu. The user is prompted for a particular company and year (e.g. British Petroleum in 1980). The data base is accessed and using a procedure, called the Financial Advisor, the financial data and calculated ratios for the specific record are displayed. Following this display the expert system then fires the appropriate rules and displays whether the financial status of the particular company in that year is satisfactory or unsatisfactory. The user can request a line of reasoning to determine the nature of the "unsatisfactory" diagnosis.

USING CASE TO DEFINE THE EXPERT SYSTEM

Why CASE in Expert System Definition

On running the consultation we found that Guru did not provide an explanation if a company query was 'not' unsatisfactory (or in our later implementation was 'not 'exceptional). The system would reply "don't know" in such a situation. Granted we could ask additional subquestions, such as, "Is the Current Position Unsatisfactory?", but such an approach by a typical user, could be diffucult and assumes a working knowledge of the rule structure.

In the process of defining rules, variables, and relationships in the expert system effort the lack of documentation and unsystematic approach was evident as we developed the expert system. In the construction and maintenance of computerized information systems there has been a progression in the development of systems analysis and design aids. It seems natural that this technology should be transferred to the construction and maintenance of business expert systems.

Under Guru rules are compiled to insure that all rules are logically related. No consideration is given to the actual variable/field contents of each rule and the information that is passed from rule-to-rule. Using a CASE structure the rule system can be defined; the processes within each rule can be stated; and data flows between rules specified. Given these definitions and specifications a data dictionary and other related documentation (data flow diagrams, context diagrams, etc.) can be generated. If a rule is added -or- changed the dictionary, processes, and relationships can automatically be updated.

Selecting a CASE Tool for the Financial Advisor ES

The CASE software tool selected was Excelerator, a product developed by Index Technology,Inc. Excelerator is a thorough analysis and design toolkit for developers of information systems (Topper, 1988). This package uses a variety of software design methodologies in an integrated, data-dictionary-driven environment. It has extensive reporting capabilities and project-control functions to support the development effort and to track progress.

Excelerator's role begins after the developer and user have identified the purpose and scope of the system. The product's major contributions are to aid developers in analyzing and modeling data and processes that make up the system, generating documentation and diagrams to aid users in making development and design decisions, maintaining an up-to-date documentation trail, and generating pseudocode or diagrams for translating into executable code.

Excelerator has the following seven major components: Graphics Tools -- data flow diagrams and structure charts; XLDictionary -- repository for records, diagrams, charts, and reports; Documentation Tools -- system components and relationships; Analysis Reports -- identify possible flaws or erros in system design; an Import/Export facility -- passes the XLDictionary between projects; and Utilities -- project security and control. These features allow the developer to create a complete and thorough system that is highly efficient and easy to maintain.

Applying Excelerator to the Financial Advisor ES

As a starting point in the structured analysis of the financial advisor ES a context diagram is created using Excelerator (Whitten and Bentley, 1987). It contains only one process representing all sub processes of the ES. In the context diagram the ES user is depicted as an external entity, the financial data base as a data store, and the expert rule system as a process.

The context diagram is used to 'level' or 'explode' the ES process into more detailed data flow diagrams (DFDs) that gradually reveal the system to the ES developer. The context diagram's single process is exploded into a system DFD.

The system DFD contains three processes which reflect the current position, equity, position and operating results. Each of these processes is, in turnn, exploded into second level DFDs. For example, the Current Position Process {1} is exploded into two sub processes -- Ability to Pay Short Term Obligations {1.1} and Movement of Current Assets {1.2}. This explosion process then continues to the leveled set of DFDs. For the Financial Advisor ES the lowest level

would be the computations of the various ratios -- e.g. processes for computing Current Ratio, Acid Test Ratio, and Working Capital to Total Assets Ratio as explosions of the Ability to Pay Process.

The lowest level processes are then selected and process descriptions, detailing the computations for the various ratios, are entered. (e.g. Acid Test Ratio = Current Assets / Current Liabilities.)

As the DFDs were defined each connecting data flow was identified. Following the ratio computations is the process description in the Process Descritions. The next step was to identify the data flow packets (e.g. Acid Test Ratio Value) that flows upwards. This process would continue to the highest level DFD. Adhering to these steps insures that orderly development process could take place for the expert system development described earlier.

REFERENCES

1. Liebowitz, Jay, "Expert Systems for Business Applications", Applied Artificial Intelligence, 1:307-313, 1987.

2. Sena, James A. and Smith, L. M. , "The Development of Expert Systems for Accounting", Accounting and EDP, Vo. 3, No. 2, Summer, 1987, 9 - 14.

3. Weiderhold, Gio, "Knowledge and Database Management", IEEE Software, January, 1984, 63 - 73.

4. Holsapple, Cylde. W. and Whinston, Andrew B., Business Expert Systems, Irwin, Homewood, Ill., 1987.

5. Standard and Poors Industry Surveys - Oil, November 21, 1985.

6. Reflex: The Analyst, Boreland International, Scotts Valley, Ca.

7. Expert Edge, Human Edge Software, Palo Alto, Ca.

8. Guru, Micro Data Base Systems, Inc., Lafayette, Ind.

9. "Guru: Brave New Expert Systems'," PC Magazine, May 27, 1987, 151 -163.

10. Aranow, Eric, "When is CASE the Right Choice?", Business Software Revie , April, 1988, 12 -27.

11. Bachman, Charlie, "A CASE for Reverse Engineering", Datamation, July 1, 1988, 49 - 57.

12. Whitten, J.L. and Bentley, L.D., "Using Excelerator for Systems Analysis and Design", Times-Mirror Mobley, St. Louis, 1987.

13. Topper, Andrew, "Excelling with CASE", PC Tech Journal, August, 1988, 71 - 88.

An application of Lp-norm to knowledge engineering

Chi-yin Pang
Unisys Corporation
25725 Jeronimo Road
Mission Viejo, California 92691

ABSTRACT

Complicated projects, for example performance analysis with simulation, usually require diverse areas of expertise. Expert systems are potentially helpful in all steps of these projects. However, it is not always economically feasible to develop an expert system for every step. This paper develops a system to rank the success potential of the candidate expert systems objectively.

The paper examines an evaluation "check list" used by some knowledge engineers. It points out some basic differences between the sub-check-lists. It also formally specifies the requirements of the functions for evaluating the candidate expert systems under different sub-check-lists. The mathematical function L^p-norm is proved useful for building a family of functions that fits the requirements. The function family is further generalized to accept weighting factors. This gives flexibility for expanding and modifying the "check-list". Finally, an evaluation system is built by putting the check-list in a hierarchical structure and applying the functions on different levels of the hierarchy.

The above technique is implemented on a spread-sheet. It is used to evaluate potential expert systems for performance analysis projects in a particular environment. Some results are not intuitively obvious but useful. The paper ends with pointing out future research directions.

INTRODUCTION

In recent years, there has been an explosion of expert systems. Success stories of expert systems saving money are common. The temptation is to jump on the band-wagon and start to knowledge-engineer everything in sight. Wait, are you sure that you are not spending half a million dollars in order to save two labor-months per year? Are you sure that the finished expert system will save time instead of add frustrations?

Experts in knowledge engineering realize this problem and have intuitions to pick the right expert systems to build. This is no help to the non-knowledge-engineer domain experts who want to build expert systems to stream-line their operations. They lack the intuition to pick the right systems to build. Can they apply their domain expertise systematically to pick the right systems objectively?

This paper answers the last question with a "yes." It integrates opinions of knowledge engineers and an extension of a mathematical function, the well known L^p-norm in real analysis. It builds an algorithm to evaluate candidate expert systems. The algorithm is implemented in a spread-sheet that enables easy evaluation and comparison of candidate expert systems.

The following describes:

A concrete example that shows the need for a candidate expert systems evaluator,
The evaluation guidelines used by knowledge engineering experts,
The development of the evaluation algorithm and system,
The application of the evaluation system, and
The direction of future development and research.

DIVERSE OPPORTUNITIES FOR APPLYING EXPERT SYSTEMS

Most commercial projects are full of opportunities for applying expert systems. For example, in a simulation project for analyzing the performance of system designs, expert systems could be applied to the following tasks:

* Determine the designer's problem area.
  (Performance, reliability, cost, validation, politics)
* Choose the communication tool between the designers and the modeler.
* Determine the designer's detailed questions.
* Determine the level of abstraction of the model.
* Determine the modeling technique.
  (Pencil&paper, queueing network, discrete event, etc.)
* Determine the modeling style.
  (Process view, transaction view, event driven)
* Partition the model's software functions.
* Debug the model.
* Design experiments. (The statistical aspect.)
* Select optimum system configurations.
* Select system workload.
* Determine the warm-up period.
* Determine the confidence in the statistics.
* Conduct the experiments.
* Extrapolate and draw conclusions.
* Organize the raw data.
* Graph data. (What to graph? What's the lay-out?)
* Analyze data-streams.
* Write reports.
* Measure real systems.

Researchers are building experimental expert systems to address some of the above problems. For example, (Hurrion and Amhad 1988; Lehmann, Szczerbicka and Roll 1988; Sargent and Rao 1988; Taylor and Hurrion 1988) worked on expert systems for generating models, choosing modeling techniques, verifying models, and designing experiments.

It is difficult to select the problem(s) that would benefit the most from expert systems in a particular environment. What criteria should one consider in this selection process? That is the topic of next section.

THE EXPERT'S EVALUATION GUIDELINES

(Barr 1987) gave four lists for judging whether a candidate expert system would be successful. The following reiterates the lists.

What's Known to be Engineerable
* Transfer of expertise: from expert to technician
* Policy and procedures
* Diagnosis, classification, structured selection
* Intelligent user interfaces to data and software
* Situation assessment and interpretation
* "Non-perceptual", real-time monitoring/control
* Constraint satisfaction and form checkers
* "Structured" planning and design

Pragmatic Considerations--Look For
* Identifiable and available expertise
* Routine problem solving
* Finite amount of knowledge
* Knowledge bottlenecks
* Shared terminology
* Rules of thumb or matter of policy
* Value of reliable and thorough performance
* Structured objects and hierarchies
* "Shallow" reasoning
* Test cases available
* Simpler subproblems (scoping)
* Management support
* New ways to do old jobs

What is Not So Easy
* Sensory/perceptual abilities
* Learning
* Reasoning from first principles
* Reasoning from cases
* Reasoning from analogy
* Common sense reasoning
* Ability to teach novices
* Multiple opinions
* Self-knowledge

Pragmatic Considerations--Avoid
* Perceptual skill and talent (fails telephone test)
* Volatile expertise
* Disagreing experts
* Time-sensitive problem situations
* Complicated geometrical or spatial reasoning
* Complex causal or temporal relations
* Liability issues

With the lists, the evaluation begins by having the domain experts fill in simple answers like those in Table 1.

Table 1.
Examples for Filling the Lists

Look For	Det.Warm-up ... Period	... Graph Data ...
Identifiable expertise	SortOfNo	SortOfYes
Routine problem solving	Yes	Yes
Finite amount of knowledge	Yes	Yes
Knowledge bottlenecks	No	No
Shared terminology	Don'tKnow	Don'tKnow
Rules of thumb or policy	No	Yes
Value of reliable performance	SortOfYes	SortOfNo
Structured objects	No	Don'tKnow
"Shallow" reasoning	No	Yes
Test cases available	No	Yes
Simpler subproblems	No	No
Management support	SortOfYes	SortOfYes
New ways to do old jobs	No	Yes

Once this 37x20 matrix is filled, we have a jungle of "Yes", "No", "SortOf" etc., much like Consumer Reports' car ratings. It is hard to pick the best column, the second best column etc. by merely scanning the 740 entries. We need an evaluation function that summarizes a column of 37 answers to an "average". We will build that function in the following sections.

THE SIMPLISTIC EVALUATION FUNCTION

Since we need an "average" function, why not use the arithmetic average? (All items are assigned with equal importance for now. They will be assigned with different importance later.) In order to use the arithmetic average, we convert:

Yes	to	1.0
SortOfYes	to	Somewhere between 1.0 and 0.5
Don'tKnow	to	0.5
SortOfNo	to	Somewhere between 0.5 and 0.0
No	to	0.0

Then the average of the column is viewed as the probability of success of the candidate expert system. (We need to treat each of the four evaluation lists separately, because the first two deal with the probability of success and the last two deal with the probability of failure. The four lists will be integrated in the "Evaluation System" Section. Until then, we will work with one list at a time.) This average function has a democratic property. It works well for summarizing the "Look For" list. Candidate expert systems that have more "Look For" items checked are more successful.

Unfortunately, this democratic function fails to summarize the "Engineerable" list. One check in this list should out-shine the rest. For example, a Power Amplifier Diagnostic Expert System is likely to be successful, although it has nothing to do with policy, intelligent interface, real-time monitor/control, or form checking. In this case, we need a function that reflects, "The one who yells the loudest has the say." The "maximum" function would do the trick.

Can the simple average and maximum functions solve all problems? One may object saying, "In real life, the function is a mixture of 'majority rule' and 'a yelling contest'." We will build that family of functions in the next section.

THE MODIFIED L^p-NORM EVALUATION FUNCTIONS

The sky is the limit in building mathematical functions. If we do not set up some ground rules, we will end up in a yelling contest. The following terms are used:

n The number of items in the list.
E.g. the $n=13$ for the "Look For" list.

A $= <a_0, a_1, \ldots, a_{n-1}>$ The evaluation vector of the list. E.g. the evaluation for Graph Data in the "Look For" list is $A = <0.3, 1, 1, 0, .5, \ldots, 1, 0, 0.7, 1>$.

[0,1] The unit interval from 0 to 1.
[0,1]^n The vector space of all the possible A's.

q A real number parameter for the family of functions.

E$_q$:[0,1]^n → [0,1] The family of evaluation functions to be built. It takes a vector A in [0,1]^n and maps it into [0,1]. We write "$E_q(A) = r$" if r is the evaluated result. ("E" is chosen for "Expected value" or average.)

average(A) The average function applied to A.
maximum(A) The maximum function applied to A.

The following lists the requirements of the function E_q.

Monotone E.g. $E_q(<1,.4,.7>) \leq E_q(<1,.5,.7>) \leq E_q(<1,.6,.7>)$.

Continuous No sudden jump can result from any small change in input.

Symmetric E.g. $E_q(<a,b,c>) = E_q(<c,b,a>) = E_q(<b,a,c>)$.

"n-inert" When the list expands, we don't want undesirable change in the result. E.g. $E_q(<a,a,b,b>)$ needs to be the same as $E_q(<a,b>)$.

$E_q(<a,a,...,a>) = a$ This is particularly important for $a=0$ and $a=1$.

"Encompassing" The E_q family includes the average function, the maximum function, and the "in between" functions.

Now we are ready to build the E_q family. Luckily, we don't need to build it from scratch. In measure theory and real analysis (which are the foundation of mathematical probability), there is a well-studied function called the L^p-norm (a norm in the L^p-space). In some special cases, the L^p-norm of the vector A has the form:

$$\|A\|_p = \{ \sum_{i=0}^{n-1} a_i{}^p \}^{1/p}$$

This function by itself satisfies a lot of our requirements. (The explanation and exploration of the properties of L^p-space and norm are beyond the scope of this paper. (Kingman and Taylor 1966; Loomis 1953; Rudin 1966) provide further exploration of the subject.) However, we must tailor the function to our needs. We modify the function in two steps:

$$F_p(A) = \{ (\sum_{i=0}^{n-1} a_i{}^p)/n \}^{1/p} \quad \text{for all } p>0$$

$$E_q(A) = F_{1/q}(A)$$
$$= \{ (\sum_{i=0}^{n-1} a_i{}^{1/q})/n \}^q \quad \text{for all } 0<q\leq 1$$

$$E_0(A) = F_\infty(A) = \lim_{p\to\infty} F_p(A)$$

F_p and E_q satisfies the requirements of monotone, continuous, symmetric, "n-inert", and $F_p(<a,...,a>) = E_q(<a,...,a>) = a$. Substituting $p=q=1$, we get $F_1(A) = E_1(A) = (a_0+...+a_{n-1})/n = \text{average}(A)$. The following proves that $F_\infty(A) = E_0(A) = \text{maximum}(A)$.

Suppose $a_k = \text{maximum}(a_1,a_2,...,a_{n-1})$ then

$$F_p(A) = \{ (\sum a_i{}^p)/n \}^{1/p}$$
$$\leq \{ (\sum a_k{}^p)/n \}^{1/p}$$
$$= a_k \quad \text{for all } p>0$$

Therefore

$$F_\infty(A) = \lim_{p\to\infty} F_p(A) \leq a_k = \text{maximum}(A).$$

The other inequality requires a little trick.

$$F_\infty(A) = \lim_{p\to\infty} F_p(A)$$
$$\geq \lim_{p\to\infty} F_p(<0,...,0,a_k,0,...,0>)$$
$$= \lim_{p\to\infty} \{ (0+ a_k{}^p +0)/n \}^{1/p}$$
$$= a_k \lim_{p\to\infty} (1/n)^{1/p}$$
$$= a_k = \text{maximum}(A)$$

Therefore $F_\infty(A) = E_0(A) = \text{maximum}(A)$.

We now have two families of functions, F_p and E_q, that are "Encompassing". (The definition and the proof of the "in betweenness" property is left to the reader.) The E_q family is more elegant, because q can be viewed as a weighting factor between the two extreme functions:

$$E_0(A) = \text{maximum}(A) \quad \text{and}$$
$$E_1(A) = \text{average}(A).$$

We built two families of functions that evaluate the success rate of a candidate expert system. The functions have the desirable property of including the "every one has equal say" method, the "the loudest yeller has the say" method, and all the "in between mix" methods. We start to generalize these basic functions next.

THE WEIGHTED L^p-NORM EVALUATION FUNCTIONS

So far, we have assumed that all items in an evaluation list have equal importance. This assumption has two difficulties. Firstly, different items may have different importance. For example, "Management support" may be more important than "Knowledge bottleneck." Secondly, uniform importance gives inconsistent results when the evaluation list is modified. For example, suppose we split the "Rule of thumb or matter of policy" item into two items: "Rule of thumb" and "Matter of policy". The resultant pair would have two times the importance. We need a way to "weight" the importance of each item. Then we need to enhance F_p and E_q to take these weights into account.

How should we enhance F_p and E_q? Let's try a simple example. Suppose $A=<a,b,c>$, and we want b to have 3 times the voting power, then A should be evaluated to:

$$F_p(A) = \{ (a^p+b^p+b^p+b^p+c^p) / 5 \}^{1/p}$$
$$= \{ (1a^p+3b^p+1c^p) / (1+3+1) \}^{1/p}$$

The enhancement is now clear. Just multiply the $a_i{}^p$'s by the weight and replace "n" by the sum of the weights. The enhancement is formalized below.

Let the vector $W=<w_0,w_1,...,w_{n-1}>$ be weights to the items of a list. Each w_i is a non-negative number. Previously, all w_i's are 1, meaning that each item has one unit of importance or influential power. Now, the more important items can be assigned with more weight (e.g. 2 or 3), and less important items can be assigned with less weight (e.g. 0.7 or 0.3). In fact, 0 weight can be assigned to items that we like to ignore. We enhance F_p and E_q as follows:

$$F_p(A) = \{ \sum_{i=0}^{n-1}(w_i\, a_i{}^p) / \sum_{i=0}^{n-1} w_i \}^{1/p} \quad \text{for all } p>0$$

$$E_q(A) = \{ \sum_{i=0}^{n-1}(w_i\, a_i{}^{1/q}) / \sum_{i=0}^{n-1} w_i \}^q \quad \text{for all } 0\leq q\leq 1$$

These new E_q and F_p are still monotone, continuous, $E_q(<a,...,a>)=a$, and encompassing. The n-inertness is also retained if the list is properly expanded. However, we loose the symmetry property which is exactly what weighting set out to destroy.

We have built E_q and F_p that can evaluate a candidate expert system against a given weighted list. In the following section, we will build an evaluation system that integrates the evaluation results from different lists.

THE EVALUATION SYSTEM

If we could get the desired result by putting all the evaluation items in a single list, then we would be finished. However, this cannot be done, because the four sub-lists of the evaluation items are fundamentally different. They differ from each other as follows:

	Contribute to Success	Contribute to Failure
Loudest Yeller Gets to Say	Engineerable List	Not So Easy List
Everyone Gets to Say	Look For List	Avoid List

How do we get one evaluation number out of these four lists? We know how to evaluate each individual list. So the problem becomes: "How do we get one number out of the four evaluated results?" One answer is: Apply the evaluation function again. The multi-level application of the E_q or F_p function does the trick. A general form of a total evaluation is:

$$E_q(<E_{q0}(EL),E_{q1}(LFL),1-E_{q2}(NSEL),1-E_{q3}(AL)>)$$

Where EL, LFL, NSEL, and AL are the vectors corresponding to the "Engineerable" list, "Look For" list, "Not So Easy" list, and "Avoid" list respectively. The simple trick of "$1-E_{q2}(NSEL)$" and "$1-E_{q3}(AL)$" turn probabilities of failure to probabilities of success. The q's can be tuned to get to right kind of function for evaluating a list. For example, if we want to use the average (or E_1) and maximum (or E_0) functions, the form of the evaluation would be:

$$E_1(<E_0(EL),E_1(LFL),1-E_0(NSEL),1-E_1(AL)>)$$

We have accomplished what we set out to do -- build a system to rank the candidate expert systems. In the next section, we discuss the experience of using such a system.

THE APPLICATION OF THE EVALUATION SYSTEM

Using the algorithm developed earlier, a spread sheet is built to rank the candidate expert systems for performance analysis, and some results are computed. These results are preliminary, because the weights (all 1's) are not tuned, and the evaluation system lacks some of the possible improvements mentioned later.

Table 2 highlights the results of two sets of q's. The "Select optimum system configurations" comes out ahead. Before I used this method, I thought that "Graph data" was a good candidate. However, the evaluation gives it a relatively low mark. Apparently, that is due to its requirement of visual perception. The system points out some intuition errors. Even without parameter tuning, accurate input data estimates, and enhancements, the system is a useful tool.

Table 2.
Results for Performance Analysis Problems

for $<q,q0,q1,q2,q3>=<1.0,.1,1.0,.1,1.0>$
for $<q,q0,q1,q2,q3>=<1.0,.2,.5,.2,.5>$

.36	.36	Determine the designer's problem area.
.47	.45	Choose the communication tool.
.60	.60	Determine the designer's detail questions.
.62	.60	Determine the level of abstraction of the model.
.69	.74	Determine the modeling technique.
.65	.61	Determine the modeling style.
.70	**.72**	Partition of the model's software functions.
.67	.63	Debug the model.
.63	.61	Design experiments.
.75	**.71**	Select optimum system configurations.
.65	.60	Select system workload.
.60	.56	Determine the warm-up period.
.72	**.67**	Determine the confidence in the statistics.
.61	.58	Conducting the experiments.
.59	.55	Extrapolate and draw conclusions.
.72	**.69**	Organize the raw data.
.61	.58	Graph data.
.70	**.72**	Analyze data-streams.
.56	.54	Write reports.
.60	.57	Measure real systems.
.63	.61	AVERAGE OF THE ABOVE

CONCLUSION

We have systematically built an evaluation system that applies the expert's check lists and a mathematical function with some appropriate properties. This evaluation system can replace the subjective, "seat of the pants", approach. In this sense, we have met our objective -- to be objective.

FUTURE RESEARCH DIRECTIONS

During the development, many potential improvements were discussed with my colleagues. Such as:

* Financial Analysis List: Since the basic question is "will it save money?", a list or new techniques should be added to deal with finance more directly.

* Consider Other Average Functions: Would harmonic mean be more appropriate than L^p-norm? How about the functions that compute the confidence factors in expert systems?

* Is E_q "The Unique" Correct Function: We have set some criteria (or axioms) for the evaluators. We found that F_p and E_q satisfy the criteria, but are they the only functions that satisfy the criteria?

* What is the Significance of the Parameter q: When q=.5 or p=2, F_2 resembles the distance function in Euclidean n-space. Is there some physical interpretation of the parameter q? What kind of average is E_q?

The above topics are not fully investigated yet. They are potential directions for research and development.

ACKNOWLEDGEMENTS

Discussions with Ted Zahn were the prime motivation for this research. He has given original ideas, moral support, and even final editorial polishings for this paper. Cecil Reames had also given helpful suggestions. I also gratefully acknowledge the support of my management for this work.

REFERENCES

Barr, A. 1987. *Managing Knowledge Systems Development*. A tutorial in 1987 IEEE WESTEX, 22-25.

Hurrion, R.D. and A. Amhad. 1988. "Automatic model generation using a Prolog model-base." In *SCS 1988.* 137-144.

Kingman, J.F.K. and S.T. Taylor. 1966. *Introduction of Measure and Probability*. Cambridge Univ. Press, London.

Lehmann, A; H. Szczerbicka; and G. Roll. 1988. "Application of expert systems in INT^3: An interactive, intelligent and integrated PC modelling environment." In *SCS 1988.* 49-54.

Loomis, L.H. 1953. *An Introduction to Abstract Harmonic Analysis*. Van Nostrand, Princeton, New Jersey.

Rudin, W. 1966. *Real and Complex Analysis*. McGraw-Hill, New York.

Sargent, R.G. and M.J. Rao. 1988. "An experimental advisory system for operational validity." In *SCS 1988.* 245-250.

SCS 1988. *Proceedings of the 1988 SCS (Society for Computer Simulation) Multiconference on Artificial Intelligence and Simulation (San Diego, CA, 3-5 Feb. 1988)*, T. Henson ed.

Taylor, R.P. and R.D. Hurrion. 1988. "An expert advisor for simulation experimental design and analysis." In *SCS 1988.* 238-244.

Simulation and AI, 1989
©1989 by the Society for Computer
Simulation International
ISBN 0-911801-44-8

Artificial intelligence research: a proper subset of
simulation methodology

G. Arthur Mihram, Ph. D.
P.O. Box № 1188   and
Princeton, N.J. 08542

Danielle Mihram, Ph. D.
Elmer H. Bobst Library
New York University
N.Y. City, N.Y. 10012

ABSTRACT

The set of artificial intelligence [AI] models is
shown to be a (proper) subset of the set of all simulation models. Furthermore, with the goal of AI research set at providing a scientifically credible model
of the mind at work making a decision, we invoke the
literature of operational research, of computing science, of statistical computing, and of industrial engineering to show that AI research can be achieved by
having its practitioners adhere rigidly to our established simulation methodology.

In particular, if our own simulation methodology
possesses all the attributes necessary for determining
the scientific credibility of any algorithmic simulation model, then the aforementioned subset relationship immediately implies that AI researchers, properly
behaved, can know how to establish the scientific credibility of their own research.

An exemplary AI model is a bibliographic retrieval programme, as used in more and more libraries and
research organisations. These are actually AI models
of the librarian (or researcher) seeking to locate references on a specified logical combination of topics.

We note also the pertinence of simulation methodology to the Strategic Defense Initiative [SDI] program by showing that the core of the SDI is to be an algorithmic computer programme which will in actuality
be a simulation model (an artificial intelligence programme) of the Office of the Presidency at work in arriving at a decision as to whether, when, and how forcefully to respond militarily to a perceived missile
attack on the United States of America.

INTRODUCTION

We hope to contribute directly to this Simulation
and Artificial Intelligence Conference by establishing,
and then noting the importance of, the subset relationship connecting artificial intelligence [AI] programmes and simulation models. We show that any AI programme is in actuality a simulation model, yet that
there exist algorithmic simulations which are not AI
models, thereby establishing the mathematical relationship of the proper subset.

We shall then review the histories of operational
research, of computing science, of statistical computation, and of industrial engineering in order to illustrate their scientific goals. The achievement of
these goals is ideally satisfied by the characteristics of our simulation methodology, but, in so discus-
sing the subject, we reveal cases which show how algorithmic simulations need not all be AI research
programmes.

We relate immediately our already well-establish-
ed simulation methodology not only to:

(A) the understanding of how the mind works, but also
to

(B) the Scientific Method itself;

indeed, both are related in a quite biological manner.
This linkage concretely connects artificial intelligence research to biology, since, after all, AI research
is that human activity devoted to providing models of
the (real) mind, of real intelligence, at work making
a decision.

We turn then to examples of now commonplace computer programmes which are in actuality AI models. In
particular, the bibliographic retrieval programmes,
frequently used by or under the supervision of a research or reference librarian, are actually AI models of
the librarian seeking to locate references for a researcher who has supplied a certain logical combination of
topical interests.

Indeed, the "automation" of libraries provides a
sequence of AI models: a software package used to maintain the card catalog is in reality an AI model of the
library's chief cataloguer at work, busily updating the
catalog and the library's shelf list; software packages
which maintain the circulation records of the library
in actuality simulation [AI] models of the circulation
librarian; and, book purchasing and journal subscription activities, now being computerised in major libraries, are becoming AI models of the acquisition librarian at work.

We conclude with a discussion of the pertinence of
simulation methodology to the Strategic Defense Initiative [SDI] program. This is particularly evident when
one realises that the SDI program's core will be a set
of computer simulation programmes which collectively
serve as an AI model of the Office of the Presidency of
the United States of America at work when faced with a
decision as to when, whether, and how forcefully to respond militarily to a perceived missile attack on the
country.

This connexion of the SDI program with the biological nature of the Scientific Method gives added meaning to the established (Mihram, 1975) survival function
of the Scientific Method itself.

THE SUBSET RELATIONSHIP

Presidential candidate (Mondale 1984) in the second
Presidential debate noted: "One final point: The most
dangerous aspect of this [the SDI] proposal is [that]
for the first time we would delegate to computers the
decision as to whether to start a war [Emphasis added]:"
In expressing his concern about leaving the decision
about entering a war (more correctly, to responding to
the threat of the same) to a computer, Mondale, without
realising it, was asking simulationists how they determine whether a computer programme's decision should be
believed: i.e., about simular credibility(Mihram '74).

It is the computer programme (software), rather than the computer itself (hardware), which will be making the SDI decision. We shall first review the result (Mihram and Mihram 1985) that computer programming, being algorithmic, is not mathematics. Then, we show that any AI programme is an algorithmic simulation model. We return, at the end of the paper, to the SDI example.

Computer Programming ≠ Mathematics

Artificial intelligence [AI] research is that human discipline seeking to construct scientifically credible models of the (adult, human) mind making a decision. But, any computer programme is an algorithm, which earlier (Wheatley & Unwin 1972) has been recognised to be nothing more than a recipe for making a decision. Thus, the algorithm (i.e., computer programming), by its very nature, shows great promise for AI research.

Indeed, programming is distinctly different from mathematics. The distinction is linguistic, is grammatical. For example, the sentence, 'X = X + DX', means different things to differing ears: for the mathematician, the statement could anywhere in his arguments be replaced by its absolute equivalent, "∀X, DX = 0"; yet, for a computer programmer, the statement provides a sequence of second-person commands, telling the robot (the computer) to assign to the location (which it has assigned the name, X) the value of the sum that it is now instructed to find in the locations, X and DX.

One could have a Ph. D. in pure mathematics and not be expected to know the meaning of the statement, "If (X.EQ.Y) GO TO ab"; whereas, this statement is perfectly well understood by the computer programmer as a (conditional) command directing the computer as to which command to follow next.

Any AI Programme is A Simulation Model

Furthermore, since any computer programme, declared by its author to be an "AI programme" or an "expert system", is merely a set of one or more algorithms carrying out a decision process, it follows that any AI programme is a simulation model. It matters not that a number of software packages are now available to assist one in constructing an AI model (or an expert system); all that these packages accomplish is to facilitate the writing of the decision algorithm(s) for their user: they allow one to define decision rules and/or chains, thereby creating a resultant algorithm, that which the AI model or expert system purports to represent as a mimicry, a simulation, of a decider/expert:

$$\{\text{AI programmes}\} \subseteq \{\text{simulation models}\} .$$

THE CONTRIBUTING DISCIPLINES

The advent of the computer has indeed led to the contemporary effort to mime the mind (Sayre and Crosson 1963). During the past thirty or forty years, a number of academic and research disciplines have embraced the computer, yet are only more recently becoming aware that they are to become simulationists: simulation practitioners.

For example, operational research [OR] was initially conceived—in a wartime scenario—as the science of men and machines in interaction. Being a science, it has dealt with the search for the very explanation for the behaviour of systems of interacting men and machines. However, if an operational researcher is to capture scientifically the dynamics of such systems,

he is discovering that algorithmic programming, rather than mathematics, is better suited to the task because the representation of the dynamics of such systems inevitably require the description of the human deciders in the system being modelled. But, deciders are ideally described by algorithms, rather than via mathematical relationships.

Indeed, the Operations Research Society of America (McCallum and Bodin 1987) now describes itself as "the application of scientific principles to assist the decision-maker in making a rational and intelligent decision." The pertinence of the algorithm, as opposed to mathematical expressions, is becoming more evident to operational researchers.

Similarly, even computer scientists seem to be more aware of the exceptional value of the algorithm, despite the predisposition of some (Ralston 1984) to mathematics. Such a predisposition probably accounts for the disparaging, though quite unfounded, remarks (Ralston 1986) which have been made regarding the capability of computer scientists to contribute to the accomplishment of the SDI's mission. Computer scientists are, however, becoming quite aware (Mihram 1977) of the distinctive advantage which computer programming is providing science generally: No longer can mathematics be viewed as the language of science, though any reflective reader of Darwin's ORIGIN OF THE SPECIES would have earlier dismissed any such notion anyway.

Statistical computation has rather naturally arisen as an academic discipline concomitant with the increasing dispersal of electronic digital computers. But, as has been pointed out (Mihram 1986), at the end of such statistical computations, one can programme an additional algorithm which advises of the statistician's decision (recommendation): that which he would himself make if he had examined the computed statistics. In effect, any such programme is an AI model, a simulation, of the working statistician and his analysis.

Furthermore, industrial (and systems) engineers have found that the description of the sequential and conditional operations in a manufacturing process is ideally accomplished by means of computer programmes. Probably the industrial engineers have been the most cognizant of the pertinence of algorithms vis-a-vis mathematics to their work. Probably the earliest of the revelations that computer programmes are better suited than mathematics to the AI research program appeared in their literature (Mihram 1980).

Yet, the industrial engineer's efforts do illustrate that there exist simulations (i.e., algorithmic models) which are not AI programmes. For example, an algorithmic model of a production activity, such as a weaving or knitting machine, does not necessarily require the mimicry of any human (or animal, or living) decider. Hence, not every simulation model is an AI programme, though every AI programme will indeed be an algorithmic simulation model; the mathematical relationship of the proper subset is thus established:

$$\{\text{AI programmes}\} \subset \{\text{simulation models}\} .$$

THE MIND: AI's FIRST REQUIREMENT

If, however, AI is to be a successful research program, we note that there are two requirements to be met: viz., (A) and (B) of the Introduction. The first (A) is that we must understand how the mind works if we are to be able to construct a scientifically credible model of the mind at work.

Yet, the literature of operational research has described (Mihram 1973) how well we understand the decision-making of the individual mind, particularly in view of its being the adult's (perfected) acquisition of mental model-building abilities in his/her adolescence.

In this regard, the nature of the process by which the child, as an element of Nature, learns the fundamentals of logical relationships before reaching puberty (adolescence) has been expounded well (Inhelder & Piaget 1968). The adolescent is then well equipped to formulate speculations, or to build mental models among his neural recordings, via mental assertions that are conducted under the logical patterns that he has developed as a child from parental supervision, from exposure to Nature, and from religious and educational instruction, though the omnipotent power of television broadcasting to this end must now be acknowledged (Mihram 1975). At adolescence, virtually every examined individual (child) was observed by Inhelder & Piaget to be constructing mental models, particularly to describe the nature and structure of the human society into which he is about to enter as an adult.

Inhelder and Piaget reveal rather strikingly the virtually "programmable" nature of the human mind. Just as they have understood how the child's mind, somewhat like an "infantile scientist", develops its abilities, two centuries ago (Condillac: 1746 to 1792) concluded that an adult's orderly mental process follows the sequence: sensation; attention; comparison; and judgement, the 'sum' (result) of which Condillac calls reflexion; then, understanding (or mental modelling) becomes the essentially sequential result of reflexion, followed by imagination and reasoning.

It is indeed puzzling that so many AI researchers have overlooked Condillac, whose works include clear refutations of the earlier notions of Descartes, whose opinions seem somehow still to be confusing AI researchers as to the separability of the mind from the soul. Some AI researchers (Newell, e.g.) have at last conclu-

ded (Waldrop 1988) that, even if the human mind should happen to have components or separations, these must all be centrally organised in order to produce behaviour: one mind must mind all such minds; it is that very 'self' naming itself 'I'.

The upbringing of a child prepares him to deal 'logically' with concrete or manipulable objects. This childhood preparation in logic has been essentially mapped by Piaget and his colleagues into a mathematico-logical context; the child develops the concepts of sets, relationships, and logical structures, so that, at the time of adolescence, he is equipped to deal with the formation of logical patterns (in other words, he is prepared to construct logical mental models). If the adolescent's educational upbringing has included training in the use of tools or writing instruments, then he is equipped to construct, as an adult, one of Man's models, or explanations, of his natural surroundings.

Thus, the human mind can be viewed as a _programmable_ (though not as a _programmed_) instrument, somewhat analogously to the digital computer. Neural recordings, with a child's logical structure stored among them, are capable at adolescence of making associations, logico-mathematical deductions, and mental models, particularly with respect to societal structure and the organisation of his personality. Thus, the child who is exposed both to more encounters with nature and to greater mental discipline shall likely be prepared better as a _model-builder_ while an adolescent and, subsequently, as a _decision-maker_ while an adult.

The cybernetic structure by which a scientist builds models has been described as a feedback mechanism (Mihram 1975) which depicts the dynamic process by which his models are both communicated to, and controlled by, his peers, adversaries, and colleagues. This functional model of the procedure by which scientists establish their explanations' credibility can also be represented, in a quite isomorphic fashion, as the procedure by which Human Knowledge is acquired and accumulated historically.

Indeed, this feedback structure also describes the _learning process_ of the individual adolescent (and, later, of the adult). It consists of six fundamental stages:

0. _Extant Knowledge_: the current state of the individual's neural recordings;
I. _Associative Reflexion_: the mental comparison, or association, of the extant neural recordings;
II. _Hypothetical Conjecture_: the formulation of a mental model upon available neurons in the brain;
III. _Logical Verification_: mental comparison of the conjecture with the extant knowledge so as to ensure its logical rectitude;
IV. _Empirical Validation_: the examination of the hypothetical conjecture's compatibility (or that of any precisely deduced conclusion reached therefrom) with Nature (including of course, the conjecturer's society), particularly with those about which the conjecture centers; and,
V. _Extended Knowledge_: the verified and validated conjecture is added to the neural recordings (Null Stage), available for use in further mental modelling, learning, and decision-making.

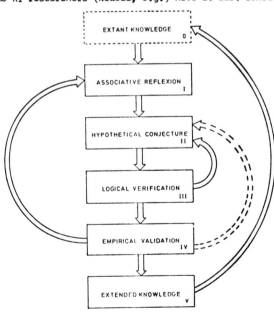

THE LEARNING PROCESS

Figure 1

The cybernetics of the adolescent's learning process is depicted in Figure 1, wherein one may note that any hypothetical conjecture's failure to pass some test of logical verity (III) implies that the mind return to the preceding stage (II), there to come forth with a rectified hypothetical conjecture.

Once a logically verified conjecture is deemed by the mind to be present ('stored') in the brain of the conjecturer, it is then subjected by the mind to tests against nature. The failure of such a validity test implies typically that the learner must have somewhere possessed an inadequate exposure to nature before hypothesising the conjecture originally: a return to Stage I (Associative Reflexion) is then required before a newly formed (i.e., rectified) hypothetical conjecture can emanate and be itself subjected to its own logical verification before itself being tested empirically against nature (and, of cours, society). It is nonetheless logically possible that a conjecture that is incompatible with empirical evidence can be rectified by the conjecturer's returning directly to formulate a new hypothetical conjecture (Stage II), much as one corrects a grammatical construction in a written statement so as to make it compatible with a reality of Nature; hence, the secondary (inner) feedback loop for a failed empirical validation is depicted in Fig.1.

Again, the cybernetic structure by which the individual constructs mental models (Figure 1) is stage-by-stage and feedback loop-by-feedback loop isomorphic to the six-stage model-building process (the Scientific Method) by which we collectively accumulate knowledge, via the editing and reviewing process, in our museums and libraries worldwide (Mihram 1975; and Mihram & Mihram 1971). It is as though, by building museums and libraries, we have been constructing a physical model of the human (individual) brain and its mind (cf. Mihram 1979).

The pertinence of Figure 1 to decision theorists and AI researchers emanates from its near-algorithmic capability to depict as an operational procedure one's learning, his decision-making process. The attempt to explain, and therefore to understand, the operation of the human mind requires that a credible model of the learning process be provided. AI researchers shall likely succeed in attaining their goal by the construction of algorithmic (i.e., simular) models of the dynamic and stochastic variety: Models will be composed of a set of decision algorithms, of simulation models.

Indeed, we received a communication from a leader in the operational research community, complimenting our 1971 paper (Cyert 1974): the propositions about human learning in that paper are verified, he noted, by psychological research into the learning process.

THE SCIENTIFIC METHOD: AI's SECOND REQUIREMENT

As we have noted above, the diagrammatic description (Figure 1) of the individual's mental model-building process proves to be identical to the earlier established (Mihram & Mihram 1971) diagrammatic depiction of the Scientific Method. A lengthier discussion of the Scientific Method has appeared in our literature of simulation methodology (Mihram 1975; Mihram & Mihram 1985) and so will not be pursued or repeated here.

Let it suffice for this writing to note that this near-algorithmic description of the Scientific Method was learned from our own established procedure for constructing credible algorithmic, machine-directed, models: from our simulation methodology (Mihram 1972). We have been enabled to learn, by observing simulationists at work, how Science has had to conduct itself over the centuries in the quest for truths of the nature of the world about us.

Thus, both the ingredients, (A) and (B), are quite well in hand for the guidance of AI researchers.

We know adequately well how the mind works (reaches decisions) and know that this can be ideally represented algorithmically; furthermore, by adhering meticulously to our six-stage model-building process, AI research shall surely attain its goal of constructing scientifically credible models of the mind as its work.

A NOTE OR TWO ASIDE

This process will not achieve immediately the ultimate goal: a computer programme as ingenuous as the entire mind and brain. But, as more and more decision processes are modelled, more and more experts are mimed via algorithms, the likely -to-be-achieved striking resemblances among these should lead to more and more general understandings of the operation of the brain and its mind. Much like the centuries of observation and modelling of the strange planetary motions were required before Newton's understanding of them via gravitational forces, we shall perhaps require decades of observation and modelling of minds before the major breakthrough in the cognitive sciences obtains.

Another important note needs to be made aside: The two six-stage model-building processes (The Learning Process, Figure 1; the Scientific Method, as Figure 5.2 of Mihram 1972) have a quite interesting biological foundation. Figure 1 represents the survival-seeking mechanism employed by any of the species of ('higher') animals who possess neural memory and recollection capabilities. But, these neural/mental mechanisms are outgrowths of the earlier chemico-genetic model-building process by which not only animals but also plant species seek to ensure their survival (Mihram & Mihram 1986).

In this sense also, then AI research, following the guidelines of simulation methodology, will be quite solidly founded biologically. This result, re the survival motivation for all scientific activity (including AI researchers) imposes an ethical constraint on our modelling freedoms.

EXAMPLE I: THE AI LIBRARIANS

As noted above [and expounded earlier at greater length (Mihram & Mihram 1985)], the "automation" of the activities in our larger academic and research libraries is accomplished, in actuality, via software programmes. But, every computer programme is actually a simulation model (of something, of some decision-filled process) and, being a model of a librarian at work, these particular software packages actually constitute AI programmes of a librarian (or researcher).

Again, the automation of the circulation desk at a library means that the library has opted to use an algorithmic, an AI, model of the circulation librarian. Similarly, the purchase and implementation of one of the software packages facilitating the purchasing of titles for the library implies that the library possesses an AI model of its acquisition librarian/clerk. And, the ongoing replacement of the card catalogs with computer terminals is the installation of an "AI catalog-searcher".

Emulation, or Simulation, in the Library?

Of more interest to those of us engaged in research in simulation methodology is the evolution of machine-readable data bases and their access via telecommunication networks. The programmes, often accessible via a "subscription", permit one (usually the librarian) to search the allowable data base(s) in order to retrieve citations of publications or artworks pertaining to one's research quest.

These programmes, if deemed to be simulation models of the reference librarian who is assisting an inquisitive reader/researcher, can be seen to be nowadays, in reality, *emulation models*: they permit much better searching than the reference librarian of earlier times would provide.

The earlier librarian would often be constrained by a list of subject headings (as typified by the Library of Congress's subject headings) or by controlled vocabularies (e.g., the E.R.I.C. THESAURUS). However, the evolution of these "bibliographic retrieval" programmes has provided KWIC (Key Words In Context) and now KWOC (Key Words Out of Context) capabilities. Whereas the KWIC mechanism allows a librarian/researcher to have the computer look through its accessible data bases so as to find every appearance of a specified term (or keyword, or, sometimes, their natural derivatives) or a specified logical combination of terms, the KWOC mechanism provides the researcher/librarian with "descriptors" from a "controlled vocabulary", a thesaurus by which suggested related terms are returned to the researcher so as to suggest further or alternative searching strategies.

The librarian of old did not have the possibility (or the option) to conduct KWIC searches, and she/he did not always have the time, or the subject expertise, to execute KWOC searches of the printed "data bases" (card catalogues, periodical listings, e.g.) available to her/him; thus, these new bibliographic retrieval packages constitute not only an AI model of the reference librarian at work but also an *emulation*, better than just a simulation, of her/his work. Furthermore, this "AI librarian" may be now searching through both computer-readable bibliographic data bases and machine-readable textual data bases (containing abstracts and/or full original texts).

The Library's Role in Making Simulation Scientific

An AI researcher might well ask, having accepted the major theme of the present paper (viz., that simulation methodology possesses all the attributes necessary for AI researchers to model with scientific credibility the mind at work on one or more decisions), why simulation methodology itself seems to be falling short of attaining the goal of credibility. We had pointed out earlier, in the literatures of industrial engineering, operational research, and statistical computation (Mihram and Mihram 1980; Mihram 1988; Mihram & Mihram 1987) several institutional mechanisms which, though readily implementable, remain not yet established in the working environment of simulationists.

Not only does our simulation methodology require an editorial policy which ensures that *both* an algorithmic, machine-readable model *and* the natural language report describing it are reviewed before the report is published but also we require dictionaries, language-by-language, of our simulation programming languages.

We also require that machine-readable models which we simulationists and AI researchers author be housed in libraries, or archives. Doing so, however, is creating considerable difficulty for libraries who seek, of course, to abide by the copyright laws. Computer programmes, once borrowed from a library's holdings, are rather readily duplicated and, though xerographic machines pose the same threat to printed materials, this poses to any library aware of any such activity the threat of litigation.

We suggest that libraries who do hold/shelve computer programmes have their institution's computer centre encrypt each of their machine-readable holdings in such a way that the encrypted (the circulating) copy can only be dis-encrypted by "knowledgeable" computers within the university/institution. The responsibility for maintaining the secrecy of the encryption 'keys' becomes that of the library/institution, but could be interpreted to mean that it is only the illicitly minded, though certainly clever, user of a software programme (and *not* the library) who is guilty of any violation of copyright restrictions. (Similarly, a chemical coding of inks might somehow have been used to prevent printed materials from duplication by any xerographic machine equipped with chemical sensors.)

EXAMPLE II: THE STRATEGIC DEFENSE INITIATIVE (SDI)

The degree of scientific credibility of the SDI's computer programmes has prompted quite emotional (e.g., Ralston 1986) outbursts from persons who should, by their earlier titular positions in computer science organisations, know better. Whether such outbursts be the result of their "worshipping a false god" (i.e., treating mathematics as if it be the only language which can convey truths of the world about us) or a disguise for ulterior political motives is left for each of us to resolve personally. However, as noted above, the core of the SDI programme is to be a set of computer programmes which collectively represent a simulation, an AI, model of the Office of the Presidency at work deciding when, whether, and how forcefully to respond militarily to a perceived missile attack.

The matter was adroitly raised by Commander Offutt of the SDI Organisation, in the keynote address of the 1986 Summer Computer Simulation Conference, by noting the pertinence of our simulation methodology to the SDI program.

CONCLUSIONS

We have reviewed the literature of our sister disciplines (operational research/management science; statistical computation; computer science; and industrial/systems engineering) to conclude that the literature of simulation methodology reveals how AI research can be conducted scientifically: viz., via our own methodology. AI research is a special case of the application of simulation methodology.

Not only has our own six-stage model-building process revealed what is, in a near-algorithmic fashion, the Scientific Method but also this model-building process is one-to-one isomorphic to the learning process, the very mental model-building process which AI researchers seek to understand fully.

Most importantly, we recognise that adherence to the Scientific Method in simulation methodology and, therefore, in AI research is of *ethical* importance: After all, the model-building process of Science is nothing more than our own (previously, unknowing) mimicry of the chemico-genetic, then chemico-neural, model-building process by which all survival on Earth has to date been assured.

REFERENCES

Cyert, Richard M. 1974. Personal communication from the Past President of the Institute of Management Science (20.VIII.1974).

Condillac, Etienne Bonnot, Abbe de. 1746 to 1792. PHILOSOPHICAL WRITINGS OF ETIENNE BONNOT, 2 vols. F. Philip and H. Lane, translators. Hillsdale, NJ: Erlbaum (1987): pp. 367-72; 423-35; and 542-48.

Inhelder, B. and J. Piaget. 1968. GROWTH OF LOGICAL THINKING FROM CHILDHOOD TO ADOLESCENCE. NY: Basic Books: pp. 346-48.

McCallum, Charles J. (Jr.) and L.D. Bodin. 1987. CAREERS IN OPERATIONS RESEARCH, p. 1. Baltimore, Md. 21202-9990: Oper. Res.Soc. America.

Mihram, Danielle and G. Arthur Mihram. 1971. "Human Knowledge: The Role of Models,Metaphors, and Analogy." INT'L J GEN SYSTEMS 1: 41-60 and 281 (1974).

Mihram, G. Arthur. 1972. SIMULATION: STATISTICAL FOUNDATIONS AND METHODOLOGY. Orlando, FL: Academic Press.

Mihram, G. Arthur. 1973. "Simulation: Methodology for Decision Theorists." pp. 320-27 of ROLE AND EFFECTIVENESS OF THEORIES OF DECISION IN PRACTICE, DJ White and KC Bowen, eds. London: Hodder and Stoughton (1975).

Mihram, G. Arthur. 1975. AN EPISTLE TO DR. BENJAMIN FRANKLIN. Pompano Beach, FL: Exposition-University Press (1974).

Mihram, G. Arthur. 1977. "Making Sure Computer Scientists Are Scientists." COMMUN ASSOC COMPUT MACHIN 20: 120ff and 452.

Mihram, G. Arthur. 1979. "Human Memory and the Brain." AMERICAN SCIENTIST 67: 394.

Mihram, G. Arthur. 1980. "Algorithmic Models: The Key to Artificial Intelligence." PROC 12th ANNUAL SOUTHEASTERN SYMPOSIUM ON SYSTEM THEORY, 349-53. NY: Institute of Electrical and Electronic Engineers.

Mihram, G. Arthur. 1986. "Artificial Intelligence, Statistical Computation, and Simulation Methodology: Distinctions and Likenesses." PROC, STATIST COMPUTAT SECT, 125-29. Alexandria, VA: Amer Statist Assoc.

Mihram, G. Arthur. 1988. "Making A.I. a Science: Simulation Methodology Revisited." ORSA/TIMS BULLETIN No 25, p. 266.

Mihram, G. Arthur and Danielle Mihram. 1980. "Simulation Programming Languages: Publishing, Dictionaries, Archives." p. 497 of PROC, FALL INDUSTRIAL ENG'G CONFER (Minneapolis). Amer. Inst. Industrial Engineers.

Mihram, G. Arthur and Danielle Mihram. 1985. "Credibility: Every Computer Programme is a Simulation Model." PROC, 18th HAWAII INT'L CONFER SYSTEM SCIENCES, pp. 306-16 [02.VII.1984].

Mihram, G. Arthur and Danielle Mihram. 1986. "C.P. Snow's Two Cultures are One: Ethical Implications." pp. F31-F43 of MENTAL IMAGES, VALUES, AND REALITY, J.A. Dillon, ed. Louisville, KY: Soc Gen Systems Reasearch.

Mihram, G. Arthur and Danielle Mihram. 1987. "A.I.: Institutional Measures to Ensure Credibility." p. 38 of STATISTICS IN THE INFORMATION AGE. Alexandria, VA: American Statistical Association (1986).

Mihram, G. Arthur et al. 1974. "Bibliography on Simular Credibility." SIMULATION, XI.1974: p. vi.

Mondale, Walter F. 1984. "Answer to Question on SDI." WASHINGTON POST, 22.X.1984: p. A12, Col. 4.

Ralston, A. 1984. "First Course in Computer Science Needs a Mathematics Co-requisite." COMMUN ASSOC COMPUT MACHIN 27: 1002-1004.

Ralston, A. 1986. "Letter to the Editor." NY TIMES, 16.I.1986: p. A22.

Sayre, K.M. and F.J. Crosson, eds. 1963. THE MODELING OF MIND. N.Y.: Simon & Schuster.

Waldrop, M.M. 1988. "Toward a Unified Theory of Cognition." SCIENCE 241: 27.

Wheatley, D.M. and A.W. Unwin. 1972. ALGORITHM WRITER'S GUIDE. London: Longman.

*

* · *

Simulation and AI, 1989
©1989 by the Society for Computer
Simulation International
ISBN 0-911801-44-8

Converting knowledge representation between rules and frames

A. Martin Wildberger, Ph.D.
Chief Computer Scientist
General Physics Corporation
6700 Alexander Bell Drive
Columbia, MD 21046

ABSTRACT

The two most common representations of knowledge in expert and other knowledge-based systems are rules and frames. Rules are usually expressed as antecedent and consequent, phrased as "if....then". This approximation to a natural language format is close to the way in which subject matter experts tend to describe their approach to a problem. Rules also make it relatively easy to automate explanations of the reasoning for a less expert user. Rules, however, are difficult to organize in a systematic way. When large numbers of rules are used, they sometimes cause unforeseen and undesirable effects.

Frames, on the other hand, are essentially the same structures as are used in most "object-oriented" computer programming languages. They tend to force a formal approach to the knowledge base which enhances consistency and efficiency, but their meaning is not intuitively obvious to most users.

Several expert system development tools make use of both modes of knowledge representation (for instance, NEXPERT[TM] from Neuron Data and S-1[TM] from Teknowledge), but these rely on the knowledge engineer (the developer) to decide what relations hold between the two representations.

A simple and practical method is presented for converting any set of rules to a set of frames (objects). This procedure will reveal inconsistencies, redundancies and areas of incomplete categorization. A method is also presented for converting a set of frames (objects) into a set of rules. This conversion method generates rules that can be used to explain automatically the reasoning of a system that uses these frames for its knowledge base. Both these procedures can be automated.

An extended example of the two procedures, included in the actual presentation, can be obtained from the author.

KNOWLEDGE REPRESENTATION BY RULES

The most common representation of knowledge currently used by expert system shells and similar tools is derived from simple implication statements used in the propositional calculus of mathematical logic. They are formally known as "Production Rules" and take the form:

$$Pattern\ A \longrightarrow Action\ B,$$

which is read: "Pattern A produces action B".

The tools that employ rules to represent knowledge usually express them as antecedent and consequent, phrased as "if....then". This approximation to a natural language format is close to the way in which subject matter experts tend to describe their approach to a problem. In fact, production rules were initially viewed as a model of human understanding (Newell 1973). Expressing knowledge in the form of rules makes it relatively easy to automate explanations of the expert system's reasoning for a user. Suppose we start with the following rules (excerpted from the example rulebase used in the actual presentation).

RULE_1: if the event is formal and the time is evening,
then wear a formal style suit.

RULE_2: if wearing a formal style suit,
then wear a black suit, a black tie, a white shirt and black shoes.

RULE_3: if the event is business and the time is workday,
then wear a business style suit or a sport coat

RULE_4: if wearing a business suit,
then wear shoes, a shirt, and a tie.

From these rules alone, the system can conclude that a formal event in the evening requires black shoes. It can defend that conclusion by citing the first two rules listed above and noting that the other two rules do not apply. The conclusion can be reached directly by forward chaining, or by backward chaining with a goal of "shoe color" and interrogating the user as to the time and nature of the event.

Rules, however, are difficult to organize in a systematic way. When large numbers of rules are used, they sometimes cause unforeseen and undesirable effects. In a large rulebase, it is difficult to ensure that all possible situations are either explicitly addressed or that the standard default mechanisms do not produce unacceptable results. The four rules excerpted above do not even begin to address all the possibilities that they raise. For instance, they say nothing about the color of the attire for the business day. Since only black and white colors are explicitly mentioned, either might logically be made the default, resulting in a conclusion that is, at the very least, inappropriate!

KNOWLEDGE REPRESENTATION BY FRAMES

Frames have also been proposed as models of actual human thinking (Minsky 1974). Frames have "slots" and "facets" whose values may be relatively static information or procedures (often called demons) which manipulate that information and/or are triggered by changes to it. Frames are essentially the same structures as are used in many currently popular "object-oriented" computer programming languages, such as Smalltalk, C++, Objective-C and ADA. Terminologies differ, but objects are generally thought to possess both data and the procedures for operating on it. These procedures, often called behaviors or methods, are the only way to affect that object's data. Objects can only be accessed from other objects via messages. Some of the structure, values, and behavior of an object may be inherited from more general objects. Languages that support this paradigm usually delay binding data to procedures until at least compile time, and preferably until execution.

The use of frames (objects) to represent knowledge tends to force a more formal approach to the construction of a knowledge base than does the use of rules. This approach enhances consistency and operating efficiency, but the "meaning" of a frame or a set of frames is not intuitively obvious to most users of a knowledge based system. Furthermore, since literally anything can be an object, the use of objects (frames) does not guarantee that the knowledge represented by them is complete, important, or even pertinent.

Since the four rules excerpted above are very incomplete (although not inconsistent), there are many possible frames that could be used to represent the same "knowledge" that they contain. For instance, a frame OUTFIT could be defined with slots for each article of clothing, and another frame SETTING could be defined with slots for time, event and a pointer to the appropriate instance of OUTFIT. The particular formalism used here to specify frames is of no consequence. It is purposely oversimplified in order to emphasize the problems being illustrated.

```
frame: OUTFIT has slots:
  SUIT with facets:
      COLOR (BLACK, WHITE, UNSPECIFIED),
      STYLE (FORMAL, BUSINESS, SPORT).
  SHOES with facets:
      COLOR (BLACK, WHITE, UNSPECIFIED).
  SHIRT with facets:
      COLOR (BLACK, WHITE, UNSPECIFIED).
  TIE with facets:
      COLOR (BLACK, WHITE, UNSPECIFIED).

frame: SETTING has slots:
  TIME with facets:
      TIME_PERIOD (EVENING, WORKDAY).
  EVENT with facets:
      ACTIVITY (FORMAL, BUSINESS).
  OUTFIT with facets:
      POINTER (FORMAL_OUTFIT, BUSINESS_OUTFIT,
               SPORT_OUTFIT).
```

Just defining these generic frames (or object classes) forces us to recognize that COLOR is incompletely specified by these four rules alone. When we try to use this representation for a parti-cular case, the nature of the missing "knowledge" becomes very clear. To operate in a knowledge base defined by these two generic frames, we need to build concrete instances of each. Building all possible such instances is equivalent to forward chaining in a rulebased system. However, it need only be done once. Thereafter, the equivalent of backward chaining can be accomplished by systematic retrieval based on the specified goal and its constraints.

If we want to find out what tie to wear to a formal event, the following two specific frames (object instances) are pertinent.

FORMAL_SETTING has TIME with TIME_PERIOD (EVENING), EVENT with ACTIVITY (FORMAL), OUTFIT with POINTER (FORMAL_OUTFIT).

FORMAL_OUTFIT has SUIT with COLOR (BLACK), STYLE (FORMAL), SHOES with COLOR (BLACK), SHIRT with COLOR (WHITE), TIE with COLOR (BLACK).

On the other hand, if we inquire about the proper shoes for business, the incomplete constraints are clear from the following three specific frames.

BUSINESS_SETTING has TIME with TIME_PERIOD (WORKDAY), EVENT with ACTIVITY (BUSINESS), OUTFIT with POINTER (BUSINESS_OUTFIT, SPORT_OUTFIT).

BUSINESS_OUTFIT has SUIT with COLOR (UNSPECIFIED), STYLE (BUSINESS), SHOES with COLOR (UNSPECIFIED), SHIRT with COLOR (UNSPECIFIED), TIE with COLOR (UNSPECIFIED).

SPORT_OUTFIT has SUIT with COLOR (UNSPECIFIED), STYLE (SPORT).

Not only does this reveal the problem of unspecified shoe color previously noted, but it also allows the possibility of not wearing shoes at all, provided that one wears a sport coat rather than a business suit!

COMBINED REPRESENTATIONS

Several expert system development tools make use of both modes of knowledge representation (for instance, NEXPERT^{TM} from Neuron Data and S-1^{TM} from Teknowledge), but these rely on the knowledge engineer (the developer) to decide what relations hold between the two representations. This ad hoc combination provides a high degree of flexibility and a potential for increased clarity by allowing different aspects of the knowledge to be represented by the more appropriate structure. However, these tools give the knowledge engineer little guidance in how to use each representation to benefit the other, so that the overall structure of the knowledge base tends to become even more diffuse and complex than a purely rule-based system.

NEXPERT, for instance, encourages the knowledge engineer to build what it calls "knowledge islands" of rules and objects (frames) which are largely self-contained. It provides built-in approaches to navigating between these islands depending on the degree of isolation that the developer desires. These bridges are useful in guiding the process of non-monotonic reasoning by which trial hypotheses can be proposed and tested automatically. However, the engineer must select the bridging approach to use and must control its operation by explicit references in the rules.

In addition, once an attribute of an object has been defined, whenever new rules are entered that reference it, NEXPERT can automatically build new relationships into the objects that contain it. In this case, the developer must periodically review what NEXPERT has added to the knowledge representation to ensure that it is actually what was meant.

CONVERSION OF RULES TO FRAMES (OBJECTS)

This section outlines a relatively simple method for converting any set of rules to a set of frames (objects). It is an algorithmic procedure that can be automated. It can be used systematically to point out possible inconsistencies, redundancies and areas of incomplete categorization in the set of rules being converted.

The steps outlined below can be adapted to a variety of formats for frames and rules. In order to meet space constraints, relatively simple formats have been selected. The terminology of "objects" is used because it seems to have wider applicability and appears to be replacing the terminology of frames in most applications.

For the purpose of this description, we define object classes (generic frames) as sets of attributes (slots/facets). An instantiation of such an object class is a set of values for its attributes along with their certainty factors (CF). Attributes may be multi-valued, where the multiple values represent a set of alternatives (logical "or"). A list of values held simultaneously (logical "and") can be handled by defining multiple attributes. Each value has its own associated CF. The CF's are positive and treated as percentages. The default is 100% (absolutely certain).

Rules are limited to structures of the type:

```
if X is Y with CF at least L, and
    (U is V with CF at least M, or
     U is W with CF at least N)
then A is B with CF P, and
    (C is D with CF Q, or
     C is E with CF R)
```

More complex logical relations can always be reduced to this form. For instance, the structure "or (F and G)" can be achieved by using two separate rules with the structure specified above.

The underlying concept in this method of conversion is to let the entire rulebase define a single object class whose attributes are all the names used on the left hand side of all the assertions contained in the premises and the conclusions of all rules. For example, using only the four rules excerpted above, we might construct the object class: PROPER_ATTIRE with attributes: SUIT_WORN, SHOES_WORN, SHIRT_WORN, TIE_WORN,

SUIT_STYLE, SUIT_COLOR, SHOE_COLOR, SHIRT_COLOR, TIE_COLOR, TIME_PERIOD, EVENT_TYPE.

Based on this single object class, a set of object instances are then instantiated, one for each rule in the rulebase. The assertions in both the premises and conclusions of each rule are used to assign values and CF's to the attributes named in that rule. The rest of the attributes for that particular object instance are treated as "unknown". For example, based only on the first rule, we would define the object instance RULE_1 with attribute values:

        SUIT_WORN = yes,
        SHOES_WORN = unknown,
        SHIRT_WORN = unknown,
        TIE_WORN = unknown,
        SUIT_STYLE = formal,
        SUIT_COLOR = unknown,
        SHOE_COLOR = unknown,
        SHIRT_COLOR = unknown,
        TIE_COLOR = unknown,
        TIME_PERIOD = evening,
        EVENT_TYPE = formal.

Based on the second rule, we would define the object instance RULE_2 with attribute values:

        SUIT_WORN = yes,
        SHOES_WORN = yes,
        SHIRT_WORN = yes,
        TIE_WORN = yes,
        SUIT_STYLE = formal,
        SUIT_COLOR = black,
        SHOE_COLOR = black,
        SHIRT_COLOR = white,
        TIE_COLOR = black,
        TIME_PERIOD = unknown,
        EVENT_TYPE = unknown.

Based on the third rule, we would define the object instance RULE_3 with attribute values:

        SUIT_WORN = yes,
        SHOES_WORN = unknown,
        SHIRT_WORN = unknown,
        TIE_WORN = unknown,
        SUIT_STYLE = business, sport
        SUIT_COLOR = unknown,
        SHOE_COLOR = unknown,
        SHIRT_COLOR = unknown,
        TIE_COLOR = unknown,
        TIME_PERIOD = workday,
        EVENT_TYPE = business.

Based on the fourth rule, we would define the object instance RULE_4 with attribute values:

        SUIT_WORN = yes,
        SHOES_WORN = yes,
        SHIRT_WORN = yes,
        TIE_WORN = yes,
        SUIT_STYLE = business,
        SUIT_COLOR = unknown,
        SHOE_COLOR = unknown,
        SHIRT_COLOR = unknown,
        TIE_COLOR = unknown,
        TIME_PERIOD = unknown,
        EVENT_TYPE = unknown.

The following steps, partially illustrated in the accompanying examples, describe how to construct and combine these object instances so as to eliminate redundancies.

1. Make a tentative object instance for each rule, entering a value of "unknown" for all attributes not mentioned in the rule. [See the four examples above.]

2. Combine into a single object instance all sets of object instances that differ only in having known versus unknown values for some attributes. Enter the known values in the resulting new object instances. Mark all object instances that are used in combinations, but do not delete them yet. They can be used in any number of combinations.

For example, we could combine the object instances RULE_1 and RULE_2, defined above, into RULE_1&2 with attribute values:
SUIT_WORN = yes,
SHOES_WORN = yes,
SHIRT_WORN = yes,
TIE_WORN = yes,
SUIT_STYLE = formal,
SUIT_COLOR = black,
SHOE_COLOR = black,
SHIRT_COLOR = white,
TIE_COLOR = black,
TIME_PERIOD = evening,
EVENT_TYPE = formal.

On this same basis, the object instances RULE_3 and RULE_4, defined above, cannot be combined into a single rule because they differ in the value(s) assigned to the attribute SUIT_STYLE.

In order to illustrate the reuse of object instances, let us assume a fifth rule:

RULE_5: if the event is formal and the time is afternoon,
then wear a formal style suit.

Based on this new rule, we would define the object instance RULE_5 with attribute values:
SUIT_WORN = yes,
SHOES_WORN = unknown,
SHIRT_WORN = unknown,
TIE_WORN = unknown,
SUIT_STYLE = formal,
SUIT_COLOR = unknown,
SHOE_COLOR = unknown,
SHIRT_COLOR = unknown,
TIE_COLOR = unknown,
TIME_PERIOD = afternoon,
EVENT_TYPE = formal.

We can then combine RULE_5 with RULE_1 and RULE_2 (separately) to form both RULE_1&5 and RULE_2&5. The latter would have attribute values:
SUIT_WORN = yes,
SHOES_WORN = yes,
SHIRT_WORN = yes,
TIE_WORN = yes,
SUIT_STYLE = formal,
SUIT_COLOR = black,
SHOE_COLOR = black,
SHIRT_COLOR = white,
TIE_COLOR = black,
TIME_PERIOD = afternoon,
EVENT_TYPE = formal.

3. Combine any sets of object instances that differ only in their values for one attribute. Include all its different values, making that attribute multi-valued. Mark all object instances that are used in combinations, but do not delete them yet. They can be used in any number of combinations.

On the basis of this step, we can combine the object instances RULE_1&2 and RULE_2&5 into an object instance FORMAL_ATTIRE with attribute values:
SUIT_WORN = yes,
SHOES_WORN = yes,
SHIRT_WORN = yes,
TIE_WORN = yes,
SUIT_STYLE = formal,
SUIT_COLOR = black,
SHOE_COLOR = black,
SHIRT_COLOR = white,
TIE_COLOR = black,
TIME_PERIOD = evening, afternoon,
EVENT_TYPE = formal.

Note that RULE_3 and RULE_4 still cannot be combined on the basis of step 3 because, for instance, attribute SHIRT_WORN is "unknown" in the one object and "yes" in the other.

4. Repeat step 3 using both the original object instances and those created by combining. Continue until no more combining can be done.

In the example being used for illustration, no further combining is possible.

5. Delete all marked object instances.

In the example being used for illustration, this leaves us with three object instances: FORMAL_ATTIRE, RULE_3, and RULE_4.

If this process resolves all "unknown" attributes, the remaining object instances may be viewed as constituting a partition into categories of a multi-dimensional space defined by the rules (Wildberger, 1984). There is no a priori justification for the particular "distance measure" between tentative object instances that was used to create this partition, but the categories are the minimum set that still retains the finest distinctions implied by the knowledge represented in that rulebase. Further reductions can be made by lumping together object instances that differ in their values for two, three, or more, attributes. However, this will throw away some of the distinctions made by the rules. It is preferable to retain all the categories, and use these less stringent "distance measures" when searching for a "best match" to a set of attribute values proposed for analysis by a user.

In the example being used for illustration, it is clear that the resulting categories do not cover completely the universe of discourse that is implied by the set of attributes in the object class. RULE_3 and RULE_4 simply have too many unknowns. What is more important, however, is that object instances with "unknown" values for one or more of their attributes do not partition the space defined by the object class. Instead, they each describe a partition of a space of lower dimensionality embedded in the space of the object class. Thus, object instance RULE_4 defines a five dimensional hyperplane in the eleven dimension space of PROPER_ATTIRE. RULE_3 defines another four dimensional hyperplane in that same space which has only two dimensions in common with RULE_4.

Note that an "unknown" value is not the same as "don't care" or "any" value. "Any" means that the attribute is multi-valued and that its values encompass all those admitted as possible for that attribute. If we were to substitute "any" for "unknown" everywhere in RULE_3 and RULE_4, we could combine them into a hypothetical ANY_ATTIRE with attributes:

> SUIT_WORN = yes,
> SHOES_WORN = yes, no,
> SHIRT_WORN = yes, no,
> TIE_WORN = yes, no,
> SUIT_STYLE = business, sport,
> SUIT_COLOR = black, white,
> SHOE_COLOR = black, white,
> SHIRT_COLOR = black, white,
> TIE_COLOR = black, white,
> TIME_PERIOD = workday, evening, afternoon,
> EVENT_TYPE = business, formal.

Then, ANY_ATTIRE could be combined with FORMAL_ATTIRE to produce a single object instance ALL_ATTIRE with attributes:

> SUIT_WORN = yes,
> SHOES_WORN = yes, no,
> SHIRT_WORN = yes, no,
> TIE_WORN = yes, no,
> SUIT_STYLE = business, sport, formal,
> SUIT_COLOR = black, white,
> SHOE_COLOR = black, white,
> SHIRT_COLOR = black, white,
> TIE_COLOR = black, white,
> TIME_PERIOD = workday, evening, afternoon,
> EVENT_TYPE = business, formal.

This results in a single category for the entire space, and fails to make any distinction between clothing to be worn regardless of the time and the event.

EXTRACTION OF RULES FROM FRAMES (OBJECTS)

This section outlines a relatively simple method for converting a set of frames (objects) into a set of rules. It is an algorithmic procedure that can be automated. This conversion method generates rules that can be used to explain automatically the reasoning of a system that uses these frames for its knowledge base.

Start with any object class (generic frame), as defined above, and a set of object instances (specific frames) instantiated from it. If one or more of its attributes are known to be the "goals" sought by the user of this knowledge base, construct a single rule whose conclusion asserts that the goal attributes have the values contained in that object instance and whose premises assert that all the other attributes also have the values contained in that object instance.

If it is not known which attribute is the goal, generate one rule for every attribute in each object instance, such that the attribute and its value are asserted in the rule's conclusion while all the other attributes and their values are asserted in the rule's premises. This approach makes no assumptions as to the order of implication within the object. The object instance is taken to mean: this is a set of attribute/values that are always found together. Clearly, any external information about the direction of implication should be used to eliminate those rules that do not reflect it correctly. If the object-oriented knowledge base is being used for advice, then the user can be asked to specify the goal attribute(s). This establishes the direction of implication to be used in deriving rules from the objects in order to "explain" the analysis performed by the knowledge based system.

If we started with the three object instances (FORMAL_ATTIRE, RULE_3, and RULE_4) that resulted from the simple example above, we could derive the same Rules 3 and 4 with which we started, and we could derive from FORMAL_ATTIRE a rule such as:

RULE_FORMAL_ATTIRE: if the event is formal and the time is either afternoon or evening,
then wear a formal suit with a black tie, a white shirt, and black shoes.

However, if we have no extrinsic reason for selecting the particular attributes to be used in the premises and conclusions, other "rules" would also have to be derived, such as:

RULE_3': if a business suit or a sport coat is being worn during the workday,
then the event is business related.

RULE_4': if a suit, shoes, shirt, and tie are being worn,
then the suit is business style.

In an interactive "expert system", it would always be clear which alternative "rule" to generate as "explanation". The appropriate rule would have premises that embodied the knowledge provided ("volunteered") by the user. Its conclusion would embody goals specified by the user or sub-goals generated as hypotheses by the system.

SUMMARY

A simple and practical method has been presented for converting any set of rules to a set of frames (objects). This procedure will reveal inconsistencies, redundancies and areas of incomplete categorization. A method is also presented for converting a set of frames (objects) into a set of rules. This conversion method generates rules that can be used to explain automatically the reasoning of a system that uses these frames for its knowledge base. Both these procedures can be automated.

REFERENCES

Minsky, M., "A Framework for Representing Knowledge," <u>MIT AI Memo 306</u>, Cambridge, MA, June 1974.

Newell, A., "Production Systems: Models of Control Structures," <u>Visual Information Processing</u>, Academic Press, New York, 1973.

Wildberger, A.M., "Application of Artificial Intelligence to Operator Assistance", <u>New Technology in Nuclear Power Plant Instrumentation and Control</u> (Washington, DC, Nov. 28-30), pp 295-301, Instrument Society of America, Research Triangle Park, NC, 1984.

Simulation and AI, 1989
©1989 by the Society for Computer
Simulation International
ISBN 0-911801-44-8

Qualitative/quantitative time constraint analysis for the generation of simulation scenarios

Kenneth H. Otwell

Martin Marietta Laboratories
1450 South Rolling Road
Baltimore, Maryland 21227

ABSTRACT

Although temporal information has always been used in simulations, researchers in artificial intelligence (AI) have only recently focused on the development of logics and algorithms for analyzing time constraints. However, temporal reasoning techniques from AI can provide significant benefits to the development of simulations. We have developed and implemented a temporal reasoning testbed which analyzes time constraints specified in a hybrid qualitative/quantitative interval language and deduces the strictest constraints between each pair of interval endpoints. A tool such as this can aid simulation development as well as interact with a simulation during runtime. Limitations of the AI approach and consequent redirections towards simulation paradigms are discussed.

INTRODUCTION

Development of discrete event simulations requires the specification of event orderings and durations. Many simulations use this information to generate or schedule events at runtime in relation to prior events, often using predefined numerical distributions to generate timings. However, there are logical constraints on event sequences, which are normally embedded in the event generation mechanism. For example, in simulations of physical systems, effects necessarily follow (or perhaps coincide with) their causes. In complex scenarios, a multitude of constraints must be analyzed to determine their temporal ramifications, especially when the time constraints admit multiple, mutually exclusive interpretations.

Simulation development requires the analysis of time-related constraints prior to their incorporation. The use of temporal reasoning techniques from artificial intelligence (AI) can significantly reduce simulation development time by detecting any inconsistencies among the time constraints before they are embedded in a simulation, thus reducing the need for manual analysis. There is also great potential for the incorporation of temporal reasoning techniques from AI in the simulation itself to automatically propagate time constraints that arise from event generation during runtime. In this paper, we focus on the issue of constraint preprocessing.

A major concern of temporal reasoning in AI is the determination of the strictest boundaries with respect to when events can occur, or have occurred, and when facts can be true or false. Recent research in AI has produced two central paradigms for representing and reasoning with time: an interval-based approach (Vilain 1982; Allen 1983; Allen and Hayes 1987; Ladkin 1986a,b) and a point-based one (McDermott 1982; Dean 1986a). These are discussed briefly below.

Drawing on this research, we have developed and implemented a temporal reasoning testbed in Common Lisp. It incorporates point-based constraint propagation implemented within a modified assumption-based truth maintenance system. (The implementation includes many ideas from Dean's Time Map program (Dean 1986a).) It accepts time boundary constraints in an extended interval-based language that includes qualitative and quantitative constraints, translates the interval constraints into canonical point constraints, and solves for the set of strictest constraints between all time points by polynomial-time constraint propagation. The deduced constraints are translated back to the interval language for answering queries.

TEMPORAL REASONING IN AI AND SIMULATION

Background

A reasonable case can be made that simulation is ahead of AI in the use of temporal information for analyzing scenarios; for example, little work has appeared in the AI literature regarding probabilistic occurrences of events, probabilistic characterizations of event durations, or reasoning about continuous change (although, these areas are quickly growing). On the other hand, work in AI has perhaps produced a better understanding of the foundations of temporal reasoning, resulting in logics and algorithms for analyzing constraints on temporal boundaries.

Issues regarding event coordination and analysis of event interactions are becoming increasingly important for AI as the complexity of problems being addressed by AI research increases, especially in the areas of planning for multiple agents and in unpredictable environments, and modelling the actions of other intelligent agents. Where the focus of simulation has been to predict the interactions and results of a given set of events, AI has "traditionally" been more concerned with the generation of events to achieve a given set of goals and with understanding the reasons why a given set of events has occurred.

Early time-related research in AI focussed on searching through the space of possible event sequences to produce plans for converting an initial state into a desired (goal) state. Systems such as STRIPS (Fikes and Nilsson 1971) and Hacker (Sussman 1973) deal with problem decomposition and efficient search techniques. Logic formalisms were developed along these same lines, with roots in Modal Logic (Kripke 1971), and Situation Calculus (McCarthy and Hayes 1969), to analyze and clarify the semantics of these reasoning processes. These early systems were limited in their expressiveness of time constraints -- temporal information was merely a byproduct of event (or situation) orderings. However, it was found that significant computational benefits could accrue if the ordering of events was delayed until conflicts between them were detected (Sacerdoti 1974). Furthermore, researchers became interested in problems involving overlapping events. These two developments led to a focus on the analysis of temporal constraints as a general issue separate from a particular planning framework, and has produced temporal reasoning theories and algorithms that are applicable to many problem domains that use temporal information, including simulation.

Interval-based Approach

Formulations for interval-based temporal reasoning have been developed and extended by several researchers, e.g., (Allen 1983; Allen and Hayes 1987; Ladkin 1986a,b; Vilain 1982). The prototypical interval language utilizes the 13 interval relations presented in Table 1.

Table 1. The 13 Interval Ordering Relations

Relation (Inverse)	Illustration
X before Y (after)	XXX YYY
X meets Y (met-by)	XXXXYYY
X overlaps Y (overlapped-by)	XXXX YYYY
X starts Y (started-by)	XXX YYYYYY
X during Y (contains)	XXX YYYYYYY
X equals Y (equals)	XXX YYY
X finishes Y (finished-by)	XXX YYYYY

The standard interval language allows only pairwise disjunctions, which are represented as a vector of mutually exclusive disjunctive relations between two intervals, e.g., [**X** (before during after) **Y**] specifies that interval **X** is before, during, or after interval **Y**. It does not allow disjunctions of the form [(**X** before **Y**) | (**Q** after **R**)], where **X** and **Q** or **Y** and **R** can represent different intervals. We will refer to this as the "classic" interval language. It is fairly intuitive and very useful for expressing ordering relations between events.

Allen (Allen 1983) developed a polynomial-time algorithm for propagating constraints in the classic interval language. However, while the algorithm is sound, it is not complete due to the exponential resources required for propagating some disjunctions, e.g., a complete analysis of [**X** (before after) **Y**] produces two mutually exclusive interpretations that should be considered separately. The distinction between interval disjunction types that enables some to be completely propagated in polynomial time is more easily seen in the point-based representation discussed below.

Point-Based Approach

Point-based approaches to the analysis of temporal constraints have been developed and utilized by (McDermott 1982; Dean 1986a,b) and others. In this framework, events are represented by their beginning and ending points, and their time constraints are analyzed by propagation between time points. For purely qualitative reasoning, where only ordering information is considered, there are three point relations, i.e., before, after, and equivalence. The set of interval disjunctions that can be completely propagated in polynomial time can be mapped to conjunctive constraints in the point language because omission of constraints between subsets of endpoints is implicit disjunction between all alternatives. All constraints specified in the conjunctive point language can be propagated soundly and completely in polynomial time and the results are isomorphic to results from the interval propagation. Thus, the point-based analysis is simpler and easier to implement, although it is still prone to the same combinatoric problems with arbitrary disjunctions.

Qualitative, time-order languages have been extended to metric time, i.e., the inclusion of numeric constraints between times, primarily in the point-based languages, e.g., (Dean 1986a). We illustrate these capabilities in the presentation of our test-bed temporal reasoning system.

TEMPORAL REASONING TESTBED

Point-based Temporal Reasoning Formulation

Although an interval-based representation is more natural for specifying the types of constraints that we are interested in (because we are generally concerned with events and facts that are associated with time intervals), we formalize our system in a point-based representation. Since interval constraints can be mapped to equivalent point constraints, we use the interval representation for specifying constraints and the point representation for the actual reasoning.

We first define a set of time points, $P = \{p_1, p_2, ...\}$, a set of temporal distance constraints, $C = \{c_1, c_2, ...\}$, and a set of distance values, $D = \{d_1, d_2, ...\}$. Each c_i is equivalent to a maximum distance constraint between an ordered pair of points, and takes the form: (p_i, p_j, d_k). Values in D are two-place coordinates, with the first coordinate taken from the reals and the second from $\{0, 1\}$. The real coordinate determines quantitative distances between points, and the second determines qualitative orderings. That is, $(\mathbf{r},1)$ denotes a maximum distance that is strictly less than $\mathbf{r}$, and $(\mathbf{r},0)$ denotes a maximum distance less than or equal to $\mathbf{r}$. We define $\mathbf{D}$ as closed over addition, with addition of the second coordinate defined as the boolean OR, as follows:

(A1) $\forall \mathbf{r_i},\mathbf{r_j} \cdot ((\mathbf{r_i},0) + (\mathbf{r_j},0) => (\mathbf{r_i} + \mathbf{r_j},0))$ &
$\qquad ((\mathbf{r_i},0) + (\mathbf{r_j},1) => (\mathbf{r_i} + \mathbf{r_j},1))$ &
$\qquad ((\mathbf{r_i},1) + (\mathbf{r_j},1) => (\mathbf{r_i} + \mathbf{r_j},1))$.

We also define a binary relation, $<\mathbf{S}$, for strictness of constraints such that "$\mathbf{c_i} <\mathbf{S}\ \mathbf{c_j}$" means "$\mathbf{c_i}$ is less strict than $\mathbf{c_j}$." $<\mathbf{S}$ forms a partial order over the constraints, and is defined by the following two axioms (for clarity, we show only the distance values from constraint expansion in A2 -- which points are being constrained is irrelevant.)

(A2) $\forall \mathbf{r_i},\mathbf{r_j} \cdot ((\mathbf{r_i},0) <\mathbf{S} (\mathbf{r_i},1))$ &
$\qquad \neg((\mathbf{r_i},0) <\mathbf{S} (\mathbf{r_i},0))$ &
$\qquad \neg((\mathbf{r_i},1) <\mathbf{S} (\mathbf{r_i},1))$ &
$\qquad ((\mathbf{r_i} > \mathbf{r_j}) => ((\mathbf{r_i},0) <\mathbf{S} (\mathbf{r_j},0)))$ &
$\qquad\qquad ((\mathbf{r_i},1) <\mathbf{S} (\mathbf{r_j},0)))$ &
$\qquad\qquad ((\mathbf{r_i},0) <\mathbf{S} (\mathbf{r_j},1)))$ &
$\qquad\qquad ((\mathbf{r_i},1) <\mathbf{S} (\mathbf{r_j},1))))$

(A3) $\forall \mathbf{c_i},\mathbf{c_j} \cdot (\mathbf{c_i} <\mathbf{S} \mathbf{c_j}) => \neg(\mathbf{c_j} <\mathbf{S} \mathbf{c_i})$.

Constraints ordered only by the second coordinate can be converted to equality by the addition of $(\mathbf{r},1)$ to both sides. However, the axioms do provide precisely the semantics we require; for instance, "less than 5" added to "less than 6" produces "less than 11," as intended, and "less than 5" added to "less than or equal to 6" also produces "less than 11," as intended. We maintain that "less than 6" is a stricter upper bound than "less than or equal to 6," even though the relative strictness can be eliminated under addition. Dean (Dean 1986a,b) uses a similiar concept for the second coordinate; however, he defines integer addition for the second coordinate that produces semantics such as "less than less than 11," which we do not require.

We can specify both upper and lower boundaries on the distances between time points with this representation, since minimum and maximum distance constraints are interchangeable by the following axiom (the constraint types are labeled here for clarity; minimum distance constraints are not used elsewhere):

(A4) $\forall \mathbf{p_i},\mathbf{p_j},\mathbf{d_k} \cdot$
$\qquad$ min-distance$(\mathbf{p_i},\mathbf{p_j},\mathbf{d_k}) <=>$ max-distance$(\mathbf{p_j},\mathbf{p_i},-\mathbf{d_k})$;
$\qquad$ where $-(\mathbf{r},0) = (-\mathbf{r},0)$ & $-(\mathbf{r},1) = (-\mathbf{r},1)$.

Thus, we do not require the constraint types in the point language and use only the implicit maximum distance constraints.

We require only one propagation axiom since we have only one constraint type:

(A5) $\forall \mathbf{p_i},\mathbf{p_j},\mathbf{p_k},\mathbf{d_l},\mathbf{d_m} \cdot (\mathbf{p_i},\mathbf{p_j},\mathbf{d_l})$ & $(\mathbf{p_j},\mathbf{p_k},\mathbf{d_m})$
$\qquad\qquad => (\mathbf{p_i},\mathbf{p_k},\mathbf{d_l} + \mathbf{d_m})$.

Thus, with this axiom, we are able to perform a sound and complete constraint propagation over all constraints specified with the language.

<u>Interval-based Constraint Specification Language</u>

Our implementation accepts constraints specified in an extended interval-based language, and translates these into the point-based representation for analysis. First, we include the classic interval language without disjunctions. Nondisjunctive qualitative relations from the classic interval language can easily be translated into our maximum distance constraints between endpoints. For illustration, we use begin($\mathbf{X}$) and end($\mathbf{X}$) to represent the beginning and ending points, respectively, of the interval $\mathbf{X}$. The translation is readily apparent from the following examples:

(I1) $\forall \mathbf{X},\mathbf{Y} \cdot (\mathbf{X}$ before $\mathbf{Y}) <=> ($begin$(\mathbf{Y}),$ end$(\mathbf{X}), (0,1))$

(I2) $\forall \mathbf{X},\mathbf{Y} \cdot (\mathbf{X}$ starts $\mathbf{Y}) <=> ($begin$(\mathbf{Y}),$ begin$(\mathbf{X}), (0,0))$ &
$\qquad\qquad ($begin$(\mathbf{X}),$ begin$(\mathbf{Y}), (0,0))$ &
$\qquad\qquad ($end$(\mathbf{Y}),$ end$(\mathbf{X}), (0,1))$.

We also assume this interval definition throughout:

(I3) $\forall \mathbf{X} \cdot (end(\mathbf{X}),$ begin$(\mathbf{X}), (0,0))$

which allows interval durations to be zero or greater, but not negative. (We ignore the issue of open or closed endpoints for our present discussion.)

We extend the interval algebra to include quantitative distances by adding eight 4-tuple distance constraints to represent minimum and maximum distances between pairs of interval endpoints. We actually require only the four maximum distance constraints or the four minimum distance constraints for completeness, but including all eight increases clarity. The additional interval constraints are defined by their translation to the point algebra, as follows:

(I4) $\forall \mathbf{X},\mathbf{Y},\mathbf{r} \cdot (\mathbf{X}$ maximum-distance $\mathbf{Y}\ \mathbf{r})$
$\qquad\qquad <=> ($end$(\mathbf{X}),$ begin$(\mathbf{Y}), (\mathbf{r},0))$

(I5) $\forall \mathbf{X},\mathbf{Y},\mathbf{r} \cdot (\mathbf{X}$ minimum-distance $\mathbf{Y}\ \mathbf{r})$
$\qquad\qquad <=> ($begin$(\mathbf{Y}),$ end$(\mathbf{X}), (-\mathbf{r},0))$

(I6) $\forall \mathbf{X},\mathbf{Y},\mathbf{r} \cdot (\mathbf{X}$ maximum-duration $\mathbf{Y}\ \mathbf{r})$
$\qquad\qquad <=> ($begin$(\mathbf{X}),$ end$(\mathbf{Y}), (\mathbf{r},0))$

(I7) $\forall \mathbf{X},\mathbf{Y},\mathbf{r} \cdot (\mathbf{X}$ minimum-duration $\mathbf{Y}\ \mathbf{r})$
$\qquad\qquad <=> ($end$(\mathbf{Y}),$ begin$(\mathbf{X}) (-\mathbf{r},0))$

(I8) $\forall \mathbf{X},\mathbf{Y},\mathbf{r} \cdot (\mathbf{X}$ maximum-begins $\mathbf{Y}\ \mathbf{r})$
$\qquad\qquad <=> ($begin$(\mathbf{X}),$ begin$(\mathbf{Y}), (\mathbf{r},0))$

(I9) $\forall \mathbf{X},\mathbf{Y},\mathbf{r} \cdot (\mathbf{X}$ minimum-begins $\mathbf{Y}\ \mathbf{r})$
$\qquad\qquad <=> ($begin$(\mathbf{Y}),$ begin$(\mathbf{X}), (-\mathbf{r},0))$

(I10) $\forall \mathbf{X},\mathbf{Y},\mathbf{r} \cdot (\mathbf{X}$ maximum-ends $\mathbf{Y}\ \mathbf{r})$
$\qquad\qquad <=> ($end$(\mathbf{X}),$ end$(\mathbf{Y}), (\mathbf{r},0))$

(I11) $\forall \mathbf{X},\mathbf{Y},\mathbf{r} \cdot (\mathbf{X}$ minimum-ends $\mathbf{Y}\ \mathbf{r})$
$\qquad\qquad <=> ($end$(\mathbf{Y}),$ end$(\mathbf{X}), (-\mathbf{r},0))$.

We also allow simplifications of I6 and I7 that take only the first interval argument and presume the second interval to be the same as the first; this provides for concise specification of constraints on the duration of a single interval. Figure 1 illustrates the temporal relations that are constrained with this language.

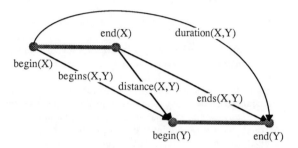

Figure 1. The Four End-Point Relations

Since our purpose in developing the interval representation is to provide for a natural specification of constraints, we allow only quantitative distance constraints in I4 through I11. All qualitative constraints that require the two distance coordinates are already specifiable with the classic interval relations. Note that a maximum distance that is strictly less than some real value other than zero cannot be specified in our interval language without postulating an additional interval; however, since few situations appear to require such a constraint, and since it would place an unnecessary burden on users to explicitly include the two-place coordinates in the interval language, we have chosen to keep it simple by hiding the two-place coordinates from the user.

Constraint Propagation Algorithm

Our algorithm is derived from well-known, polynomial-time algorithms for propagating conjunctive constraints (Freuder 1978; Mackworth and Freuder 1985; Dean 1986a; Vilain and Kautz 1986).

The basic algorithm propagates each input constraint separately to completion. Constraints are taken from an agenda and propagated only if they are stricter than all existing ones between the same two points. The updates are incremental as new constraints are added, since the algorithm guarantees that the strictest boundaries between points, determined by previous constraints, are known. However, if the agenda is ordered by decreasing strictness of constraints, it is usually more efficient to accumulate as many new constraints on the agenda as possible before propagation. (We discuss this heuristic further after presenting the algorithm.) The algorithm generates the strictest bounds between all pairs of points, and, for each new constraint, terminates in time bounded by the square of the number of points. Constraints "between" the same point are not propagated because a single point is maximally constrained, by definition, to be equivalent to itself (anything stricter is trapped as a contradiction). We justify these properties, and describe the algorithm, with the following informal proof:

It is not necessary to propagate constraints through cycles. Propagating a constraint in cycles would result in one of: 1) a nonstrictest constraint if the sum of constraints in a cycle is greater than zero, 2) a redundancy if the sum of constraints in a cycle is equal to zero, or 3) an inconsistency if the sum of constraints in a cycle is less than zero because points in the cycle would be forced to end before they started. (This property allows inconsistencies to be easily detected.)

Assume that the strictest constraints between points derivable from all previously input constraints are known. Consider the propagation of an input constraint between the ordered pair of points p and q. The input constraint is required to be propagated if and only if it is stricter than an existing one between p and q. A stricter constraint between any other ordered pair of points can be derived from the input constraint by the propagation axiom A5 only if the input constraint is included in a directed path from the first point in the pair to the second.

The constraints from each point disjoint from (p,q) to p and the constraints from q to all points disjoint from (p,q) cannot be made stricter by the input constraint, because that would require cyclic propagation.

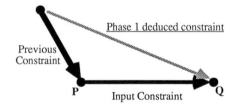

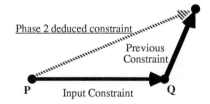

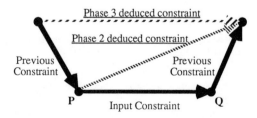

Figure 2. The Three Propagation Phases

122

Constraint propagation is performed in three phases, where the first phase consists of applying axiom A5 with the input constraint as the first of the two left-hand side constraints, the second phase consists of applying A5 with the input constraint as the second of the two left-hand side constraints, and the third phase consists of applying A5 with the constraints deduced under phase two in the left-hand side. That is: the first phase generates a constraint from p to each point with a constrained distance from q; phase two generates a constraint to q from each point with a constrained distance to p; and phase three generates a constraint between pairs of points disjoint from (p,q) by utilizing results from phase two (see Figure 2). (An equivalent phase three can be formulated by utilizing the results from phase one instead of those from phase two.) Cycles are not propagated and nonstrictest constraints are discarded.

Phases one and two each generate at most N - 2 constraints, where N is the number of points, because there are at most N - 2 constraints from each point in the input constraint to all other points, excluding the other point in the input constraint. Since each of these is generated with a single application of axiom A5, phases one and two complete in time bounded by $O(N)$. (Constraint indexing by ordered pairs of points, e.g., use of arrays to store constraints, eliminates any need for pattern matching.) Phase three generates at most $(N - 2)(N - 3)$ constraints, because there are at most N - 3 points that the N - 2 phase two constraints can be propagated with. Since each constraint deduced in phase three requires only one application of A5, phase three completes in time bounded by $O(N^2)$.

No additional propagation is necessary, because constraints between all points connected by paths through (p,q) have been deduced by considering the strictest constraint path through (p,q). Thus, the entire algorithm completes in time bounded by $O(CN^2)$, where N is the number of time points and C is the total number of input constraints.

Our implementation is slightly more complex than this description: to avoid needless third-phase propagation, we use a variant propagation axiom for phase three that combines the results from phases one and two and generates isomorphic phase-three constraints but not any redundant or nonstrictest ones.

It is extremely rare for an input constraint to generate a new constraint between every pair of points that is stricter than the existing ones. To further decrease the occurrence of such "pathological" behavior, the agenda is ordered so that the strictest constraints are propagated first. However, since constraints can contain negative distances, new constraints that are stricter than an existing one for an ordered pair of points might be created by propagation, defeating our ordering heuristic. In a completely ordered set of points, half of the constraints must be negative or zero, and half must be positive or zero; thus, the ordering heuristic is very useful for reducing the average runtime.

Our implementation also extends the basic algorithm by incorporating a simplified assumption-based truth maintenance system (ATMS) for detecting and handling inconsistencies. We do not describe the ATMS here due to space limitations; issues regarding the maintenance of dependency relations between conclusions and the detection of inconsistencies have been presented at length elsewhere (e.g., (Doyle 1979; DeKleer 1984,86). We are currently extending the ATMS to enable the implementation to include the propagation of disjunctions with no duplicate propagation of nondisjunctive constraints under alternative interpretations.

DISCUSSION

It is difficult to define "average" sets of time constraints for testing the time-complexity behavior of our algorithm. However, our experience with a small number of test cases indicates that the computation time increases with the size of the input much less than the upper bound computed above would indicate.

Our implementation does not yet handle disjunctions or their sometimes mutually exclusive interpretations. Such capabilities are needed in many cases. For example, if it is known only that two events cannot intersect, then two orderings are possible and both should be considered. While it is relatively straightforward to implement this capability, the combinatorics of the computations can quickly become overwhelming. The primary utility of this capability, from the AI perspective, is the ability to determine optimal event sequences for achieving goals. Weaker, but still useful, is the capability to search through the space of possible interpretations until an acceptable one is found -- pruning inconsistent combinations of disjuncts and selecting the first combination encountered that satisfies some minimal time or effort criterion.

As mentioned above, AI techniques for plan generation have been developed that depend on delaying the imposition of order constraints between events (or actions) to reduce the combinatorics inherent in considering multiple potential orderings. Unfortunately, the effect of many events cannot be determined without considering the context in which they occur, which requires knowledge of what has transpired prior to the event occurrence and thus reintroduces the need to examine possible orderings (Dean and Boddy 1987). One of the strengths of simulation is the ability to search through just such "interpretation spaces" to determine the consequences. However, time-constraint analysis of an interpretation prior to simulation could determine the strictest constraints and prune logically inconsistent alternatives to ensure that the simulations would contain only a valid set of temporal choices. It appears that AI and simulation have much to offer each other in this area.

ACKNOWLEDGEMENTS

I am indebted to Brian Haugh for his invaluable contribution to the temporal reasoning formalism, although I am solely responsible for any errors in reporting it. I wish to thank Steve Jameson, whose dedication and programming skill permitted the development of our testbed implementation on schedule. I also wish to express gratitude to Judy Marcus, who discovered all of the terrible typos and lousy language, even the stuff that got left in.

REFERENCES

Allen, J. 1983. "Maintaining Knowledge about Temporal Intervals." *Communications of the ACM* 26, no. 11 (Nov.): 832-843.

Allen, J. and P. Hayes. 1987. "Moments and Points in an Interval-Based Temporal Logic." Technical Report TR-180. Departments of Computer Science and Philosophy, University of Rochester, Rochester, NY. (Dec.)

Dean, T. 1986a. "Temporal Imagery: An Approach to Reasoning about Time for Planning and Problem Solving." Research Report YALEU/CSD/RR-433. Department of Computer Science. Yale University. New Haven, CT. (Oct.) (Doctoral dissertation.)

Dean, T. 1986b. "Large-Scale Temporal Data Bases for Planning in Complex Domains." Technical Report CS-86-15. Department of Computer Science. Brown University. Providence, RI. (Jul.)

Dean, T. and M. Boddy. 1987. "Incremental Causal Reasoning." In *Proceedings of the Sixth National Conference on Artificial Intelligence* (AAAI-87, Seattle, WA, Jul. 13-17). AAAI, Menlo Park, CA., 196-201.

DeKleer, J. 1984. "Choices Without Backtracking." In *Proceedings of the Fourth National Conference on Artificial Intelligence* (AAAI-84, Austin, TX, Aug. 6-10). AAAI, Menlo Park, CA., 79-85.

DeKleer, J. 1986. "An Assumption-Based Truth Maintenance System," *Artificial Intelligence* 28, no. 2 (Mar.): 127-162.

Doyle, J. 1979. "A Truth Maintenance System," *Artificial Intelligence* 12, no. 3 (Nov.): 231-272.

Fikes, R.E. and N.J. Nilsson. 1971 "STRIPS: A New Approach to the Application of Theorem Proving to Problem Solving." *Artificial Intelligence* 2, nos. 3,4: 189-208.

Freuder, E. 1978. "Synthesizing Constraint Expressions," *Communications of the ACM* 21, no. 11 (Nov.): 958-966.

Kripke, S. 1971 "Semantic Considerations on Modal Logic." in *Reference and Modality*, L. Linsky, ed. Oxford University Press, London, UK, 63-72.

Ladkin, P. 1986a. "Time Representation: A Taxonomy of Interval Relations." In *Proceedings of the Fifth National Conference on Artificial Intelligence* (AAAI-86, Philadelphia, PA, Aug. 11-15). AAAI, Menlo Park, CA., 360-366.

Ladkin, P. 1986b. "A Representation for Collections of Temporal Intervals," *Proceedings of the Fifth National Conference on Artificial Intelligence*, (AAAI-86, Philadelphia, PA, Aug. 11-15). AAAI, Menlo Park, CA., 367-371.

McCarthy, J. and P. Hayes. 1969. "Some Philosophical Problems from the Standpoint of Artificial Intelligence," in *Machine Intelligence* 4, B. Meltzer and D. Michie, eds. Edinburgh University Press, Edinburgh, 463-502.

McDermott, D. 1982. "A Temporal Logic for Reasoning About Processes and Plans," *Cognitive Science* 6, no. 2: 101-155.

Mackworth, A. and E. Freuder. 1985. "The Complexity of Some Polynomial Network Consistency Algorithms for Constraint Satisfaction Problems," *Artificial Intelligence* 25, no. 1 (Jan.): 65-74.

Sacerdoti, E. D. 1974. "Planning in a Hierarchy of Abstraction Spaces," *Artificial Intelligence* 5, no. 2: 115-135.

Sussman, G. J. 1973. "A Computational Model of Skill Acquisition." Technical Report 297, AI Laboratory, Massachusetts Institute of Technology, Boston, Mass. (Doctoral dissertation.)

Vilain, M. 1982. "A System for Reasoning About Time." In *Proceedings of the National Conference on Artificial Intelligence* (AAAI-82, Pittsburgh, PA, Aug. 18-20). AAAI, Menlo Park, CA, 197-201.

Vilain, M. and H. Kautz. 1986. "Constraint Propagation Algorithms for Temporal Reasoning." In *Proceedings of the Fifth National Conference on Artificial Intelligence* (AAAI-86, Philadelphia, PA, Aug. 11-15). AAAI, Menlo Park, CA, 377-382.

Simulation International
ISBN 0-911801-44-8

Knowledge-based generation of multi-level models for troubleshooting computer network performance

Jean-Louis Fléchon   and   John A. Zinky
jflechon@BBN.COM   jzinky@BBN.COM
(617) 873-3134   (617) 873-2561

BBN Communication Corp.
150 CambridgePark Rd.
Cambridge, MA 02238

ABSTRACT

The Automatic Network Troubleshooter (ANT) demonstrates the benefits of combining AI and modeling techniques in a diagnostic problem. ANT incorporates an expert system that quickly identifies the cause of throughput bottlenecks in large computer networks. It produces a causal model of the bottleneck process, which is analyzed to determine appropriate corrective actions. The heart of the expert system's knowledge base is a specification of the protocol hierarchy, which is interpreted by different task specialists. The level of detail of the model can be adjusted by combining submodels. The search for a simple model is guided by heuristic knowledge, and relies on a general scheme for generating and testing simplification hypotheses. The current prototype, written in Prolog, demonstrates that the total troubleshooting time can be reduced from several weeks to several hours.

INTRODUCTION

Computer networks are complex systems and consequently are very hard to troubleshoot. This paper presents the Automatic Network Troubleshooter (ANT), a system designed to diagnose performance problems in large-scale networks and to find adequate remedies without human intervention [ZF89]. The focus of the current system is to identify throughput bottlenecks caused by bad configuration parameter settings or lack of network resources. Such problems are noticeable when large file transfers become excessively slow. ANT achieves this goal by merging expert system and modeling techniques.

This paper focuses on the importance of the expert system used by ANT in the troubleshooting process. The next section, "Expert System Description", describes the system itself and addresses the issues of knowledge representation, specialized languages, search technique and relationship to the overall process. The results are presented in the following section, both in terms of implementation and performance. Finally our experience with ANT and the future project directions are outlined in the conclusion.

Expert Systems and Diagnostic Problems

Diagnostic problems lend themselves very well to the use of expert systems. Even when they are very complex, there is generally an existing body of expert knowledge that can be readily exploited. Examples of expert systems capable of troubleshooting network faults abound. For instance, a description of a successful expert system currently operating in networks can be found in [ST88].

Typically, diagnostic expert systems fall into two categories. The first includes systems using "shallow" theories of the domain, generally in the form of heuristic rules associating symptoms with probable faults. In the context of networks, [Mar88] describes a rule-based expert system dealing with physical faults such as noisy lines. Very often these systems have most success in well-defined domains, for example by focusing on certain classes of protocols [Hit88] or certain types of equipment [Lei88].

In the second category we find expert systems based on "deep" theories of the system analyzed, i.e., models of its structure and behavior. These systems deduce the cause of failures by reasoning from first principles. Examples of this technique are common, especially in digital electronics troubleshooting [Dav85, Gen85].

ANT belongs to each category: it uses expert knowledge, represented as heuristic rules, but it also relies on an extensive model of communication, addressing both structure and behavior. The originality of ANT is that it is not an expert system itself: it only uses an expert system to generate a simple model describing the network behavior at a particular time. This model then becomes the focus of the troubleshooting process, which is carried out in a more traditional way using sensitivity analysis [ZE88]. Sensitivity analysis is acceptable only because this simple model can be generated. The number of parameters typically drops from about 150, which is out of reasonable range for the analysis, to less than 10.

EXPERT SYSTEM DESCRIPTION

Architecture

Figure 1 describes the general architecture of the system. The knowledge used by ANT is partitioned into different compartments, each under the supervision of a specialist. The system is regulated by a modeling manager which is in charge of producing the best model for a given situation. A similar specialization of tasks in a diagnostic expert system is described in [Bar85]. During the search, the modeling manager relies on the specialists to form new assumptions, to build the current model, to execute it, and to evaluate it. The specialists can interact with each other when they need information that falls outside of their expertise domain while satisfying a query.

The modeling manager is itself supervised by the troubleshooting manager whose role is to call the modeling manager upon detection of a performance problem, to analyze the model it produces, and to formulate recommendations to fix the problem. The

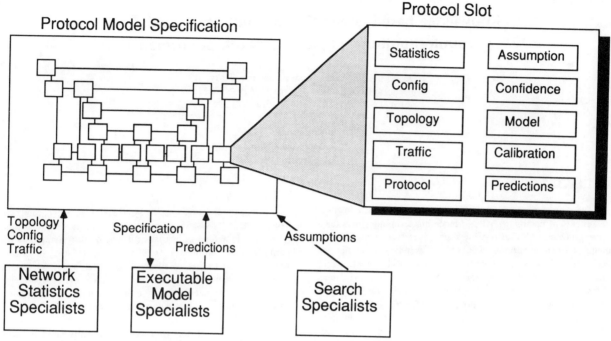

Protocol Model Specification

Protocol Slot

Statistics	Assumption
Config	Confidence
Topology	Model
Traffic	Calibration
Protocol	Predictions

Topology
Config
Traffic

Specification

Predictions

Assumptions

Network Statistics Specialists

Executable Model Specialists

Search Specialists

Figure 1: Model Extraction from Knowledge Base

troubleshooting manager is fairly simple in its current form. We will not describe it further.

There are currently six specialists in ANT:

- The **network topology specialist** maintains and interprets information on network devices and their connections. It has an interface with actual network data.

- The **statistics specialist** is concerned with the collection of network measurements (traffic and response, such as throughput and delay). It also interacts directly with the network (Figure 2).

- The **protocol specialist** deals with abstract protocol knowledge, including hierarchical protocol layering, peer-to-peer interfaces, and services offered by each protocol layer. This specialist needs to interact frequently with the topology specialist: the actual implementation of the X.25 protocol in a given network is represented as a combination of topology and protocol layering knowledge. In addition to this basic abstract knowledge, the protocol specialist also embodies protocol meta-knowledge encoded as rules. These rules allow arbitrary navigation within the protocol layers. For example, tracking down potential faults is achieved through a protocol subspecialist able to "interpret" the protocol layering in a strict hierarchical way.

- The **model specialist** is responsible for the construction of an appropriate model each time the modeling manager needs a new model (Figure 3). It includes a "warehouse" of elementary submodels used as building blocks. A complete model is obtained by linking together these building blocks in a pattern that corresponds to the protocol layers as indicated in Figure 4. The model specialist's task is to ensure that assumptions about fault locations are translated into corresponding models.

- The **heuristic search specialist** encompasses heuristic knowledge from experienced network troubleshooters. The encoded rules relate network measurements to potential fault locations.

Knowledge Representation

The knowledge representation vehicle in the ANT system is based on first-order predicate logic. Elementary components of the knowledge base are either **simple relationships** or **rules**, mainly expressed as Horn clauses. The use of Logic Programming makes it possible to reduce procedural knowledge to a strict minimum with the huge benefit of producing a system that can be maintained and developed for the most part by domain experts. Expert knowledge can be entered declaratively, without specific order and without dependency on the rest of the knowledge base. Procedural knowledge is mainly restricted to the inference engine and the user-interface code.

Below are some examples of simple relationships, preceded by comments:

```
/* length of the netaa packet: 160 bits (globally) */
config(netaa_length, global, 160).
```

```
/* node n88 is next node after node n89 */
next_node(n88, n89).
```

Rules have many different patterns in the system. Here are examples from three different specialists:

```
/* Troubleshooting rule:
If the first subnet link utilization is low (< 30%), the model for the
service offered by the physical layer to the level 2 trunk layer (data
side) can be simplified */
for [topology(source_node(Ns)), topology(subnet_link(1,data,L))]:
```

126

if (utilization(L) < 0.30) then
simplify [(service(out,trunk_l2,physical,Ns), data)].

/* Topology rule:
A source link is a physical link connecting a source host and a
source node */
source_link(L) :-
    source_host(H),
    source_node(N),
    physical_link(H, N, _, L).

/* Calibration rule:
For any link, the data packet length on that link is the sum of the
data length and the data header */
for [topology(link(L))] :
data_packet_length(L) := data_length(L) + data_header(L).

In addition to regular rules, the knowledge base also contains some **meta-rules** that can operate on these basic rules. One good example occurs with the calibration formulas which are used to dimension submodels according to traffic measurements and network configuration parameters, such as line speeds, timers, and packet component sizes.

Calibration formulas are introduced in the knowledge base as part of the expert knowledge, but they need to be interpreted in different ways according to the situation. For example, when building a model, the model specialist needs the value of each calibration parameter used by the model. When analyzing a given model, the troubleshooting manager needs to know which parameters in the calibration formulas are tunable. Therefore the knowledge base is equipped with special interpreters that deliver various information about the calibration formulas. As an example this toplevel rule evaluates a formula:
value(Var, V) :-
    for Defs : Var := Expression,
    definitions(Defs),
    value(Expression, Val),
    V is Val, !.

Specialized Languages

The ANT project makes extensive use of specialized languages, or **little languages**, as termed by J. Aho ("Languages and Their Compilers", talk at MIT, 4/21/88), so that non-programmers can introduce their own knowledge into the system in a natural way, thus achieving complete separation between the knowledge and its use. In addition, these languages are as independent as possible, so that several persons can enter their knowledge into the system or write dedicated interface programs, knowing little or nothing about other expertise domains.

ANT uses Prolog operators [CM84] as an efficient way of interpreting expert and user knowledge and storing it as Horn clauses.

Below is a list of the domains for which user-accessible little languages were devised along with some examples.

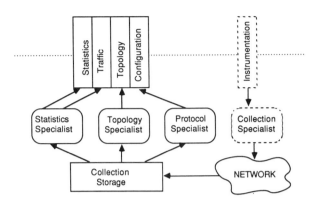

Figure 2: Network Statistics Specialists

Case-specific knowledge. Three separate languages allow users to enter specific or generic relationships to describe the network topology, the formatted statistics, and the configuration parameters. Below are examples in each category:

- **Topology language** (example of a specific relationship):
  source host h3 attached_to node n88.

- **Measurement language:**
  for node n88: packet_rate := 2.7.

- **Configuration language** (example of a generic relationship):
  for any_node: fast_tick := 0.0256.

Expert knowledge. Three languages help represent protocol, submodels, and troubleshooting expertise. Combined with the declarative style of the knowledge base architecture, these languages make it possible for different experts to increment the knowledge base independently. It should be noted however that one of them, the protocol language, is referred to by the other two. Following is an overview of these languages:

- **Protocol language:** This language allows an expert to describe multiple protocol layers (as in the OSI model) as a set of elementary building blocks, or protocol slots. Slots belong to one of the categories:

  - processing units

  - services (offered by one layer to another)

  - peer-to-peer interfaces, which can be either physical for the bottom layer, or logical for all others

The complete set of connections between these slots is derived from their description by a specialized protocol model interpreter, and does not have to be stated explicitly by the expert. Here are some examples of statements about protocol slots:

sending processing_unit (layer x25_l3, at source_host).
service (from x25_l2 to local_l3, at source_node).
interface (layer x25_l2, from source_host to source_node).

- **Submodel language**: This language describes the warehouse of submodels. As described previously, submodels are associated with protocol slots. Each slot is represented by one out of several submodels, whose number depends on the level of detail available for that particular slot. In the current system, there are only one detailed and one simple model available for each slot. The submodel language associates submodels with their position in the protocol, and describes their form according to the level of detail. Since simple models have no effect on the input they receive, they are not described explicitly, as detailed models are. The detailed submodels in the current system are **queue** or **delay** models.

  Here is an example of the statement expressing the detailed model for the physical link between the source host and the source node as a delay model with a service time:

  detailed model for
  interface (physical, from source_host to source_node):
  delay with service_time.

- **Troubleshooting language**: This language serves two purposes. The first is to help formalize expert knowledge on network troubleshooting. The second is to ease the transfer from the expert to the knowledge base. Each rule describes a set of conditions which the expert recognizes as characteristic of some abnormal network behavior, and associates with these conditions the level of detail the expert recommends for an appropriate subset of the model. Since submodels are either simple or detailed, the expert's recommendation, when a given pattern is recognized, is a list of submodels, some to be simplified and others to be detailed.

  An interpreted version of a troubleshooting rule was given in the knowledge representation subsection. Here is the user version of the same rule:

  if (utilization(subnet_link(1, data side) < 0.30)
  then simplify
  [(service(from physical to trunk_l2, at source_node),
  data side)].

Search Technique

The search mechanism, or inference engine, is designed to produce a simple model in a minimum amount of time. The process is composed of two phases: **pattern matching** and **model simplification**.

Pattern Matching. During this phase, all heuristic troubleshooting expertise encoded in the knowledge base is applied. When a pattern can be matched among the data, the action part of the rule is carried out. It produces an assumption marking for each protocol slot mentioned. A slot marked with the assumption "simple" means the bottleneck does not occur in this slot according to the expert's encoded opinion, whereas a slot marked with the assumption "detailed" suggests this slot could be a bottleneck.

Since several rules may be applied that would mark the same slot with possibly different conclusions, the marking is in fact a degree of evidence toward simplification. A rule leaning toward simplification increases the degree of evidence, initially set at 0, because no opinion has been formed yet, whereas a rule suggesting a detailed model decreases it.

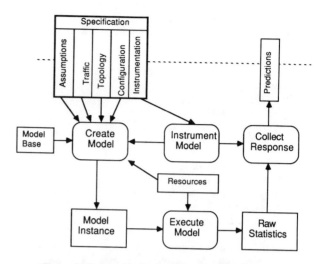

Figure 3: Executable Performance Model Specialist

This process mimics the way an expert would build a first impression when considering the network performance and the measurements at hand, except that here it is done more thoroughly.

Model Simplification. The use of heuristic knowledge is only one part of the process. During the next phase, the actual model simplification is carried out in a systematic way, using a trial-and-error approach which exploits the hierarchical structure of the problem.

The process starts by executing the full model in its most detailed version, in order to ensure that the network behavior can be reproduced. Two criteria are used to confirm the model's accuracy: the predicted delay along the path considered and the predicted network throughput must be close enough to the measured values (10% for throughput and 30% for delay [LZGS84]).

Once we are sure that at least the most complicated model can predict the network behavior, we start simplifying it. The simplification proceeds in a top-down manner from the highest protocol layers to the lowest ones. The hierarchy can be described as follows. Processing units (the boxes in Figure 4) and services between layers (the vertical lines) are terminal elements in the tree. Peer-to-peer interfaces (the horizontal lines) are non-terminal nodes in the tree (except for the physical interfaces). They stand for everything below them including the service offered to the processing units located at each end of the interface.

Each simplification cycle focuses on all the components at one layer, resulting from the expansion of a logical peer-to-peer interface at the layer immediately above. The idea is to try some assumptions about simplification of these components, generate the corresponding model, run it, and exploit the results. If the model still predicts the behavior, the assumptions are validated. We then proceed to the first logical interface that needs to be detailed at the current layer, and we expand it. If the model is inaccurate, we review the assumptions and start again.

128

Validating an assumption means that if the submodel for that particular component was detailed, then the detailed version will be kept in the final model. A simple submodel is validated the same way, but, in addition, simplification of a logical interface is propagated to all the protocol slots implementing that interface.

The first assumptions exploit the pattern matching results by following their recommendations. If the assumptions need to be reviewed, then only one element at a time is modeled as simple and tested. If the resulting model is inaccurate, the detailed model for that component is validated. For each layer, the search proceeds breadth-first. But each exploration of a logical interface proceeds depth-first.

At the end, the model simplification yields a confirmed marking for each slot in the protocol layering, therefore producing a complete specification of the executable model.

Integration into the Overall Troubleshooting Process

Given a set of network measurements, the troubleshooting manager uses the expert system previously described to generate the specification of a simple executable model of the network behavior. Once this model is known, it is analyzed using a technique called **sensitivity analysis**.

Each parameter of the complete model is in turn slightly modified and the effect observed on the predicted network throughput. The **sensitivity** of each parameter is defined as: percent increase in throughput divided by percent increase in parameter, for small (10%) parameter variations. A sensitivity of 1 means that throughput is very sensitive to the parameter, of 0 that it is not sensitive at all, and of -1 that it is adversely sensitive (in other words, the parameter would have to be decreased).

The final output of the troubleshooting process is a list of all relevant network parameters, found by the expert system, with their sensitivity to throughput. The analyst can now decide which parameter achieves the best compromise in terms of throughput increase and economic feasibility. For example, some parameters such as line bandwidth may bring the best results, but may be expensive and/or difficult to change.

RESULTS

Implementation

The system was implemented in Prolog, mainly because first-order predicate logic is a well-defined mathematical support for knowledge representation. The search mechanism is currently encoded using a procedural view of Prolog. However, further work on this system will include a formalization of the meta-rules governing the search in order to allow users to modify them at will.

The Prolog language was also chosen for the ease it provides in building rapid prototypes: it allowed us to develop in a short time and in a concise manner very sophisticated features, for example multiple interpreters for the calibration formulas. The prototype as it stands now represents about 6 man-months of work.

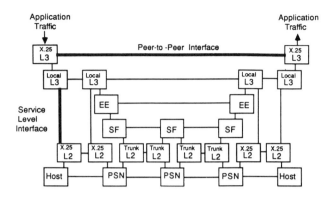

Figure 4: X.25 Protocol Hierarchy

The language portability was abundantly exploited: ANT was developed concurrently on Symbolics Lisp machines and on a VAX with the same version running on either of these machines. A single switch was devised to turn on or off the user-interface facilities specifically developed for the Lisp machine. In addition, the same system version has been successfully ported to an IBM-PC. Porting time is on the order of an hour for standard Prolog implementations.

Performance

The ANT prototype was designed to detect throughput bottlenecks in very simple networks. It was tested on a laboratory network which was intentionally misconfigured in several ways. In each case ANT was able to converge on the solution within a few minutes with Symbolics-Prolog and to suggest all the corrective measures that were expected. The search space that was explored when looking for the simple model contained over 2^{30} combinations.

If we include the time necessary to prepare the input to the system from raw data directly measured on the network, the total time spent to troubleshoot the network is systematically on the order of an hour. This compares very favorably to the estimated time a performance analyst would spent on this type of problem, which could take as long as several weeks.

CONCLUSION AND FUTURE WORK

The ANT project was initially conceived as a feasibility study. It has been very successful at demonstrating how AI and modeling techniques can be closely integrated to produce a powerful troubleshooting system. The approach, which consists in generating an executable performance model of the faulty system with the help of an expert system, is very general and can easily be applied to any domain where hierarchically-structured models are readily available.

ANT's encouraging results have generated a lot of interest for the approach. Work is currently underway to produce a faster system, to integrate the whole debugging cycle from problem detection to problem correction, and to extend the number and type of performance problems that can be solved automatically for arbitrary topologies and traffic patterns. In addition another heuristic specialist will be added in order to devise the best troubleshooting strategy given the recommendations of the current system and a set of economic constraints. In the long-term, ANT is destined to support automatic capacity management in networks.

REFERENCES

References

[Bar85]   Eric Barrielle. Applications des Techniques de l'Intelligence Artificielle au Diagnostic de défauts des Circuits Imprimés. Ecole Nationale Supérieure des Télécommunications, December 1985. Doctor of Engineering Thesis.

[CM84]   William F. Clocksin and Christopher S. Mellish. *Programming in Prolog*. Springer-Verlag, second edition, 1984.

[Dav85]   Randall Davis. *Qualitative Reasoning about Physcial Systems*, chapter Diagnostic Reasoning Based on Structure and Behavior, pages 347–410. MIT Press, 1985.

[Gen85]   Michael R. Genesereth. *Qualitative Reasoning about Physcial Systems*, chapter The Use of Design Descriptions in Automated Diagnosis, pages 411–436. MIT Press, 1985.

[Hit88]   Bruce Hitson. Knowledge-Based Monitoring and Control: An Approach to Understanding the Behavior of TCP/IP Network Protocols. In *SIGCOMM*, ACM, August 1988.

[Lei88]   Melisse Leib. *Intelligent Gateway Troubleshooter*. ANM Technical Note 7, BBN, April 1988.

[LZGS84] Edward D. Lazowska, John Zahorjan, G. Scott Graham, and Kenneth C. Sevcik. *Quantitative System Performance*. Prentice-Hall, 1984.

[Mar88]   Todd E. Marques. A Symptom-Driven Expert System for Isolating and Correcting Network Faults. *IEEE Communications Magazine*, 6–13, March 1988.

[ST88]   William Sayles and Jack Thomas. Finding and Fixing Network Faults with an Expert System. *Data Communications*, 149–165, June 1988.

[ZE88]   John A. Zinky and Joshua Etkin. Troubleshooting Computer Network Performance using Executable Models. Submitted to Networks and ISDN, August 1988.

[ZF89]   John A. Zinky and Jean-Louis Fléchon. An Automated Network Troubleshooter for Throughput Bottlenecks in Computer Networks. Submitted to AI in Government Conference, 1989.

Simulation and AI, 1989
©1989 by the Society for Computer
Simulation International
ISBN 0-911801-44-8

Analysis of the delay behavior of synchronous state machines in the context of their intended use

Angela Sutton

Department of Engineering, University of Aberdeen, Aberdeen, AB9 2UE, Scotland *and*
Schlumberger Technologies Laboratory, 3340 Hillview Ave., Palo Alto, CA 94304
Sutton@spar.slb.com

Abstract

Exhaustive circuit simulation is both expensive and may exercise impossible paths and mutually impossible streams of transitions that could not occur during the circuit's actual use. An investigation of the speed of a circuit may therefore find the slowest path to be one that could not occur in practice; In such a case, the estimate of the worst-case delay through the circuit would be pessimistic.

In this paper we describe a system which is capable of overcoming these problems and of performing only that simulation which is necessary in order to deduce a synchronous state machine's worst case delay and critical path. We do so by performing simulation in the context of a state machine's intended use, and by maintaining full data-dependency.

Data-dependency considerations, although somewhat expensive, are important; They account for the fact that the logical transitions that occur at the outputs of gates that are connected in series are sometimes mutually exclusive, and thus for the fact that the slowest transition of EVERY gate's output along a path cannot necessarily occur when a stream of data is propagated down that path. Additionally, a less pessimistic and less expensive speed estimate can be obtained if we do not simulate the affect of propagating data that will not occur during the machine's use. We can further prune our simulation by considering the Boolean functionality of the gates comprising the state machine and by identifying previous simulation results that can be re-used.

1 INTRODUCTION

We describe a system which obtains an estimate of the worst-case delay behavior of a synchronous state machine circuit and which utilizes knowledge of the state machine's intended use as a means both of obtaining a less pessimistic speed estimate and of pinpointing the critical path more accurately.

Our timing simulation process can be summarized as follows:

1. Separate the logic of the state machine into groups (which we call *"logic blocks"*), each of which is responsible for driving a flip-flop or primary output of the machine.

2. Algorithmically generate only those input stimuli*, to each logic block, that can occur during its normal use. Only the input stimuli, so generated, need be used to drive our simulator.

3. Perform simulation which maintains FULL data-dependency.

Our consideration of the circuit's behavior ensures that our simulator propagates only that data which can occur during the circuit's normal use. Knowledge of the following is used to infer only those transitions that can occur at the gate outputs, and affords a means both of maintaining full dependency and of pruning the simulation:

- Boolean functionality of the individual logic gates
- Gate connectivity
- Signal directionality

---

*logical transitions that can occur simultaneously at a logic block's inputs

We will describe the algorithm responsible for generating the input stimuli to our simulator and will compare the total number of input stimuli that we expect to yield with the number that we would have used, had we performed exhaustive simulation.

The simulation is effected using our so-called "history-based" algorithm. The history of a gate port is the complete set of {time-of-transition-of-port-signal, logical-value-of-signal-after-transition} pairs that describes the port's behavior during a given clock cycle of the state machine. We further define the "history-of-interest" of a port to be that part of the port's history which we have not established cannot have an impact upon the primary-output. The mechanism for deriving the history-of-interest will be described and is a technique by which we can achieve significant pruning of the number of simulation calculations that we need perform. We also describe the complete circuit simulation algorithm.

2 THE NEED FOR DATA-DEPENDENCY AND USE-CONSIDERATIONS

Data-dependent timing analysis takes account of the dependency between the *direction of the transitions* that can occur at the outputs of gates that are interconnected, when data is propagated through those gates. It is important to do so because the speed of a transition at a gate's ports depends upon the *direction* of that transition. Such data-dependent analysis also takes account of the *direction in which data may propagate* through circuit components, thus preventing impossible signal paths (e.g. impossible paths backwards through a gate) from being exercised.

Moreover, it is important that we simulate the affect of propagating actual *data* through the circuit for two reasons:

1. Spurious intermediate gate outputs (hazards) may occur in response to spurious input data. Hazards contribute a delay, yet their occurrence at a particular gate's output cannot be predicted from knowledge of the logical transitions occurring at the logic block's primary inputs and a Boolean equation describing that gate's output in terms of the logic block's primary inputs.

2. In some gate architectures, transitions are effected by conducting current through transistors lying on parallel paths[†], and the speed of a transition in a given direction can depend upon how many gate inputs support the transition by turning or holding the parallel transistor paths ON.

Both the number of gate inputs supporting a transition and the presence of hazards can only be deduced from the actual values and times of arrival of the gate input data.

Static (data-independent) timing estimators do not propagate data. They can make safe speed estimates only by making the false assumption that all gates always exhibit their longest delay. The result is a pessimistic worst-case delay estimate and possibly a false critical path. Since static timing estimators perform no data propagation, they are unable to exploit the existence of impossible input stimuli. Hence it would be impossible to render a static timing analyzer use-dependent. Examples of such analyzers include STA (Murphy *et al.* 1985), MTA

[†]True of many CMOS gates

(Hofmann and Kim 1987), DASP (Toyoshima *et al.* 1986), TI-LOS (Fishburn and Dunlop 1985), Timing Analyzer (Hitchcock 1982).

The effectiveness of Min-Max speed estimation (Miczo 1986) relies upon the assumption that some gates contribute a non-zero minimum delay. This is incorrect because any gate whose output does not change in response to its logic block's primary input stimulus effectively contributes no delay because the gate's output is immediately stable.

A less pessimistic speed estimate results if we consider data-dependencies. Timing estimators such as Crystal (Ousterhout 1983) (Ousterhout 1984) (Ousterhout 1986), the work of Benkowski (Benkoski *et al.* 1987), TV (Jouppi 1983b) (Jouppi 1983a), do so to a limited extent, but have little appreciation of the circuit's intended use; None has an automatic means of determining the circuit's valid input stimuli. Some allow the user to manually specify impossible paths but, unlike our simulator, none detects these paths automatically.

2.1 USE-CONSIDERATIONS

Whereas data-dependent analysis is significantly more accurate than static analysis, both fail to fully account for the intended use of the circuit. If the worst-case delay that they compute corresponds to the propagation of impossible data through a circuit then it follows that such a speed estimate will be pessimistic.

Significant work in the domain of circuit use consideration has been performed by Brand (Brand and Iyengar 1986b) (Brand and Iyengar 1986a). Brand's timing analyzer can deduce the interrelationships of any signals in the circuit that have a common source and can use this information to eliminate some non-functional paths. Unlike our system, this system uses static timing analysis, and impossible input stimuli cannot therefore be accounted for. The intended use of a circuit has also been exploited in the work of (Shirley 1986) and (Bryant 1988) for the purpose of test pattern generation.

3 STATE MACHINE SIMULATION

To perform synchronous state machine simulation, we first partition the state machine logic into *logic blocks*, as depicted in Figure 1. We then determine the possible input stimuli to each logic block, and use these input stimuli to drive our data-dependent simulator.

We estimate the speed of each logic block, using the ideas presented in Sections 4.1, 5.3 and 5.2 to achieve some pruning of the search space of {network path, input stimuli} pairs that need be traversed.

4 POSSIBLE INPUT STIMULI

4.1 Number Of Possible Input Stimuli

Consider the logic block of Figure 1(a) with n primary inputs, f of which are feedback inputs and e of which are external inputs. Hence the number of potential input stimuli is:

$$n = e + f \tag{1}$$

Without any consideration of the intended use of the logic block, we would consider the total number, C_{pot}, of potential transition combinations* to be given by the product of the number of potential input combinations, 2^n, and the number of different input combinations, 2^n-1, that each input combination could change to. Hence:

$$C_{pot} = 2^n(2^n - 1) = 2^{2(e+f)} - 2^{e+f} \tag{2}$$

In a state machine, only certain *valid present state to next state transitions* can occur. The factors which constrain the total number of ways that valid state changes can be induced are the *number of*:

1. *valid feedback input combinations*, **N**, which is also equal to the total number of states of the machine.

2. *valid external input combinations*, **E**.

---
*i.e., the number of input stimuli

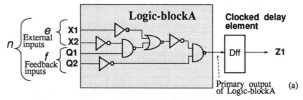

(a)

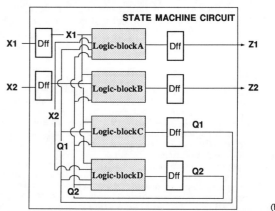

(b)

Figure 1: A state machine circuit and one of its logic blocks. The logic block has n inputs, e of which are external inputs and f of which are feedback inputs.

3. *self loops that can occur when the machine is initially in a valid state*. A *self loop* is an occasion where no state change occurs when a certain external input combination is applied. We define $k(st)$ to be the number of self loops that occur when a finite state machine is initially in state st.

In (Sutton 1989), we show that, for any logic-block of a state machine, the number of input stimuli is given by C_g:

$$C_g = NE^2 - \sum_{st=1}^{N} k(st) \tag{3}$$

Note that the above parameters are bound as follows:
$$1 \leq N \leq 2^f \qquad 0 \leq E \leq 2^e \qquad 0 \leq k(st) \leq E$$
and hence the maximum value of Equation 3 is given by $C_{g,max}$:

$$C_{g,max} = 2^{f+2e} \tag{4}$$

For a state machine, $C_{g,max}$ can be no greater than the number, C_{pot}, of potential input stimuli expressed in Equation 2.

4.2 Determination Of Input Stimuli

In the previous section, we saw that the *number* of input stimuli to be used to drive our simulator can be dramatically reduced by taking each logic block's intended use into account. We derive the input stimuli that could occur during the circuit's normal use from the finite state machine's behavioral specification: a state table.

Consider the state table depicted by Table 1(a). We determine each possible input stimulus:

$$(e1, f1) \longrightarrow (e2, f2) \tag{5}$$

This change in the inputs of a logic block is illustrated in Figure 2. The prefixes, e and f denote external inputs and feedback inputs respectively. If st is a state currently under consideration, $(e1, f1)$ are those values of the inputs which cause the state machine to adopt a state st from any of its

(a)

Present state		Next state caused by e			
State	State code	e=00	e=01	e=10	e=11
1	00	1	1	2	2
2	01	1	1	3	3
3	11	2	1	**4**	3
4	10	**3**	**2**	**3**	**1**

(b)

Present state		Next state caused by e		e1	
State	State code	e=00	e=01	e=10	e=11
1	00	1	1	2	2
2	01	1	1	3	3
3	**f1** 11	2	1	④	3
4	10	**3**	**2**	**3**	**1**

Achieve state *st*

(c)

Present state		Next state	e2 caused by e		
State	State code	e=00	e=01	e=10	e=11
1	00	1	1	2	2
2	01	1	1	3	3
3	11	2	1	**4**	3
4	**f2** 10	**3**	②	**3**	**1**

Change state from state *st* to one of *st*'s next states

Table 1: Determination of a possible input stimulus.

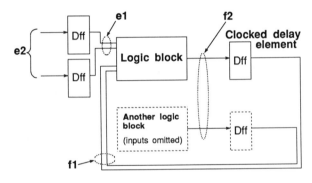

Figure 2: An input stimulus $(e1, f1) \longrightarrow (e2, f2)$ occurs when the clocked delay elements are clocked.

valid present states (either a different state or the same state, *st*). (e2, f2) are the inputs which cause the state machine to change its state *from* state *st* to any of its valid next states.

Table 1(b) shows the procedure for deducing a particular (e1, f1) when the state, *st*, under consideration is state 4.

1. We first locate an *st* entry (i.e. a **4** entry) in the "next state caused by e" portion of the state table.

2. (e1, f1) are the logic block inputs that lead to the occurrence of this entry (i.e., lead to the state machine's arrival in state *st*). Hence:

   • *e1* is the set of external inputs that heads the column in which the entry appears, i.e. **e1=10**

   • *f1* is the set of feedback inputs that encodes the 'present state' lying in the same row as the entry, i.e. **f1=the state code of state 3 = 11**

(e2, f2) are the logic block inputs which cause state *st* to be exited or cause a self loop back to state *st*. Hence we must consider the conditions under which, if *st* were the present

state, the state machine could change state or could self-loop. Table 1(c) depicts one such situation.

The steps that are then taken to determine (e2, f2) are as follows:

1. Detect a situation in the state table for which state *st* is the present state by locating the state table row in which *st* is the present state, i.e., the row whose present state is 4.

2. Consider a valid transition from state *st* to any one of the next states, i.e., a transition from state 4 to, say, state 2 *.

3. (e2, f2) are the logic block inputs which cause the transition from state 4 to state 2. Hence:

   • *e2* is the set of external inputs that heads the column in which the 'next state'=2 entry appears, i.e., **e2=01**

   • *f2* is the set of feedback inputs that encodes the current 'present state', state *st*, i.e. **f2=the state code of state *st* = state code of 4 = 10**

Bearing the above procedure in mind, a formal definition of *e1, f1, e2* and *f2* is:

(e1, f1) = Logic block inputs that cause the state machine to attain state *st*.

e1 = The binary value of external inputs that leads to a next-state entry of value *st* in the state table.

f1 = The state code of the present-state that leads to a 'next state' entry, *st*, in the state table. This is the 'present state' of the row where *st*'s state table entry appears.

(e2, f2) = Valid logic block inputs when *st* is the present state, i.e., the logic block inputs which cause the state machine either to exit state *st* or to self-loop back to the same state *st*.

e2 = Binary value of external inputs which leads to a transition from the state *st* to one of its next states.

f2 = State code of the state *st*.

An input stimulus only occurs if at least one logic block undergoes a transition, i.e., if:

$$e1 \neq e2 \text{ and/or } f1 \neq f2 \qquad (6)$$

The overall algorithm for determining all $(e1, f1) \longrightarrow (e2, f2)$ transitions that can occur during a logic block's normal use is as follows and is exemplified by the table entries marked in bold type in Table 1(a).

For each state (*st*) e.g. state 4
  For each entry *st* in the next-state portion of the table
    e.g. the 4 in the present-state=3 row
    Let e1 = value of *e* heading the column in which the entry appears e.g. **e1=10**
      f1 = state code of the present state of the row in which the entry appears e.g. **state code of state 3**
  l1 = list of (e1, f1) combinations.
    e.g. ((10, 3's state code))
  For each *next-state* of *st* e.g. next-states=3,2,3,1
  Let e2 = value of *e* heading a next-state's respective column
    e.g. when *next-state* =3 then e2 =00
        when *next-state* =2 then e2 =01
        when *next-state* =3 then e2 =10
        when *next-state* =1 then e2 =11
    f2 = state code of *st* e.g. 4's state code = 10.
  l2 = list of (e2, f2) combinations
    e.g. ((00, 4's state code) (01, 4's state code) (10, 4's state code)(11, 4's state code))
Pair each member of l1 with each member of l2.
Eliminate pairs for which no inputs change.

In the example, the process of pairing each member of l1 with each member of l2 produces the following transitions of $(e1, f1) \longrightarrow (e2, f2)$ when *st*=4:

(10, 3's state code) $\longrightarrow$ (00, 4's state code)
(10, 3's state code) $\longrightarrow$ (01, 4's state code)
(10, 3's state code) $\longrightarrow$ (10, 4's state code)
(10, 3's state code) $\longrightarrow$ (11, 4's state code)

---

* we could have chosen a transition to state 1 or to either one of the two instances of state 3, in which case, (e2, f2) would be different. It should be noted that, since there are four next state columns in the state table, there are four valid (e2, f2) pairs for each (e1, f1) pair.

Valid transitions $(e1, f1) \longrightarrow (e2, f2)$ involve (e, f) pairs for which Equation 6 holds. All of the four transitions above abide by Equation 6 and are therefore valid transitions.

5 HISTORY-BASED SIMULATION WITH PRUNING

We have considered the number of *input stimuli* that can occur during the use of the logic blocks of a state machine. We could, at this point, perform delay analysis by simulating the behavior of each logic block when each one of its valid input stimuli is applied. However, this may involve multiple evaluations of the same delays associated with certain parts of their networks of gates. Moreover, one of the inputs of a gate, G, can, in certain circumstances, block the effects of G's other inputs. In such situations, we can eliminate from the analysis the network feeding the other inputs of G, reasoning that their action cannot influence the *time* at which G's final output transition or the logic block's final primary output transition occurs.

5.1 Sensitive inputs and the Dominant Logic Value
We now define the terms *Dominant logic value* and *Sensitive input*. These terms were introduced in the paper (Abramovici et al. 1983) on fault detection. We found them to be useful in the domain of timing analysis because they allowed us to describe the conditions under which a gate's final output transition occurred.

We say that a gate input X is sensitive if, by complementing its logical value, we cause the gate output to change.

*For a given gate, the dominant logic value (DLV) is the logical value that a gate input X must adopt in order to render the gate output independent of the the logical value of all of the other inputs. Note that the same gate input X will only be sensitive if all other inputs to the gate have value $\overline{DLV}$. * Certain types of gate (e.g. inverters) have no DLV.*

Boolean function of gate	Dominant Logic Value	Logical value of output when an input adopts Dominant Logic Value
NAND	0	1
AND	0	0
NOR	1	0
OR	1	1
NOT	None	Not applicable

Table 2: The Dominant Logic Value of some types of logic gate.

Table 2 shows the dominant logic value (DLV) of several types of logic gates. It also indicates the value that the gate output will adopt when a single input attains the DLV.[†] We utilize the DLV concept to justify pruning our simulation.

5.2 Subpath Elimination Using A Sensitized Path Technique
Our timing analysis technique involves the calculation of cumulative delays along paths within logic blocks. *We will define the cumulative delay of a gate output to be the delay from the time that the logic block's primary inputs first begin to change, to the time that the gate output attains its stable value.* The cumulative delay, t_{cum}, associated with the output of a gate is also given by:

$$t_{cum} = \text{(Time that the last gate input transition to affect the output completes)} +$$
$$\text{(Delay of gate output's final transition)} \quad (7)$$

When calculating the cumulative delay associated with a particular gate output, we are therefore only interested in the time that the last input transition to affect the output completes.

---
[*]because, if one of those other inputs were of value DLV, then it would itself block the affects of X, automatically rendering X insensitive. $\overline{DLV}$ denotes the logical inverse of DLV.

[†]For such an output *transition* to occur, all other inputs must have had a value $\overline{DLV}$.

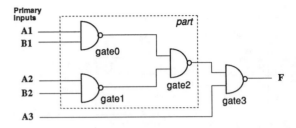

Figure 3: A circuit for which we can avoid the multiple evaluation of the delays incurred by gates within a region, *part*.

In circuits comprising logic gates we can, under certain conditions, deduce an upper bound to this completion time, before the particular gate's input histories are all known. We term the upper bound to the completion time the cut-off time of the gate.

The cut-off time, symbolized by t_{cutoff}, of a gate G is the time of completion of the transition at one of its inputs that would cause its output to attain a stable value, if that output has not attained a stable value already. The cut-off time is the earliest time 'known so far' that an input transition would cause the output to stabilize. The cut-off time is dynamically updated as more information about G's input histories are deduced.

We update the cut-off time if any of the conditions below is satisfied, because each condition would cause the gate output to stabilize, if it is not subsequently found to have done so already.

1. X undergoes its final transition $\overline{DLV} \longrightarrow$ DLV and all other known gate inputs have a logical value of $\overline{DLV}$.

2. X undergoes an intermediate transition $\overline{DLV} \longrightarrow$ DLV at a time when all other known gate inputs have a logical value of $\overline{DLV}$. Before X's logical value reverts to $\overline{DLV}$, some other input(s) adopt(s) and retains the DLV up until the time when all inputs have stabilized. We will refer to this situation as a **DLV continuum**.

A more general algorithm, *prune-input-subpaths*, is responsible for curbing the investigation of the behavior of the other inputs feeding a gate G at times later than that at which the last input transition to affect the output occurs. The algorithm is defined as follows:

When a transition occurs at an input to a gate G at time t and causes the output of G to undergo a transition to a stable value, then that input is declared to be the last input of G to affect the output of G and all transitions occurring in the paths, $\{P\}$, feeding the other inputs of G need no longer be analyzed if they occur at a time $> t$.

5.3 Avoiding multiple evaluation of paths

Gate	External input name	IS1	IS2
gate0	A1	$0 \longrightarrow 1$	$0 \longrightarrow 1$
	B1	1	1
gate1	A2	1	1
	B2	0	0
gate3	A3	$0 \longrightarrow 1$	1

Table 3: Two input stimuli to the circuit of Figure 3. Note that the subset of input stimuli that form inputs to gate0 and gate1 are the same for both.

We analyze the delay response of each logic-block to each of its valid input stimuli. When analyzing the impact of a particular input stimulus, we may sometimes re-use some of the results that we obtained previously from the analysis of the impact of a another input stimulus.

Some subset, S, of the logic block's input stimulus may be identical to that of one of its other input stimuli. Suppose S drives a particular part, *part* of the logic block. We economize effort by avoiding multiple evaluations of the delay associated with the gates comprising *part*. For example, suppose *part* of Figure 3 is driven, in turn, by each of the two sets of valid input stimuli, IS1 and IS2, described in Table 3.

In both sets, *gate0*'s and *gate1*'s joint input stimuli are identical and both the associated history*, {H}, describing the transitions that occur within *part*, and the delay between the primary inputs and *gate2*'s output, *D*, need only be calculated once for the two input stimuli.

For the collection of input stimuli {IS1, IS2}, we avoid the multiple evaluation of subpaths driving *gate2*'s output by caching the cumulative delay, *D*, and history, {H}, that result from their common {A1,B1,A2,B2} stimuli.

5.4 History-Based Simulation Algorithm

Our history-based algorithm performs data-dependent timing analysis. It prunes all transition calculations that it has determined need not be calculated any more, i.e., it prunes those logical transitions that occur later than the cut-off times of the gates that they drive. The algorithm performs the delay-behavior-caching of intermediate results that can be re-used, an idea presented in Section 5.3. It also calculates, stores and uses *histories* of the logical transitions that occur within each logic block at each of the gate inputs and outputs.

We will define the **history** *of a gate port to be the list of* {*Time-at-which-node-first-adopted-logical-value, logical-Value*} *pairs* (Henceforth referred to as (T, V) pairs) *that occur at that port during a given clock cycle. The history of a port fully describes the time and direction of all of the transitions that occur at that port during that clock cycle. The* (T,V) *pairs are chronologically-ordered and the first* (T,V) *pair,* (T_1, V_1), *states the initial value of a port at the beginning of the analysis. Hence the history of a port that remains stable when an input stimulus is applied to its logic block's primary inputs is specified by a list:* $((T_1, V_1))$.

Of course, for a given primary input stimulus, not all transitions within a logic block have an impact upon cumulative delay of the primary outputs.

We therefore further define the **history-of-interest** *of a gate input or output port to be the part of the history which we have not established cannot have an impact on the logic block's output history.*

Our algorithm propagates each input stimulus through a logic block by generating the history-of-interest of each gate's output port from the history-of-interest of that gate's inputs. A gate output's history-of-interest can be computed only when sufficient information about its inputs' histories (i.e., their histories-of-interest) are known. The algorithm recognizes the conditions under which the gate output can no longer change in response to an input change (the *prune-input-subpaths* algorithm). The history-based algorithm maintains a queue of *gates* for which the output history can now be computed without error.

Our history-based algorithm will be described with reference to the example of Figure 4. We will see that the *prune-input-subpaths* algorithm can sometimes be applied, and that we can easily avoid the multiple evaluation of certain subpaths which have the same subset of primary input stimuli. The pseudocode for the history-based algorithm is then listed.

With respect to the circuit of Figure 4, the history-based simulation algorithm proceeds as follows:

1. For each logic block, select a primary input stimulus from the valid stimuli generated by the technique described in Section 4.2. Suppose the logic block output is *Y1*.

2. Compute the histories of all logic block primary inputs.

3. Initialize the queue to be a list of gates whose input histories are all known. Hence all gates that are driven only by the primary inputs of the logic-block are placed on the queue; Suppose that the queue is:

    (gate2 gate1 gate3)

4. Compute the history-of-interest of the output of the first gate of the queue, namely that of NOR gate *gate2*'s output

*The idea of a history of the dynamic behavior of a gate input or output is described more fully in Section 5.4

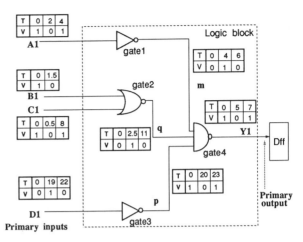

Figure 4: A logic block which illustrates the history-based speed estimation algorithm.

q. The cut-off time of *gate2* is 8ns because *gate2*'s input, *C1*, stabilizes to *gate2*'s DLV at that time. The history-of-interest of *gate2*'s output is generated from the complete histories-of-interest of its inputs. The stable output of *gate2* is first achieved at a time $t = 11ns$ and forms an input *q* to *gate4*. Since the analysis of *gate2* is complete, we remove its name from the queue.

5. The history-of-interest of *q* allows us to establish that an input, namely *q*, to the NAND gate, *gate4*, achieves a stable value of the DLV of that NAND gate at a time $t=11ns$. The cut-off time of *gate4* is therefore updated to 11ns.

6. The histories-of-interest of the inputs *m* and *p* of *gate4* are not yet known. Hence we cannot yet place *gate4* on the queue.

7. The next gate in the queue is *gate1*. Gate1's output, *m*, stabilizes to the DLV of *gate4* at a time t=6ns. Hence the cut-off time, t_{cutoff}, of *gate4* is updated to 6ns. *Gate4* cannot be put on the queue because the history-of-interest of its input *p* has not yet been computed. *Gate1* is removed from the queue.

8. The next gate in the queue is *gate3*. Gate3's output history-of-interest is computed. It does not lead to a DLV continuum at the inputs of *gate4*. Hence *gate4*'s cut-off time is not updated. Since the histories-of-interest of all of *gate4*'s inputs are now known, *gate4* is put on the queue. *Gate3* is removed from the queue.

9. *Gate4* is the next gate on the queue. The history-of-interest of *gate4*'s inputs are computed by removing that part of their known histories that occurred prior to *gate4*'s cut-off time, t_{cutoff} =6ns. The history-of-interest of *gate4*'s output is then computed. The primary output, *Y1*, under investigation has been reached and computation of the delay between it and the primary inputs for the particular primary input stimulus terminates.

10. The worst-case delay of 7ns, that would result if that particular input stimulus were applied, is saved, as are the intermediate histories-of-interests associated with each gate's ports. The latter can be re-used, as described in Section 5.3, during the computation of the delay associated with other input stimuli.

11. We repeat the process for all input stimuli. Suppose that the critical path exhibited its slowest delay when the data illustrated in Figure 4 was propagated. To locate the critical path, we would trace back from the primary output, *Y1* through the single trail of connections that form the 'last gate input to affect their gate's output'. We trace back from *Y1*, through *gate4*. Since *m* is the last input to affect

135

```
For each input stimulus (I) to be applied to circuit
    For each logic block primary output, PO,
        Initialize the value of each gate's cut-off time, t_cutoff to ∞
        Derive the history of each of the primary inputs feeding PO
        Create a queue, queue, of those gates driven solely by primary
        inputs and whose input histories are therefore all known.
        If behavior-delay-caching is to be performed, then:
            update port histories from relevant previous analyses
            and update the queue
            For the gate, gate, currently at the front of the queue
            Compute the history-of-interest of each of gate's input
            ports from the port's history and knowledge of gate's
            cut-off time, t_cutoff.
            Compute history-of-interest of gate's output port, GO.
            If: GO stabilizes to the DLV of any gate driven-gate
            that it drives at a time prior to the cut-off time of
            driven-gate or in such a way that a DLV continuum occurs:
                Update the t_cutoff of that gate, driven-gate, with the
                time that the last transition of GO occurred.
            If: histories-of-interest of all input ports of any gate,
            driven-gate, that GO drives directly are all known
            Then: push driven-gate onto the rear of queue.
        Remove gate's name from queue.
        If: the primary output PO of the circuit is reached.
        Then: Return the time that that output stabilized
            minus the time that the clock that gated the
            primary input transitions went low. This is
            the delay, D1, from the primary inputs to PO.
    If: all input stimuli have been analyzed,
    Then: Worst-case-delay of logic block= the maximum, M, of
    these delays, D1
Deduce critical path by tracing back from the primary output
to a primary input via a path that follows a trail of last gate
input, GI, to affect its gate's output.
```

Figure 5: Pseudocode for the history-based algorithm

gate4's output, we trace back along m to gate1. The last
input to affect gate1's output is A1. Hence the critical path
is the trail from A1 through gate1 and then gate4 to Y1.

The pseudocode of the **history-based algorithm** is illustrated in Figure 5.

6 CONCLUSION

Both static and data-dependent delay analysis fail to take
account of the intended use of the circuit under analysis. If the
slowest delay that they compute corresponds to an occasion
involving the propagation of impossible data through a circuit
then the speed estimate will be pessimistic and a false critical
path may be detected. We have presented a means of arriving
at a less pessimistic speed estimate, i.e., an estimate which tells
us that we can safely clock our circuit faster. Our technique
affords a more reliable means of locating the critical path.

It is necessary to analyze the propagation of data through
the logic of the circuit under scrutiny. The first reason for
this is that a gate's delay depends upon both the direction of
the gate's input and output transitions (if any) and upon the
status of the gate's other inputs at the time of these transitions.
The second reason is that, when gate's are connected in a path
and data is propagated down that path, individual gate output
transitions may be mutually exclusive.

We performed our delay analysis using a history-based algorithm. We reflected the intended use of a synchronous state
machine by determining only the input stimuli that could occur *during its actual use* and by then feeding those stimuli to
a data-dependent timing analyzer, capable of simulating the
propagation of data through the state machine logic. We used
knowledge of the conditions under which a gate input transition is the last to affect the gate's output as a means of pruning
the simulation.

We generated all valid input stimuli to our simulator automatically. These input stimuli could be used to drive any
simulator (e.g. SPICE (Nagel 1975)) that has the ability to
simulate the propagation of real data.

Acknowledgements
Many thanks to Bic Schediwy, Tim Spracklen, John Mo-
hammed, Dipti Mohapatra, and Dan Carnese for guiding this
work, and to Steve Rubin and Schlumberger for facilitating it.
Neil Hunt assisted greatly with the formatting of this paper.

References
Abramovici, M., P. R. Memon, and D. T. Miller.
1983. Critical path tracing– an alternative to fault simulation. In *20th IEEE Design Automation Conference.*

Benkoski, J. *et al.* 1987. Efficient algorithms for solving
the false path problem in timing verification. In *IEEE
ICCAD.*

Brand, D. and V. S. Iyengar. 1986. *Timing Analysis
Using Functional Analysis.* Technical Report, IBM T.
J. Watson Center, Yorktown Heights, New York 10598,
USA.

Brand, D. and V. S. Iyengar. 1986. Timing analysis
and functional relationships. In *IEEE ICCAD.*

Bryant, R. E. 1988. Verifying a static ram design by logic
simulation. In *5th MIT Conference of Advanced Research
in VLSI.*

Fishburn, J. P. and A. E. Dunlop. 1985. TILOS: a
posynomial programming approach to transistor sizing.
In *IEEE ICCAD.*

Hitchcock, R. B. 1982. Timing verification and the timing analysis program. In *19th IEEE Design Automation
Conference.*

Hofmann, M. and J. K. Kim. 1987. Delay optimization
of combinatorial static CMOS logic. In *24th IEEE Design
Automation Conference.*

Jouppi, N. P. 1983. TV: an nMOS timing analyzer.
In *Third Caltech Conference on VLSI. Computer Science
Press.*

Jouppi, N. P. 1983. Timing analysis for nMOS VLSI. In
20th IEEE Design Automation Conference.

Miczo, A. 1986. *Digital Logic Testing and Simulation,*
pages 146–8. Harper and Row.

Murphy, B. J., J. E. Kleckner, and K. K. Tam. 1985.
STA: a mixed level timing analyzer. In *IEEE ICCAD.*

Nagel, W. 1975. *SPICE2, A Computer Program to Simulate Semiconductor Circuits.* 1975.

Ousterhout, J. K. 1983. Crystal: a timing analyzer
for nMOS VLSI circuits. In *Third Caltech Conference on
VLSI. Computer Science Press.*

Ousterhout, J. K. 1984. Switch-level delay models for
digital MOS VLSI. In *21st IEEE Design Automation
Conference.*

Ousterhout, J. K. 1986. *Using Crystal for Timing Analysis.* Electrical Engineering and Computer Science Division, University of California, Berkeley, 1986.

Shirley, M. H. 1986. Generating tests by exploiting designed behavior. In *AAAI National Conference on Artificial Intelligence.*

Sutton, A. M. 1989. *The Synthesis and Speed Analysis
of Digital Systems.* PhD thesis, University of Aberdeen,
Scotland, Department of Engineering.

Toyoshima, R. *et al.* 1986. An effective delay analysis
system for a large scale computer design. In *23rd IEEE
Design Automation Conference.*

Author Index

Author Index (continued)

NOTES